A Guide to the Good Life

A Guide to the Good Life

The Ancient Art of Stoic Joy

William B. Irvine

2009

OXFORD
UNIVERSITY PRESS

Oxford University Press, Inc., publishes works that further
Oxford University's objective of excellence
in research, scholarship, and education.

Oxford New York
Auckland Cape Town Dar es Salaam Hong Kong Karachi
Kuala Lumpur Madrid Melbourne Mexico City Nairobi
New Delhi Shanghai Taipei Toronto

With offices in
Argentina Austria Brazil Chile Czech Republic France Greece
Guatemala Hungary Italy Japan Poland Portugal Singapore
South Korea Switzerland Thailand Turkey Ukraine Vietnam

Published by Oxford University Press, Inc.
198 Madison Avenue, New York, NY 10016

www.oup.com

Library of Congress Cataloging-in-Publication Data
Irvine, William Braxton, 1952–
A guide to the good life : the ancient art
of Stoic joy / William B. Irvine.
p. cm.
Includes bibliographical references and index.
ISBN 978-0-19-537461-2
1. Stoics. I. Title.
B528.I78 2008
171'.2—dc22 2008010563

7 9 8

Printed in the United States of America
on acid-free paper

In memory of Charlie Doyle,

who taught me to keep my head in the boat

even when I'm not rowing.

Contents

PART THREE
STOIC ADVICE

PART FOUR
STOICISM FOR MODERN LIVES

Acknowledgments

It takes more than an author to make a book. Allow me, therefore, to thank some of those who contributed to the realization of this work.

Thanks, to begin with, to Wright State University for providing the professional development leave during which the bulk of this book was written. Thanks also to my department for allowing me to teach, in the fall of 2005, a course on Hellenistic philosophy in which I was able to try out an early version of this book.

Thanks to those who (in most cases unwittingly) played a significant role in my "program of voluntary discomfort," including Jim McCutcheon of McCutcheon Music, Debbie Stirsman of Inner Dance Yoga Center, and my buddies at Greater Dayton Rowing Association, with a special thanks going to those who had the courage to row one seat behind me: Judy Dryer, Chris Luhn, and Michael McCarty. Thanks also to Michael for helping me explore the world of discomfort provided by the erg and for making valuable suggestions concerning the terminology used in chapter 7.

Thanks to Cynthia King, who read and commented on my manuscript. Thanks also to Bill King, who, although unwilling to admit allegiance to the Stoic credo, has nevertheless been an inspiration to this Stoic.

Thanks to numerous anonymous readers who helped me sharpen the argument of this book. Thanks also to Cybele Tom at Oxford University Press for being such a patient and persevering literary midwife.

The biggest thanks, though, goes to my wife, Jamie, for giving me the time and especially the space in which to write this book.

A Guide to the Good Life

Introduction

A Plan for Living

What do you want out of life? You might answer this question by saying that you want a caring spouse, a good job, and a nice house, but these are really just some of the things you want *in* life. In asking what you want *out of* life, I am asking the question in its broadest sense. I am asking not for the goals you form as you go about your daily activities but for your grand goal in living. In other words, of the things in life you might pursue, which is the thing you believe to be most valuable?

Many people will have trouble naming this goal. They know what they want minute by minute or even decade by decade during their life, but they have never paused to consider their grand goal in living. It is perhaps understandable that they haven't. Our culture doesn't encourage people to think about such things; indeed, it provides them with an endless stream of distractions so they won't ever have to. But a grand goal in living is the first component of a philosophy of life. This means that if you lack a grand goal in living, you lack a coherent philosophy of life.

Why is it important to have such a philosophy? Because without one, there is a danger that you will mislive—that despite all your activity, despite all the pleasant diversions you might have enjoyed while alive, you will end up living a bad life. There is, in other words, a danger that when you are on your deathbed, you will look back and realize that you wasted your one chance at living. Instead of spending your life pursuing something genuinely valuable, you squandered it because you allowed yourself to be distracted by the various baubles life has to offer.

Suppose you can identify your grand goal in living. Suppose, too, that you can explain why this goal is worth attaining. Even then, there is a danger that you will mislive. In particular, if you lack an effective strategy for attaining your goal, it is unlikely that you will attain it. Thus, the second component of a philosophy of life is a strategy for attaining your grand goal in living. This strategy will specify what you must do, as you go about your daily activities, to maximize your chances of gaining the thing in life that you take to be ultimately valuable.

IF WE WANT to take steps to avoid wasting our wealth, we can easily find experts to help us. Looking in the phone book, we will find any number of certified financial planners. These individuals can help us clarify our financial goals: How much, for example, should we be saving for retirement? And having clarified these goals, they can advise us on how to achieve them.

Suppose, however, that we want to take steps to avoid wasting not our wealth but our life. We might seek an expert to guide us: a philosopher of life. This individual would help us think about our goals in living and about which of these goals are in fact worth pursuing. She would remind us that because goals can come into conflict, we need to decide which of our goals should take precedence when conflicts arise. She will therefore help us sort through our goals and place them into a hierarchy. The goal at the pinnacle of this hierarchy will be what I have called our grand goal in living: It is the goal that we should be unwilling to sacrifice to attain other goals. And after helping us select this goal, a philosopher of life will help us devise a strategy for attaining it.

The obvious place to look for a philosopher of life is in the philosophy department of the local university. Visiting the faculty offices there, we will find philosophers specializing in metaphysics, logic, politics, science, religion, and ethics. We might also find philosophers specializing in the philosophy of sport, the philosophy of feminism, and even the philosophy of philosophy. But unless we are at an unusual university, we will find no philosophers of life in the sense I have in mind.

It hasn't always been this way. Many ancient Greek and Roman philosophers, for example, not only thought philosophies of life were worth contemplating but thought the raison d'être of philosophy was to develop them. These philosophers typically had an interest in other areas of philosophy as well—in logic, for example—but only because they thought pursuing that interest would help them develop a philosophy of life.

Furthermore, these ancient philosophers did not keep their discoveries to themselves or share them only with their fellow philosophers. Rather, they formed schools and welcomed as their pupils anyone wishing to acquire a philosophy of life. Different schools offered different advice on what people must do in order to have a good life. Antisthenes, a pupil of Socrates, founded the Cynic school of philosophy, which advocated an ascetic lifestyle. Aristippus, another pupil of Socrates, founded the Cyrenaic school, which advocated a hedonistic lifestyle. In between these extremes, we find, among many other schools, the Epicurean school, the Skeptic school, and, of most interest to us here, the Stoic school, founded by Zeno of Citium.

The philosophers associated with these schools were unapologetic about their interest in philosophies of life. According to Epicurus, for example, "Vain is the word of a philosopher which does not heal any suffering of man. For just as there is no profit in medicine if it does not expel the diseases of the body, so there is no profit in philosophy either, if it does not expel the suffering of the mind."[1] And according to the Stoic philosopher Seneca, about whom I will have much to say in this book, "He who studies with a philosopher should take away with him some one good thing every day: he should daily return home a sounder man, or on the way to become sounder."[2]

THIS BOOK IS WRITTEN for those seeking a philosophy of life. In the pages that follow, I focus my attention on a philosophy that I have found useful and that I suspect many readers will also find useful. It is the philosophy of the ancient Stoics. The Stoic philosophy of life may be old, but it merits the attention of any modern individual who wishes to have a life that is both meaningful and fulfilling—who wishes, that is, to have a good life.

In other words, this book offers advice on how people should live. More precisely, I will act as a conduit for the advice offered by Stoic philosophers two thousand years ago. This is something my fellow philosophers are generally loath to do, but then again, their interest in philosophy is primarily "academic"; their research, that is to say, is primarily theoretical or historical. My interest in Stoicism, by way of contrast, is resolutely practical: My goal is to put this philosophy to work in my life and to encourage others to put it to work in theirs. The ancient Stoics, I think, would have encouraged both sorts of endeavor, but they also would have insisted that the primary reason to study Stoicism is so we can put it into practice.

Another thing to realize is that although Stoicism is a philosophy, it has a significant psychological component. The Stoics realized that a life plagued with negative emotions—including anger, anxiety, fear, grief, and envy—will not be a good life. They therefore became acute observers of the workings of the human mind and as a result became some of the most insightful psychologists of the ancient world. They went on to develop techniques for preventing the onset of negative emotions and for extinguishing them when attempts at prevention failed. Even those readers who are leery of philosophical speculation should take an interest in these techniques. Who among us, after all, would not like to reduce the number of negative emotions experienced in daily living?

ALTHOUGH I HAVE BEEN studying philosophy for all my adult life, I was, until recently, woefully ignorant of Stoicism. My teachers in college and graduate school never asked me to read the Stoics, and although I am an avid reader, I saw no need to read them on my own. More generally, I saw no need to ponder a philosophy of life. I instead felt comfortable with what is, for almost everyone, the default philosophy of life: to spend one's days seeking an interesting mix of affluence, social status, and pleasure. My philosophy of life, in other words, was what might charitably be called an enlightened form of hedonism.

In my fifth decade of life, though, events conspired to introduce me to Stoicism. The first of these was the 1998 publication by the author Tom Wolfe of *A Man in Full*. In this novel, one character accidentally discovers the Stoic philosopher Epictetus and then starts spouting his philosophy. I found this to be simultaneously intriguing and puzzling.

Two years later I started doing research for a book about desire. As part of this research, I examined the advice that has been given over the millennia on mastering desire. I started out by seeing what religions, including Christianity, Hinduism, Taoism, Sufism, and Buddhism (and in particular, Zen Buddhism), had to say about desire. I went on to examine the advice on mastering desire offered by philosophers but found that only a relative handful of them had offered such advice. Prominent among those who had were the Hellenistic philosophers: the Epicureans, Skeptics, and Stoics.

In conducting my research on desire, I had an ulterior motive. I had long been intrigued by Zen Buddhism and imagined that on taking a closer look at it in connection with my research, I would become a full-fledged convert. But what I found, much to my surprise, was that Stoicism and Zen have certain things in common. They both, for example, stress the importance of contemplating the transitory nature of the world around us and the importance of mastering desire, to the extent that it is possible to do so. They also advise us to pursue tranquility and give us advice on how to attain and maintain it. Furthermore, I came to realize that Stoicism was better suited to my analytical nature than Buddhism was. As a result, I found myself, much to my amazement, toying with the idea of becoming, instead of a practicing Zen Buddhist, a practicing Stoic.

Before I began my research on desire, Stoicism had been, for me, a nonstarter as a philosophy of life, but as I read the Stoics, I discovered that almost everything I thought I knew about them was wrong. To begin with, I knew that the dictionary defines a *stoic* as "one who is seemingly indifferent to or unaffected by joy, grief, pleasure, or pain."[3] I therefore expected that the uppercase-*S* Stoics would be lowercase-*s* stoical—that they would be emotionally repressed individuals. I discovered, though, that the goal of the Stoics was not to banish *emotion* from life but to banish *negative* emotions.

When I read the works of the Stoics, I encountered individuals who were cheerful and optimistic about life (even though they made it a point to spend time thinking about all the bad things that could happen to them) and who were fully capable of enjoying life's pleasures (while at the same time being careful not to be enslaved by those pleasures). I also encountered, much to my surprise, individuals who valued joy; indeed, according to Seneca, what Stoics seek to discover "is how the mind may always pursue a steady and favourable course, may be well-disposed towards itself, and may view its conditions with joy."[4] He also asserts that someone who practices Stoic principles "must, whether he wills or not, necessarily be attended by constant cheerfulness and a joy that is deep and issues from deep within, since he finds delight in his own resources, and desires no joys greater than his inner joys."[5] Along similar lines, the Stoic philosopher Musonius Rufus tells us that if we live in accordance with Stoic principles, "a cheerful disposition and secure joy" will automatically follow.[6]

Rather than being passive individuals who were grimly resigned to being on the receiving end of the world's abuse and injustice, the Stoics were fully engaged in life and worked hard to make the world a better place. Consider, for example, Cato the Younger. (Although he did not contribute to the literature of Stoicism, Cato was a practicing Stoic; indeed, Seneca refers to him as the perfect Stoic.)[7] His Stoicism did not prevent Cato from fighting bravely to restore the Roman republic. Likewise, Seneca seems to have been remarkably energetic: Besides being a philosopher, he was a successful playwright, an advisor to an emperor, and the first-century equivalent of an investment banker. And Marcus Aurelius, besides being a philosopher, was a Roman emperor—indeed, arguably one of the greatest Roman emperors. As I read about the Stoics, I found myself filled with admiration for them. They were courageous, temperate, reasonable, and self-disciplined—traits I would like to possess. They also thought it important for us to fulfill our obligations and to help our fellow humans—values I happen to share.

In my research on desire, I discovered nearly unanimous agreement among thoughtful people that we are unlikely to have a good and meaningful life unless we can overcome our insatiability. There was also agreement that one wonderful way to tame our tendency to always want more is to persuade ourselves to want the things we already have. This seemed to be an important insight, but it left open the question of how, exactly, we could accomplish this. The Stoics, I was delighted to discover, had an answer to this question. They developed a fairly simple technique that, if practiced, can make us glad, if only for a time, to be the person we are, living the life we happen to be living, almost regardless of what that life might be.

The more I studied the Stoics, the more I found myself drawn to their philosophy. But when I tried to share with others my newfound enthusiasm for Stoicism, I quickly discovered that I had not been alone in misconceiving the philosophy. Friends, relatives, and even my colleagues at the university seemed to think the Stoics were individuals whose goal was to suppress all emotion and who therefore led grim and passive lives. It dawned on me that the Stoics were the victims of a bum rap, one that I myself had only recently helped promote.

This realization alone might have been sufficient to motivate me to write a book about the Stoics—a book that would set the record straight—but as it happens, I came to have a second motivation even stronger than this. After learning about Stoicism, I started, in a low-key, experimental fashion, giving it a try as my philosophy of life. The experiment has thus far been sufficiently successful that I feel compelled to report my findings to the world at large, in the belief that others might benefit from studying the Stoics and adopting their philosophy of life.

READERS WILL NATURALLY be curious about what is involved in the practice of Stoicism. In ancient Greece and Rome, a would-be Stoic could have learned how to practice Stoicism by attending a Stoic school, but this is no longer possible. A modern would-be Stoic might, as an alternative, consult the works of the ancient Stoics, but what she will discover on attempting to do so is that many of these works—in particular, those of the Greek Stoics—have been lost. Furthermore, if she reads the works that have survived, she will discover that although they discuss Stoicism at length, they don't offer a lesson plan, as it were, for novice Stoics. The challenge I faced in writing this book was to construct such a plan from clues scattered throughout Stoic writings.

Although the remainder of this book provides detailed guidelines for would-be Stoics, let me describe here, in a preliminary fashion, some of the things we will want to do if we adopt Stoicism as our philosophy of life.

We will reconsider our goals in living. In particular, we will take to heart the Stoic claim that many of the things we desire—most notably, fame and fortune—are not worth pursuing. We will instead turn our attention to the pursuit of tranquility and what the Stoics called *virtue*. We will discover that Stoic virtue has very little in common with what people today mean by the word. We will also discover that the tranquility the Stoics sought is not the kind of tranquility that might be brought on by the ingestion of a tranquilizer; it is not, in other words, a zombie-like state. It is instead a state marked by the absence of negative emotions such as anger, grief, anxiety, and fear, and the presence of positive emotions—in particular, joy.

We will study the various psychological techniques developed by the Stoics for attaining and maintaining tranquility, and we will employ these techniques in daily living. We will, for example, take care to distinguish between things we can control and things we can't, so that we will no longer worry about the things we can't control and will instead focus our attention on the things we can control. We will also recognize how easy it is for other people to disturb our tranquility, and we will therefore practice Stoic strategies to prevent them from upsetting us.

Finally, we will become a more thoughtful observer of our own life. We will watch ourselves as we go about our daily business and will later reflect on what we saw, trying to identify the sources of distress in our life and thinking about how to avoid that distress.

Practicing Stoicism will obviously take effort, but this is true of all genuine philosophies of life. Indeed, even "enlightened hedonism" takes effort. The enlightened hedonist's grand goal in living is to maximize the pleasure he experiences in the course of a lifetime. To practice this philosophy of life, he will spend time discovering, exploring, and ranking sources of pleasure and investigating any untoward side effects they might have. The enlightened hedonist will then devise strategies for maximizing the amount of pleasure he experiences. (Unenlightened hedonism, in which a person thoughtlessly seeks short-term gratification, is not, I think, a coherent philosophy of life.)

The effort required to practice Stoicism will probably be greater than that required to practice enlightened hedonism but less than that required to practice, say, Zen Buddhism.

A Zen Buddhist will have to meditate, a practice that is both time-consuming and (in some of its forms) physically and mentally challenging. The practice of Stoicism, in contrast, doesn't require us to set aside blocks of time in which to "do Stoicism." It does require us periodically to reflect on our life, but these periods of reflection can generally be squeezed into odd moments of the day, such as when we are stuck in traffic or—this was Seneca's recommendation—when we are lying in bed waiting for sleep to come.

When assessing the "costs" associated with practicing Stoicism or any other philosophy of life, readers should realize that there are costs associated with *not* having a philosophy of life. I have already mentioned one such cost: the danger that you will spend your days pursuing valueless things and will therefore waste your life.

Some readers might, at this point, wonder whether the practice of Stoicism is compatible with their religious beliefs. In the case of most religions, I think it is. Christians in particular will find that Stoic doctrines resonate with their religious views. They will, for example, share the Stoics' desire to attain tranquility, although Christians might call it *peace*. They will appreciate Marcus Aurelius's injunction to "love mankind."[8] And when they encounter Epictetus's observation that some things are up to us and some things are not, and that if we have any sense at all, we will focus our energies on the things that are up to us, Christians will be reminded of the "Serenity Prayer," often attributed to the theologian Reinhold Niebuhr.

Having said this, I should add that it is also possible for someone simultaneously to be an agnostic and a practicing Stoic.

The remainder of this book is divided into four parts. In part 1, I describe the birth of philosophy. Although modern philosophers tend to spend their days debating esoteric topics, the primary goal of most ancient philosophers was to help ordinary people live better lives. Stoicism, as we shall see, was one of the most popular and successful of the ancient schools of philosophy.

In parts 2 and 3, I explain what we must do in order to practice Stoicism. I start by describing the psychological techniques the Stoics developed to attain and subsequently maintain tranquility. I then describe Stoic advice on how best to deal with the stresses of everyday life: How, for example, should we respond when someone insults us? Although much has changed in the past two millennia, human psychology has changed little. This is why those of us living in the twenty-first century can benefit from the advice that philosophers such as Seneca offered to first-century Romans.

Finally, in part 4 of this book, I defend Stoicism against various criticisms, and I reevaluate Stoic psychology in light of modern scientific findings. I end the book by relating the insights I have gained in my own practice of Stoicism.

My fellow academics might have an interest in this book; they might, for example, be curious about my interpretation of various Stoic utterances. The audience I am most interested in reaching, though, is ordinary individuals who worry that they might be misliving. This includes those who have come to the realization that they lack a coherent philosophy of life and as a result are floundering in their daily activities: what they work to accomplish one day only undoes what they accomplished the day before. It also includes those who have a philosophy of life but worry that it is somehow defective.

I wrote this book with the following question in mind: If the ancient Stoics had taken it upon themselves to write a guidebook for twenty-first-century individuals—a book that would tell us how to have a good life—what might that book have looked like? The pages that follow are my answer to this question.

PART ONE

The Rise of Stoicism

ONE

Philosophy Takes an Interest in Life

There have probably always been philosophers, in some sense of the word. They were those individuals who not only asked questions—such as Where did the world come from? Where did people come from? and Why are there rainbows?—but more important, went on to ask follow-up questions. When told, for example, that the world was created by the gods, these proto-philosophers would have realized that this answer didn't get to the bottom of things. They would have gone on to ask why the gods made the world, how they made it, and—most vexatiously to those trying to answer their questions—who made the gods.

However and whenever it may have started, philosophical thinking took a giant leap forward in the sixth century BC. We find Pythagoras (570–500 BC) philosophizing in Italy; Thales (636–546 BC), Anaximander (641–547 BC), and Heracleitus (535–475 BC) in Greece; Confucius (551–479 BC) in China; and Buddha (563–483 BC) in India. It isn't clear whether these individuals discovered philosophy independently of one another; nor is it clear which direction philosophical influence flowed, if it indeed flowed.

The Greek biographer Diogenes Laertius, from the vantage point of the third century AD, offered an eminently readable (but not entirely reliable) history of early philosophy. According to Diogenes, early Western philosophy had two separate branches.[1] One branch—he calls it the Italian branch—began with Pythagoras. If we follow through the various successors of Pythagoras, we ultimately come to Epicurus, whose own school of philosophy was a major rival to the Stoic school. The other branch—Diogenes calls it the Ionian branch—started with Anaximander, who (intellectually, pedagogically) begat Anaximenes, who begat Anaxagoras, who begat Archelaus, who, finally, begat Socrates (469–399 BC).

Socrates lived a remarkable life. He also died a remarkable death: He had been tried for corrupting the youth of Athens and other alleged misdeeds, found guilty by his fellow citizens, and sentenced to die by drinking poison hemlock. He could have avoided this punishment by throwing himself on the mercy of the court or by running away after the sentence had been handed down. His philosophical principles, though, would not let him do these things. After his death, Socrates' many followers not only continued to do philosophy but attracted followers of their own. Plato, the best-known of his students, founded the school of philosophy known as the Academy, Aristippus founded the Cyrenaic school, Euclides founded the Megarian school, Phaedo founded the Elian school, and Antisthenes founded the Cynic school. What had been a trickle of philosophical activity before Socrates became, after his death, a veritable torrent.

Why did this explosion of interest in philosophy take place? In part because Socrates changed the focus of philosophical inquiry. Before Socrates, philosophers were primarily interested in explaining the world around them and the phenomena of that world—in doing what we would now call science. Although Socrates studied science as a young man, he abandoned it to focus his attention on the human condition. As the Roman orator, politician, and philosopher Cicero put it, Socrates was "the first to call philosophy down from the heavens and set her in the cities of men and bring her also into their homes and compel her to ask questions about life and morality and things good and evil."[2] The classicist Francis MacDonald Cornford describes Socrates' philosophical significance in similar terms: "Pre-Socratic philosophy begins . . . with the discovery of Nature; Socratic philosophy begins with the discovery of man's soul."[3]

Why does Socrates remain an impressive figure twenty-four centuries after his death? It isn't because of his philosophical discoveries; his philosophical conclusions, after all, were basically negative: He showed us what we don't know. Rather, it was the extent to which he allowed his way of life to be affected by his philosophical speculations. Indeed, according to the philosopher Luis E. Navia, "in [Socrates], perhaps more than in any other major philosopher, we come upon the example of a man who was able to integrate in his life theoretical and speculative concerns into the context of his daily activities." Navia describes him as "a veritable paradigm of philosophical activity both in thought and in deed."[4]

Presumably, some of those drawn to Socrates were impressed primarily by his theorizing, while others were most impressed by his lifestyle. Plato belonged to the former group; in his Academy, Plato was more interested in exploring philosophical theory than in dispensing lifestyle advice. Antisthenes, in contrast, was most impressed with Socrates' lifestyle; the Cynic school he founded eschewed philosophical theorizing and focused instead on advising people about what they must do to have a good life.

It is as if Socrates, on his death, had fissioned into Plato and Antisthenes, with Plato inheriting Socrates' interest in theory and Antisthenes inheriting his concern with living a good life. It would have been wonderful if these two sides of philosophy had flourished in subsequent millennia, inasmuch as people benefit from both philosophical theorizing and the application of philosophy to their own life. Unfortunately, although the theoretical side of philosophy has flourished, the practical side has withered away.

UNDER A DESPOTIC GOVERNMENT such as that of ancient Persia, the ability to write, read, and do arithmetic was important for government officials, but the ability to persuade others wasn't. Officials needed only give orders, which those under their power would unhesitatingly obey. In Greece and Rome, however, the rise of democracy meant that those who were able to persuade others were most likely to have successful careers in politics or law. It was in part for this reason that affluent Greek and Roman parents, after a child's secondary education was completed, sought teachers who could develop their child's persuasive ability.

These parents might have sought the services of a sophist, whose goal was to teach pupils to win arguments. To achieve this goal, sophists taught various techniques of persuasion, including both appeals to reason and appeals to emotion. In particular, they taught students that it was possible to argue for or against any proposition whatsoever. Along with developing pupils' argumentative skills, sophists developed their speaking skills, so they could effectively communicate the arguments they devised.

Alternatively, parents might have sought the services of a philosopher. Like sophists, philosophers taught persuasive techniques, but unlike sophists, they eschewed appeals to emotion. Also unlike sophists, philosophers thought that besides teaching their pupils how to persuade, they should teach them how to live well. Consequently, according to the historian H. I. Marrou, in their teaching they emphasized "the moral aspect of education, the development of the personality and the inner life."[5] In the course of doing this, many philosophers provided their pupils with a philosophy of life: They taught them what things in life were worth pursuing and how best to pursue them.

Some of the parents who wanted a philosophical education for their child hired a philosopher to act as live-in tutor; Aristotle, for example, was hired by King Philip of Macedon to tutor Alexander, who subsequently became "the Great." Parents who could not afford a private tutor would have sent their sons—but probably not their daughters—to a school of philosophy. After the death of Socrates, these schools became a prominent feature of Athenian culture, and when, in the second century BC, Rome came under the spell of Athenian culture, schools of philosophy started appearing in Rome as well.

THERE ARE NO LONGER schools of philosophy, and this is a shame. It is true that philosophy is still done within schools—more precisely, within the philosophy departments of universities—but the cultural role played by philosophy departments is quite unlike the role played by the ancient philosophical schools. For one thing, those who sign up for the philosophy classes offered by universities are rarely motivated to do so by a desire to acquire a philosophy of life; instead, they take classes because their advisor tells them that if they don't, they can't graduate. And if they do seek a philosophy of life, they would, in most universities, have a hard time finding a class that would offer them one.

But even though schools of philosophy are a thing of the past, people are in as much need of a philosophy of life as they ever were. The question is, Where can they go to obtain one? If they go to the philosophy department of the local university, they will, as I have explained, probably be disappointed. What if they instead turn to their local church? Their pastor might tell them what they must do to be a *good person*, that is, what they must do to be morally upstanding. They might be instructed, for example, not to steal or tell lies or (in some religions) have an abortion. Their pastor will also probably explain what they must do to have a *good afterlife*: They should come to services regularly and pray and (in some religions) tithe. But their pastor will probably have relatively little to say on what they must do to have a *good life*. Indeed, most religions, after telling adherents what they must do to be morally upstanding and get into heaven, leave it to them to determine what things in life are and aren't worth pursuing. These religions see nothing wrong with an adherent working hard so he can afford a huge mansion and an expensive sports car, as long as he doesn't break any laws doing so; nor do they see anything wrong with the adherent forsaking the mansion for a hut and forsaking the car for a bicycle.

And if religions do offer adherents advice on what things in life are and aren't worth pursuing, they tend to offer the advice in such a low-key manner that adherents might regard it as a suggestion rather than a directive about how to live and might therefore ignore the advice. This, one imagines, is why the adherents of the various religions, despite the differences in their religious beliefs, end up with the same impromptu philosophy of life, namely, a form of enlightened hedonism. Thus, although Lutherans, Baptists, Jews, Mormons, and Catholics hold different religious views, they are remarkably alike when encountered outside of church or synagogue. They hold similar jobs and have similar career ambitions. They live in similar homes, furnished in a similar manner. And they lust to the same degree for whatever consumer products are currently in vogue.

It is clearly possible for a religion to require its adherents to adopt a particular philosophy of life. Consider, by way of illustration, the Hutterite religion, which teaches its adherents that one of the most valuable things in life is a sense of community. Hutterites are therefore forbidden to own private property, the rationale being that such ownership would give rise to feelings of envy, which in turn would disrupt the sense of community the Hutterites value. (We can, of course, question whether this is a sound philosophy of life.)

Most religions, however, don't require their adherents to adopt a particular philosophy of life. As long as adherents don't harm others and don't do things to anger God, they are free to live their life as they will. Indeed, if the Hutterite religion seems both extreme and exotic to most people, it is because they can't imagine belonging to a religion that tells them how to live their life.

What this means is that it is entirely possible these days for someone to have been raised in a religion and to have taken philosophy courses in college but still to be lacking a philosophy of life. (Indeed, this is the situation in which most of my students find themselves.) What, then, should those seeking a philosophy of life do? Perhaps their best option is to create for themselves a virtual school of philosophy by reading the works of the philosophers who ran the ancient schools. This, at any rate, is what, in the following pages, I will be encouraging readers to do.

In ancient Greece, when schools of philosophy were still prominent features of the cultural landscape, there were any number of schools to which parents could send their children. Suppose we could travel back in time to 300 BC and take a thinking person's walking tour of Athens. We could begin our tour in the Agora, where Socrates a century earlier had philosophized with the citizens of Athens. On the northern side of the Agora we would see the Stoa Poikile, or Painted Porch, and holding forth there might be Zeno of Citium, the founder of the Stoic school of philosophy. This "porch" was actually a colonnade decorated with murals.

As we walked through Athens, we might come across the Cynic philosopher Crates, whose school of philosophy Zeno had once attended. Although the first Cynics met near the gymnasium of Cynosarges—hence their name—they could be found anywhere in Athens, attempting to draw (or drag, if need be) ordinary people into philosophical discussions. Furthermore, whereas parents might have willingly sent their children to study with Zeno, it is unlikely that they encouraged them to become Cynics, inasmuch as Cynic doctrines, if successfully internalized, would guarantee their child a life of ignominious poverty.

Heading northwest and leaving the city by Dipylon Gate, we would come to the Garden of the Epicureans, presided over by Epicurus himself. Whereas the Painted Porch was in an urban setting, with Stoic lectures periodically interrupted, one imagines, by noise from the street or the comments of passers-by, Epicurus's Garden had a distinctly rural feel. The Garden was in fact a working garden in which the Epicureans grew their own vegetables.

Continuing toward the northwest, about a mile from the Agora, we would come to the Academy, the school of philosophy founded by Plato in 387 BC, a bit more than a decade after the death of Socrates. Like Epicurus's Garden, the Academy would have been a striking place in which to philosophize. It was a parklike retreat, furnished with walks and fountains. On the Academy grounds were buildings, paid for by Plato and his friends. Holding forth there in 300 BC might have been Polemo, who had inherited the position of master of the school. (The Stoic philosopher Zeno, as we shall see, attended Polemo's school for a time.)

Doubling back, going through the city again, and exiting the city gates into the eastern suburbs of Athens, we would have come to the Lyceum. In this wooded area, near a shrine to Apollo Lykeios, we could see the Peripatetics, disciples of Aristotle, walking and talking, and at the head of the group might be Theophrastus.

But this is only the beginning of the educational options open to ancient parents. Besides the schools mentioned in connection with our walking tour, there were the Cyrenaic, Skeptic, Megarian, and Elian schools mentioned earlier, to which we can add several other schools mentioned by Diogenes Laertius, including the Eretrian, Annicerean, and Theodorean schools, along with the schools run by the Eudaemonists, the Truth-lovers, the Refutationists, the Reasoners from Analogy, the Physicists, the Moralists, and the Dialecticians.[6]

As it so happens, young men (and, rarely, young women) weren't the only ones to attend schools of philosophy. Sometimes fathers studied alongside their sons. In other cases, adults attended a school's lectures by themselves. Some of these adults were simply interested in philosophy; perhaps they had attended a school as a youth and now sought "continuing education" in the philosophy of life taught by that school. Other adults, though never having belonged to a school, might have attended its lectures as guests. Their motives were probably very much like the motives modern individuals have in attending a public lecture: They sought to be enlightened and entertained.

Yet other adults had an ulterior motive for attending schools of philosophy: They wanted to start their own school and listened to the lectures of heads of successful schools in order to borrow philosophical ideas they could use in their own teaching. Zeno of Citium was accused of doing just this: Polemo complained that Zeno's motive for attending lectures at the Academy was to steal his doctrines.[7]

THE RIVAL SCHOOLS OF PHILOSOPHY differed in the subjects they taught. The early Stoics, for example, were interested not only in a philosophy of life, but in physics and logic as well, for the simple reason that they thought these areas of study were inherently entwined. The Epicureans shared the Stoics' interest in physics (although they had different views about the physical world than the Stoics did) but did not likewise share their interest in logic. The Cyrenaics and Cynics were interested in neither physics nor logic; at their schools, all one was taught was a philosophy of life.

Those schools that offered students a philosophy of life differed in the philosophy they recommended. The Cyrenaics, for example, thought the grand goal in living was the experience of pleasure and therefore advocated taking advantage of every opportunity to experience it. The Cynics advocated an ascetic lifestyle: If you want a good life, they argued, you must learn to want next to nothing. The Stoics fell somewhere between the Cyrenaics and the Cynics: They thought people should enjoy the good things life has to offer, including friendship and wealth, but only if they did not cling to these good things. Indeed, they thought we should periodically interrupt our enjoyment of what life has to offer to spend time contemplating the loss of whatever it is we are enjoying.

Affiliating oneself with a school of philosophy was a serious business. According to the historian Simon Price, "Adherence to a philosophical sect was not simply a matter for the mind, or the result of mere intellectual fashion. Those who took their philosophy seriously attempted to live that philosophy from day to day."[8] And just as a modern individual's religion can become the key element of his personal identity—think of a born-again Christian—an ancient Greek's or Roman's philosophical association became an important part of who he was. According to the historian Paul Veyne, "To truly be a philosopher was to live out the sect's doctrine, conform one's conduct (and even one's attire) to it, and if need be, to die for it."[9]

Readers of this book should therefore keep in mind that although I am advocating Stoicism as a philosophy of life, it isn't the only option available to those seeking such a philosophy. Furthermore, although the Stoics thought they could prove that theirs was the correct philosophy of life, I don't (as we shall see in chapter 21) think such a proof is possible. Instead, I think that which philosophy of life a person should choose depends on her personality and circumstances.

But having made this admission, let me add that I think there are very many people whose personality and circumstances make them wonderful candidates for the practice of Stoicism. Furthermore, whatever philosophy of life a person ends up adopting, she will probably have a better life than if she tried to live—as many people do—without a coherent philosophy of life.

TWO

The First Stoics

ZENO (333–261 BC) was the first Stoic. (And by *Zeno*, I mean Zeno of Citium, not to be confused with Zeno of Elea, who is famous for a paradox involving Achilles and a tortoise, or with any of the seven other Zenos mentioned by Diogenes Laertius in his biographical sketches.) Zeno's father was a merchant of purple dye and used to come home from his travels with books for Zeno to read. Among them were philosophy books purchased in Athens. These books aroused Zeno's interest in both philosophy and Athens.

As the result of a shipwreck, Zeno found himself in Athens, and while there, he decided to take advantage of the philosophical resources the city had to offer. He went to a bookseller's shop and asked where men like Socrates could be found. Just then, Crates the Cynic was walking by. The bookseller pointed to him and said, "Follow yonder man." And so it was, we are told, that Zeno became Crates' pupil. Looking back on this time in his life, Zeno commented, "I made a prosperous voyage when I suffered shipwreck."[1]

The Cynics had little interest in philosophical theorizing. They instead advocated a rather extreme philosophical lifestyle.

They were ascetics. Socially speaking, they were the ancient equivalent of what we today call the homeless: They lived in the streets and slept on the ground. They owned only the clothing on their backs, typically one poor cloak, what the ancients refer to as "Cynic garb." Theirs was a day-to-day, hand-to-mouth existence.

When someone told Epictetus—who, although himself a Stoic, was familiar with Cynicism—that he was contemplating joining the Cynic school, Epictetus explained what becoming a Cynic would entail: "You must utterly put away the will to get, and must will to avoid only what lies within the sphere of your will: you must harbour no anger, wrath, envy, pity: a fair maid, a fair name, favourites, or sweet cakes, must mean nothing to you." A Cynic, he explained, "must have the spirit of patience in such measure as to seem to the multitude as unfeeling as a stone. Reviling or blows or insults are nothing to him."[2] Few people, one imagines, had the courage and endurance to live the life of a Cynic.

The Cynics were renowned for their wit and wisdom. When, for example, someone asked what sort of woman a man should marry, Antisthenes replied that no matter what woman he chose for his wife, he would live to regret marrying: "If she's beautiful, you'll not have her to yourself; if she's ugly, you'll pay for it dearly." Concerning our dealings with other people, he commented that "it is better to fall in with crows than with flatterers; for in the one case you are devoured when dead, in the other case while alive." He also advised his listeners to "pay attention to your enemies, for they are the first to discover your mistakes." Despite, or perhaps because of, his sharp wit, Antisthenes was described as being "the most agreeable of men in conversation."[3]

Diogenes of Sinope (not to be confused with Diogenes Laertius, who wrote a biographical sketch of him and other philosophers) was a student of Antisthenes and went on to become the most famous Cynic. In defense of simple living, Diogenes observed that "the gods had given to men the means of living easily, but this had been put out of sight, because we require honeyed cakes, unguents and the like." Such is the madness of men, he said, that they choose to be miserable when they have it in their power to be content. The problem is that "bad men obey their lusts as servants obey their masters," and because they cannot control their desires, they can never find contentment.[4]

Men's values, Diogenes insisted, had been corrupted. He pointed out, by way of illustration, that a statue, the only function of which is to please the eye, might cost three thousand drachmas, while a quart of barley flour, which when consumed can keep us alive, can be bought for only two copper coins.[5] He believed hunger to be the best appetizer, and because he waited until he was hungry or thirsty before he ate or drank, "he used to partake of a barley cake with greater pleasure than others did of the costliest of foods, and enjoyed a drink from a stream of running water more than others did their Thasian wine."[6] When asked about his lack of an abode, Diogenes would reply that he had access to the greatest houses in every city—to their temples and gymnasia, that is. And when asked what he had learned from philosophy, Diogenes replied, "To be prepared for every fortune."[7] This reply, as we shall see, anticipates one important theme of Stoicism.

The Cynics plied their trade not in a suburban setting, as Epicurus and Plato did, but on the streets of Athens, as Socrates had done. And like Socrates, the Cynics sought to instruct not only those who offered themselves as pupils but anyone at all, including those who were reluctant to be taught. Indeed, the Cynic Crates—who, as we have seen, was the Stoic philosopher Zeno's first philosophical teacher—wasn't content simply with badgering the people he encountered on the street; he also entered people's homes uninvited to admonish those within. For this habit, he became known as "the Door Opener."[8]

AFTER STUDYING WITH CRATES for a time, Zeno decided that he was more interested in theory than Crates was. He therefore came up with the idea of focusing not just on a philosophical lifestyle or a philosophical theory, but combining lifestyle with theory, the way Socrates had done.[9] The nineteenth-century German philosopher Arthur Schopenhauer summed up the relationship between Cynicism and Stoicism by observing that the Stoic philosophers proceeded from the Cynics "by changing the practical into the theoretical."[10]

Zeno therefore set out to learn philosophical theory. He went off to study with Stilpo, of the Megarian school. (Crates responded by physically trying to drag him away.) He also studied with Polemo at the Academy, and in around 300 BC, he started his own school of philosophy. In his teaching, he appears to have mixed the lifestyle advice of Crates with the theoretical philosophy of Polemo. (According to Polemo, Zeno did little more than give the doctrines of the Academy "a Phoenician make-up.")[11] Into this mix he incorporated the Megarian school's interest in logic and paradoxes.

Zeno's school of philosophy enjoyed immediate success.[12] His followers were initially called Zenonians, but because he was in the habit of giving his lectures in the Stoa Poikile, they subsequently became known as the Stoics—as, by the way, had been the poets who had formerly been in the habit of hanging out there.[13]

One thing that made Stoicism attractive was its abandonment of Cynic asceticism: The Stoics favored a lifestyle that, although simple, allowed creature comforts. The Stoics defended this abandonment by arguing that if they avoided the "good things," as the Cynics did, they thereby demonstrated that the things in question really were good—were things that, if they did not hide them from themselves, they would crave. The Stoics enjoyed whatever "good things" happened to be available, but even as they did so, they prepared themselves to give up the things in question.

ZENO'S PHILOSOPHY had ethical, physical, and logical components. Those who studied Stoicism under him started with logic, moved on to physics, and ended with ethics.[14]

Although the Stoics were not the first to do logic—Aristotle, for example, had done it before them, as had the Megarians—Stoic logic showed an unprecedented degree of sophistication. The Stoics' interest in logic is a natural consequence of their belief that man's distinguishing feature is his rationality. Logic is, after all, the study of the proper use of reasoning. The Stoics became experts on argument forms, such as "If A, then B; but

A, therefore B" or "Either A or B; but not A, therefore B." These argument forms, which are called *modus ponens* and *modus tollendo ponens*, respectively, are still used by logicians.

To understand the Stoics' interest in logic, it helps to remember that parents sent their children to schools of philosophy not just so they could learn how to live well but so they could sharpen their skills of persuasion. By teaching their students logic, the Stoics were helping them develop these skills: Students who knew logic could detect the fallacies committed by others and thereby prevail over them in arguments.

Physics was the second component of Zeno's Stoicism. Living, as they did, in a time without science, Zeno's students doubtless appreciated explanations of the world around them. And besides providing explanations of natural phenomena, as modern physics does, Stoic physics was concerned with what we would call theology. Zeno, for example, tried to explain such things as the existence and nature of the gods, why the gods created our universe and its inhabitants, the role the gods play in determining the outcome of events, and the proper relationship between people and the gods.

Ethics was the third and most important component of Zeno's Stoicism. The Stoic conception of ethics, readers should realize, differs from our modern conception. We think of ethics as the study of moral right and wrong. A modern-day ethicist might wonder, for example, whether abortion is morally permissible, and if so, under what circumstances. Stoic ethics, in contrast, is what is called eudaemonistic ethics, from the Greek *eu* meaning "good" and *daimon* meaning "spirit."

It is concerned not with moral right and wrong but with having a "good spirit," that is, with living a good, happy life or with what is sometimes called moral wisdom.[15] As the philosopher Lawrence C. Becker puts it, "Stoic ethics is a species of eudaimonism. Its central, organizing concern is about what we ought to do or be to live well—to flourish."[16] In the words of the historian Paul Veyne, "Stoicism is not so much an ethic as it is a paradoxical recipe for happiness."[17]

It is easy for modern readers to misconstrue what the Stoics had in mind by "a good life." Indeed, many readers will equate having a good life with making a good living—with, that is, having a high-paying job. The Stoics, however, thought it entirely possible for someone to have a bad life despite making a very good living. Suppose, for example, that he hates his high-paying job, or suppose that the job creates conflict within him by requiring him to do things he knows to be wrong.

What, then, must a person do to have what the Stoics would call a good life? Be virtuous! But again, "virtue" is a word that invites misunderstanding. Tell a modern reader that the Stoics advocate that she live in a virtuous manner, and she might roll her eyes; indeed, to this reader, nuns would be prime examples of virtuous individuals, and what makes them virtuous are their chastity, humility, and kindheartedness. Are the Stoics, then, advocating that we live like nuns?

In fact, this isn't at all what the Stoics have in mind when they talk about virtue. For the Stoics, a person's virtue does not depend, for example, on her sexual history. Instead, it depends on her excellence as a human being—on how well she performs the function for which humans were designed. In the same way that a "virtuous" (or excellent) hammer is one that performs well the function for which it was designed—namely, to drive nails—a virtuous individual is one who performs well the function for which humans were designed. To be virtuous, then, is to live as we were designed to live; it is to live, as Zeno put it, in accordance with nature.[18] The Stoics would add that if we do this, we will have a good life.

And for what function were people designed? To answer this question, the Stoics thought, we need only examine ourselves. On doing this, we will discover that we have certain instincts, as do all animals. We experience hunger; this is nature's way of getting us to nourish ourselves. We also experience lust; this is nature's way of getting us to reproduce. But we differ from other animals in one important respect: We have the ability to reason. From this we can conclude, Zeno would assert, that we were designed to be reasonable.

And if we use our reason, we will further conclude that we were designed to do certain things, that we have certain duties. Most significantly, since nature intended us to be social creatures, we have duties to our fellow men. We should, for example, honor our parents, be agreeable to our friends, and be concerned with the interests of our countrymen.[19] It was this sense of social duty that led the Stoic Cato to be an active player in Roman politics, even though doing so cost him his life.

Although, as I have said, the primary concern of the Stoics was with ethics—with living virtuously and thereby having a good life—they were also interested in logic and physics. By studying logic, they hoped to perform well one of the functions for which we were designed; namely, to behave in a rational manner. And by studying physics, they hoped to gain insight into the purpose for which we were designed. The Stoics came up with various metaphors to explain the relationship between the three components of their philosophy. They asserted, for example, that Stoic philosophy is like a fertile field, with "Logic being the encircling fence, Ethics the crop, Physics the soil."[20] This metaphor makes clear the central role played by ethics in their philosophy: Why worry about the soil and why build a fence unless a crop will result?

If we lived in perfect accordance with nature—if, that is, we were perfect in our practice of Stoicism—we would be what the Stoics refer to as a wise man or sage. A Stoic sage, according to Diogenes Laertius, is "free from vanity; for he is indifferent to good or evil report." He never feels grief, since he realizes that grief is an "irrational contraction of the soul." His conduct is exemplary. He doesn't let anything stop him from doing his duty. Although he drinks wine, he doesn't do so in order to get drunk. The Stoic sage is, in short, "godlike."[21]

Such godlikeness, the Stoics will be the first to admit, is exceedingly rare. For the Stoics, however, the near impossibility of becoming a sage is not a problem. They talk about sages primarily so they will have a model to guide them in their practice of Stoicism. The sage is a target for them to aim at, even though they will probably fail to hit it. The sage, in other words, is to Stoicism as Buddha is to Buddhism. Most Buddhists can never hope to become as enlightened as Buddha, but nevertheless, reflecting on Buddha's perfection can help them gain a degree of enlightenment.

CLEANTHES (331–232 BC) was a pupil in Zeno's Stoic school, and when Zeno died, he inherited leadership of the school. When Cleanthes grew old, though, he started losing students to other schools, and the future of Stoicism looked bleak. When he died, leadership of the Stoic school was passed on to his pupil Chrysippus (c. 282–206 BC), under whose leadership the school regained its former prominence.

After the death of Chrysippus, the Stoic school continued to prosper under a succession of leaders, including Panaetius of Rhodes, who is remembered in the annals of Stoicism not as an innovator but as an exporter of the philosophy. When Panaetius traveled to Rome in around 140 BC, he took Stoicism with him. He befriended Scipio Africanus and other Roman gentlemen, got them interested in philosophy, and thereby became the founder of Roman Stoicism.

After importing Stoicism, the Romans adapted the doctrine to suit their needs. For one thing, they showed less interest in logic and physics than the Greeks had. Indeed, by the time of Marcus Aurelius, the last of the great Roman Stoics, logic and physics had essentially been abandoned: In the *Meditations*, we find Marcus congratulating himself for not having wasted time studying these subjects.[22]

The Romans also made subtle changes in the Greek Stoics' ethical program. As we have seen, the primary ethical goal of the Greek Stoics was the attainment of virtue. The Roman Stoics retained this goal, but we find them also repeatedly advancing a second goal: the attainment of tranquility. And by tranquility they did not have in mind a zombie-like state. (To advocate *that* kind of tranquility, after all, would be a rejection of the rationality that the Stoics thought essential to virtuous living.) Rather, Stoic tranquility was a psychological state marked by the absence of negative emotions, such as grief, anger, and anxiety, and the presence of positive emotions, such as joy.

For the Roman Stoics, the goals of attaining tranquility and attaining virtue were connected, and for this reason, when they discuss virtue, they are likely to discuss tranquility as well. In particular, they are likely to point out that one benefit of attaining virtue is that we will thereupon experience tranquility. Thus, early in his *Discourses*, Epictetus advises us to pursue virtue but immediately reminds us that virtue "holds out the promise... to create happiness and calm and serenity" and that "progress toward virtue is progress toward each of these states of mind." Indeed, he goes so far as to identify serenity as the result at which virtue aims.[23]

Because the Roman Stoics spent so much time discussing tranquility (as a by-product of virtuous living), they create the impression that they were disinterested in virtue. Consider, for example, Epictetus's *Handbook*, also known as his *Manual* or *Encheiridion*. Arrian (one of Epictetus's students) compiled this work with the goal of providing second-century Roman audiences with an easily accessible introduction to Stoicism. Although the *Handbook* is filled with advice on what, according to Epictetus, we must do if we wish to gain and maintain tranquility, Arrian saw no need to mention virtue.

One last comment is in order on the connection for the Roman Stoics between the goal of attaining virtue and the goal of attaining tranquility. Besides asserting that the pursuit of virtue will bring us tranquility, I think the Roman Stoics would argue that the attainment of tranquility will help us pursue virtue. Someone who is not tranquil—someone, that is, who is distracted by negative emotions such as anger or grief—might find it difficult to do what his reason tells him to do: His emotions will triumph over his intellect. This person might therefore become confused about what things are really good, consequently might fail to pursue them, and might, as a result, fail to attain virtue. Thus, for the Roman Stoics, the pursuit of virtue and the pursuit of tranquility are components of a virtuous circle—indeed, a doubly virtuous circle: The pursuit of virtue results in a degree of tranquility, which in turn makes it easier for us to pursue virtue.

WHY DID THE ROMAN STOICS give the attainment of tranquility a more prominent role than their Greek predecessors did? Part of the answer to this question, I think, is that the Roman Stoics had less confidence than the Greeks in the power of pure reason to motivate people. The Greek Stoics thought that the best way to get people to pursue virtue was to make them understand what things were good: If a person understood what the truly good things were, he, being rational, would necessarily pursue them and thereby become virtuous. The Greek Stoics therefore saw little need to mention the beneficial by-products of the pursuit of virtue, including, most significantly, the attainment of tranquility.

The Roman Stoics, in contrast, apparently thought it wouldn't be obvious to their fellow Romans why they should pursue virtue. They also recognized that ordinary Romans would instinctively value tranquility and would consequently be receptive to strategies for attaining it. The Roman Stoics therefore seem to have concluded that by sugarcoating virtue with tranquility—more precisely, by pointing to the tranquility people would gain by pursuing virtue—they would make Stoic doctrines more attractive to ordinary Romans.

Furthermore, Stoic teachers such as Musonius Rufus and Epictetus had another reason for highlighting tranquility: By doing so, they made their school more attractive to potential students. In the ancient world, we should remember, schools of philosophy were in direct competition with each other. If a school taught a philosophy that people found attractive, it gained "market share," but if a school's philosophy fell out of favor with potential students, the school might have sunk into oblivion—which, as we have seen, almost happened to the Stoic school under Cleanthes.

To gain and retain students, schools were willing to be flexible in the philosophical doctrines they taught. It has been suggested, for example, that in the middle of the third century BC, the Academic and Stoic schools of philosophy, because they were losing students to the rival Epicurean school, decided to join into a philosophical alliance and modify their doctrines accordingly, with the common purpose of attracting students away from the Epicureans.[24] Along similar lines, it is conceivable that the Roman Stoics, by accentuating tranquility in their philosophy, might have been trying to attract students away from the Epicureans, who also dangled the prospect of tranquility before their students.

If it seems implausible that ancient philosophers would "bend" philosophical doctrines in an attempt to attract students, we should remember that this is precisely how many ancient schools of philosophy got started. For example, when Potamo of Alexandria decided to start a school of philosophy, he had a stroke of marketing genius: He decided that the best way to draw students was to cherry-pick from the philosophical doctrines of competing schools.[25] Those who joined his so-called Eclectic school could, he argued, gain the best that each of the competing schools had to offer. More to the point, we should remember that Zeno himself, to concoct Greek Stoicism, bent and blended the doctrines of (at least) three different philosophical schools: the Cynics, the Megarians, and the Academy.

By highlighting tranquility in their philosophy, the Stoics not only made it more attractive to ancient Romans but made it, I think, more attractive to modern individuals as well. It is unusual, after all, for modern individuals to have an interest in becoming more virtuous, in the ancient sense of the word. (We probably *should be* interested in becoming more virtuous, but the brutal truth of the matter is that most of us aren't.) Thus, tell someone that you possess and are willing to share with him an ancient strategy for attaining virtue, and you will likely be met with a yawn. Tell him that you possess and are willing to share an ancient strategy for attaining tranquility, though, and his ears are likely to perk up; in most cases, people don't need to be convinced of the value of tranquility. Indeed, if asked, he might go on at length about how his life has been blighted by tranquility-disrupting negative emotions.

It is for this reason that in the following pages I focus my attention on the Roman rather than the Greek Stoics, and it is for this reason that the primary focus of my examination of the Roman Stoics is not their advice on how to attain virtue but their advice on how to attain and maintain tranquility. Having said this, I should add that readers who follow Roman Stoic advice on attaining tranquility might thereby attain virtue as well. Should this happen, so much the better!

THREE

Roman Stoicism

THE MOST IMPORTANT of the Roman Stoics—and the Stoics from whom, I think, modern individuals have the most to gain—were Seneca, Musonius Rufus, Epictetus, and Marcus Aurelius.[1] The contributions these four made to Roman Stoicism were nicely complementary. Seneca was the best writer of the bunch, and his essays and letters to Lucilius form a quite accessible introduction to Roman Stoicism. Musonius is notable for his pragmatism: He offered detailed advice on how practicing Stoics should eat, what they should wear, how they should behave toward their parents, and even how they should conduct their sex life. Epictetus's specialty was analysis: He explained, among other things, why practicing Stoicism can bring us tranquility. Finally, in Marcus's *Meditations*, written as a kind of diary, we are privy to the thoughts of a practicing Stoic: We watch as he searches for Stoic solutions to the problems of daily life as well as the problems he encountered as emperor of Rome.

LUCIUS ANNAEUS SENECA, also known as Seneca the Younger, was born sometime between 4 and 1 BC in Corduba, Spain. Although we have more of his philosophical writings than we have of any other Stoic, he wasn't the most prolific of the Stoics. (Chrysippus was remarkably prolific, but his works have not survived.) Nor was he particularly original. Nevertheless, his Stoic writings are quite wonderful. His essays and letters are full of insight into the human condition. In these writings, Seneca talks about the things that typically make people unhappy—such as grief, anger, old age, and social anxieties—and about what we can do to make our life not just tolerable but joyful.

Seneca, like the other Roman Stoics I will discuss, was not stoically resigned to life; he was instead an active participant in it. And like these other Stoics, he was a complex individual. Indeed, even if Seneca had never written a word of philosophy, he would have made it into the history books for three other reasons. He would be remembered as a successful playwright. He would be remembered for his financial undertakings: He appears to have been a prototypical investment banker who became enormously wealthy in large part because of his financial acumen. And finally, he would be remembered for the role he played in the politics of first-century Rome; besides being a senator, he was a tutor and subsequently a principal advisor to Emperor Nero.

Seneca's involvement with the imperial court got him into trouble. When Claudius became emperor, he condemned Seneca to death for (allegedly) committing adultery with Claudius's niece Julia Livilla. The sentence was commuted to banishment and confiscation of all property, and so in the year 41, Seneca, then in his forties, was sent off to the "barren and thorny rock" that we call Corsica.[2] During this time, he read, wrote, made a study of the island—and presumably practiced his Stoicism.

In 49, Agrippina married Claudius and talked him into recalling Seneca from banishment so he could act as tutor for her son Nero, who was then eleven or twelve. Thus it was that after eight years of banishment, Seneca returned to Rome. Again ensconced in Roman society, he became, we are told, "the most renowned citizen of his time: the greatest living writer in prose and verse, the greatest name in literature since the golden age at the beginning of the century, and the favorite of the imperious empress."[3] Seneca was as surprised as anyone by his success in life: "Is it I," he asked, "born in the station of a simple knight and a provincial, who am numbered with the magnates of the realm?"[4]

When Nero became emperor, Seneca was promoted to the job of counselor. Indeed, he and Sextus Afranius Burrus, the prefect of the Praetorian guard, became Nero's inner circle. At first, Seneca and Burrus did a good job of keeping Nero's licentious tendencies in check, and the Roman empire enjoyed five years of good government. Seneca also flourished during this period: He became incredibly wealthy. This wealth has given rise to the charge that Seneca was a hypocrite, that he advocated Stoic restraint while living a life of extreme affluence. Readers need to keep in mind, though, that unlike Cynicism, Stoicism does not require its adherents to adopt an ascetic lifestyle. To the contrary, the Stoics thought there is nothing wrong with enjoying the good things life has to offer, as long as we are careful in the manner in which we enjoy them. In particular, we must be ready to give up the good things without regret if our circumstances should change.

After the death of Agrippina in 59—Nero had her killed—Nero began to chafe at the guidance of Seneca and Burrus. In 62, Burrus died, either from illness or as the result of being poisoned. Seneca realized that his days at court were numbered, and he attempted to retire from politics, pleading ill health and old age. Nero finally agreed to let him retire, but the retirement was short-lived. The counselors who replaced Seneca convinced Nero that Seneca had been involved in a conspiracy against him, and in 65, Nero ordered Seneca's death.

When the friends who were present at his execution wept over his fate, Seneca chastised them. What, he asked, had become of their Stoicism? He then embraced his wife. The arteries in his arms were slit, but because of age and infirmity, he bled slowly, so the arteries of his legs and knees were also severed. Still he did not die. He asked a friend to bring poison, which he drank but without fatal consequences. He was then carried into a bath, the steam of which suffocated him.[5]

Seneca's essay "On the Happy Life" was written for his elder brother Gallio—the same Gallio, by the way, as is mentioned in Acts 18:12–16 of the New Testament for his refusal to try St. Paul in Corinth. In this essay, Seneca explains how best to pursue tranquility. Basically, we need to use our reasoning ability to drive away "all that excites or affrights us." If we can do this, there will ensue "unbroken tranquility and enduring freedom," and we will experience "a boundless joy that is firm and unalterable." Indeed, he claims (as we have seen) that someone who practices Stoic principles "must, whether he wills or not, necessarily be attended by constant cheerfulness and a joy that is deep and issues from deep within, since he finds delight in his own resources, and desires no joys greater than his inner joys." Furthermore, compared to these joys, pleasures of the flesh are "paltry and trivial and fleeting."[6]

Elsewhere, we find Seneca telling his friend Lucilius that if he wishes to practice Stoicism, he will have to make it his business to "learn how to feel joy." He adds that one of the reasons he wants Lucilius to practice Stoicism is because he does not wish Lucilius "ever to be deprived of gladness."[7] Those who are accustomed to thinking of the Stoics as a glum bunch might be surprised by such comments, but these and other remarks make it clear that the phrase "joyful Stoic" is not an oxymoron.[8]

GAIUS MUSONIUS RUFUS, the least well-known of the four great Roman Stoics, was born in around 30 AD. Because of his family's standing, Musonius could have gone far in politics, but instead he started a school of philosophy. We know little about Musonius in part because he, like Socrates, didn't bother to write down his philosophical thoughts. Fortunately, Musonius had a pupil, Lucius, who took notes during lectures. In these notes, Lucius often begins by talking about what "he," Musonius, said in response to some question. It therefore seems likely that the lectures Musonius gave in his school weren't monologues; rather, he carried on a two-way Socratic conversation with his students. It is also likely that Musonius used these conversations both to instruct his students and to assess their philosophical progress.

Musonius was at the height of his fame and influence at the time of Emperor Nero. He apparently aligned himself with Nero's enemies—or rather, with people Nero took to be enemies. Nero had him imprisoned and subsequently banished him. (According to Tacitus, the real reason Nero banished Musonius was his envy of Musonius's fame as a philosopher.)[9]

Musonius's banishment was particularly brutal, as banishments go. In 65 AD, he was sent to the island of Gyara (or Gyaros) in the Cyclades, a group of islands in the Aegean Sea southeast of Greece. The island was desolate, bleak, rocky, and nearly waterless. The Greek geographer and historian Strabo describes it as "worthless,"[10] and Seneca mentions it in his list of the worst places on which to be exiled.[11] (This island, interestingly, was still being used as a place of banishment in the twentieth century; it is where the Greek generals sent their political opponents in the early 1970s.)[12]

On being exiled, though, Musonius did not fall into despair. He instead took an interest in Gyara and its inhabitants, mostly fishermen. He soon discovered a spring on the island and thereby made it more habitable. And whatever loneliness he might have experienced there was relieved by an influx of philosophical disciples.

After Nero's death, Musonius returned to Rome. Not long thereafter, Emperor Vespasian banished all philosophers from Rome but seems to have exempted Musonius.[13] Later, though, Musonius was again exiled. He died in around 100 AD.

ACCORDING TO MUSONIUS, we should study philosophy, since how otherwise could we hope to live well?[14] Furthermore, he says that studying philosophy should affect us personally and profoundly; indeed, when a philosopher lectures, his words should make those in his audience shudder and feel ashamed, and when he is done speaking, they should, rather than applauding him, have been reduced to silence.[15] According to Epictetus, Musonius himself apparently possessed the ability to reduce his audiences to silence, for when he spoke, his listeners felt as if he had discovered and laid before them those traits of which they were secretly ashamed.[16]

Musonius also thought the practice of philosophy required one not to withdraw from the world, as the Epicureans advised, but to be a vigorous participant in public affairs. Musonius therefore taught his students how to retain their Stoic tranquility while participating.

Besides thinking that philosophy should be practical, Musonius thought the study of philosophy should be universal. Indeed, he argued that both women and men "have received from the gods the same reasoning power." Consequently, women, like men, can benefit from education and the study of philosophy.[17] Because he held these views when he did, Musonius has been applauded by modern feminists.

Epictetus, the most famous of Musonius's students, was born into slavery sometime between 50 and 60 AD. He was subsequently acquired by Epaphroditus, secretary to Emperor Nero and later to Domitian. This must have given Epictetus exposure to the imperial court.[18] It also meant that Epictetus, although a slave, was a "white-collar" slave. Romans valued those slaves who showed signs of intelligence and initiative.

They trained them so they could make the best use of their gifts, and they subsequently put their slaves to work as teachers, counselors, and administrators.

Epictetus appears to have developed an interest in philosophy early in life. As a youth, we are told, he went around asking people whether their souls were healthy. If they ignored him, he persisted in questioning them until they threatened to beat him.[19] This behavior, to be sure, suggests that Epictetus had initially been drawn to Cynicism rather than Stoicism; the Cynics, as we have seen, proselytized in a manner that the Stoics did not. Even in his mature philosophy, we can find evidence of his respect for the Cynics.

After the death of Nero, Epictetus apparently gained freedom. He started a school of philosophy but was subsequently banished, along with all the other philosophers in Rome, by Domitian. He moved his school to Nicopolis, in what is now western Greece. After the assassination of Domitian, Stoicism regained its respectability and even became fashionable among Romans. Epictetus was by then the leading Stoic teacher. He could have moved back to Rome but chose instead to remain in Nicopolis. His school, despite its location, attracted students from around the Roman Empire.

According to the classicist Anthony A. Long, Epictetus expected his pupils to satisfy two conditions: "(1) wanting to benefit from philosophy and (2) understanding what a commitment to philosophy entails."[20] Epictetus knew that his words would be wasted on students who didn't yet recognize their own inadequacies or who weren't willing to take the steps necessary to deal with them. He describes his ideal pupil as someone who will be satisfied if he can "live untrammelled and untroubled," as someone who seeks to be "tranquil and free from turmoil."[21]

What these students could expect at one of Epictetus's lectures was not a one-way communication, from Epictetus to his students, about esoteric philosophical theories. To the contrary, he wanted his students to take his lectures personally. He wanted his remarks to strike close to home. He therefore told his students that a Stoic school should be like a physician's consulting room and that patients should leave feeling bad rather than feeling good,[22] the idea being that any treatment likely to cure a patient is also likely to cause him discomfort. His lectures were therefore, according to Long, "dialectical lessons—invitations to his audience to examine themselves."[23]

According to Epictetus, the primary concern of philosophy should be the art of living: Just as wood is the medium of the carpenter and bronze is the medium of the sculptor, your life is the medium on which you practice the art of living.[24] Furthermore, much as a master carpenter teaches an apprentice by showing him techniques that can be used to build things out of wood, Epictetus taught his students the art of life by showing them techniques that could be used to make something of their life. The techniques in question were quite practical and completely applicable to students' everyday lives. He taught them, among other things, how to respond to insults, how to deal with incompetent servants, how to deal with an angry brother, how to deal with the loss of a loved one, and how to deal with exile. If they could master these techniques, Epictetus promised, they would experience a life that was filled with purpose and dignity, and more important, they would attain tranquility. Furthermore, they would retain their dignity and tranquility regardless of the hardships life might subsequently inflict on them.

THOSE WHO READ Epictetus cannot help but notice his frequent mention of religion. Indeed, Zeus is mentioned more than anyone except Socrates. To better understand the role Zeus plays in Stoicism, consider the situation of a prospective pupil at Epictetus's school. If this person asked what one must do to practice Stoicism, Epictetus might describe the various techniques Stoics advocate. If he asked why he should practice these techniques, Epictetus might reply that doing so will enable him to attain tranquility.

So far, so good, but suppose this student had looked at other schools of philosophy and wondered why Epictetus's school was better than they were. Suppose, more precisely, he asked Epictetus what reason there was to think that the techniques advocated by the Stoics would enable him to attain tranquility. In his response to this question, Epictetus would start talking about Zeus.

We were, he would tell the student, created by Zeus. His student was likely to accept this claim, inasmuch as atheism appears to have been a rarity in ancient Rome. (Then again, what Epictetus had in mind when he referred to Zeus is probably different from what most Romans had in mind. In particular, it is possible that Epictetus identified Zeus with Nature.)[25] Epictetus would go on to explain that Zeus made us different from other animals in one important respect: We are rational, as are the gods. We are therefore a curious hybrid, half-animal and half-god.

Zeus, as it so happens, is a thoughtful, kind, and loving god, and when he created us, he had our best interests in mind. But sadly, he appears not to have been omnipotent, so in creating us, there were limits to what he could do. In his *Discourses*, Epictetus imagines having a conversation with Zeus, in which Zeus explains his predicament in the following terms: "Epictetus, had it been possible I should have made both this paltry body and this small estate of thine free and unhampered. . . . Yet since I could not give thee this, we have given thee a certain portion of ourself, this faculty of choice and refusal, of desire and aversion." He adds that if Epictetus learns to make proper use of this faculty, he will never feel frustrated or dissatisfied.[26] He will, in other words, retain his tranquility—and even experience joy—despite the blows Fortune might deal him.

Elsewhere in the *Discourses*, Epictetus suggests that even if Zeus could have made us "free and unhampered," he would have chosen not to do so. Epictetus presents us with the image of Zeus as an athletic coach: "It is difficulties that show what men are. Consequently, when a difficulty befalls, remember that God, like a physical trainer, has matched you with a rugged young man." Why do this? To toughen and strengthen you, so you can become "an Olympic victor"[27]—in other words, so you can have the best life possible. Seneca, by the way, argued along similar lines: God, he said, "does not make a spoiled pet of a good man; he tests him, hardens him, and fits him for his own service." In particular, the adversities we experience count as "mere training," and "those things which we all shudder and tremble at are for the good of the persons themselves to whom they come."[28]

Epictetus would then tell the prospective student that if he wishes to have a good life, he must consider his nature and the purpose for which God created him and live accordingly; he must, as Zeno put it, live in accordance with nature. The person who does this won't simply pursue pleasure, as an animal might; instead, he will use his reasoning ability to reflect on the human condition. He will then discover the reason we were created and the role we play in the cosmic scheme. He will realize that to have a good life, he needs to perform well the function of a human being, the function Zeus designed him to fulfill. He will therefore pursue virtue, in the ancient sense of the word, meaning that he will strive to become an excellent human being. He will also come to realize that if he lives in accordance with nature, he will be rewarded with the tranquility that Zeus promised us.

This explanation might have satisfied people in Epictetus's time, but it is likely to be off-putting to modern individuals, almost none of whom believe in the existence of Zeus, and many of whom don't believe we were created by a divine being who wanted what was best for us. Many readers will therefore, at this point, be thinking, "If I have to believe in Zeus and divine creation to practice Stoicism, then Stoicism is for me a nonstarter." Readers should therefore realize that it is entirely possible to practice Stoicism—and in particular, to employ Stoic strategies for attaining tranquility—without believing in Zeus or, for that matter, in divine creation. In chapter 20 I will have more to say about how this can be done.

"BEGIN EACH DAY by telling yourself: Today I shall be meeting with interference, ingratitude, insolence, disloyalty, ill-will, and selfishness—all of them due to the offenders' ignorance of what is good or evil."[29] These words were written not by a slave like Epictetus, whom we would naturally expect to encounter insolence and ill will; they were written by the person who was at the time the most powerful man in the world: Marcus Aurelius, emperor of Rome.

Because he was someone important, we know more about Marcus than about any of the other Roman Stoics. We also have an unusual degree of insight into his inner thoughts, thanks to the correspondence he carried on with his tutor Cornelius Fronto and thanks, also, to his *Meditations*, in which he reflects on life and his response to it.

Marcus was born in 121. He appears to have taken an interest in philosophy at an early age. One biographer describes him as a "solemn child" and relates that "as soon as he passed beyond the age when children are brought up under the care of nurses, he was handed over to advanced instructors and attained to a knowledge of philosophy."[30] At age twelve Marcus was taught by the painter and philosopher Diognetus, and he started experimenting with what sounds like Cynicism: He wore crude clothing and started sleeping on the ground.[31] His mother subsequently talked him into sleeping instead on a couch strewn with skins.[32]

As a teenager, Marcus studied with the Stoic philosopher Apollonius of Chalcedon. According to Marcus, it was Apollonius who impressed on him the need to be decisive and reasonable, taught him how to combine days full of intense activity with periods of relaxation, and taught him how, "with the same unaltered composure," to withstand sickness and pain—and in particular, Marcus notes, how to withstand the mental anguish he later experienced on losing a son. Another important influence on Marcus was Quintus Junius Rusticus, who, significantly, lent Marcus a copy of Epictetus's *Discourses.*[33] Epictetus subsequently became the single most important influence on Marcus.

Like Epictetus, Marcus was far more interested in Stoic ethics—in, that is, its philosophy of life—than in Stoic physics or logic. Indeed, in the *Meditations* he asserts that it is possible to achieve "freedom, self-respect, unselfishness, and obedience to the will of God" even though we have not mastered logic and physics.[34]

When Marcus was sixteen, Emperor Hadrian adopted Marcus's maternal uncle, Antoninus, who in turn adopted Marcus. (Marcus's father had died when Marcus was quite young.) From the time Marcus entered palace life, he had political power, and when Antoninus became emperor, Marcus served as virtual co-emperor. He didn't let this power go to his head, though; during the thirteen years he acted as Antoninus's chief lieutenant, he did not give people the impression that he longed for sole rule.[35] Furthermore, when Antoninus died and Marcus gained power, he appointed Lucius Verus joint emperor. This was the first time the Roman Empire had two emperors.[36]

As Roman emperors go, Marcus was exceptionally good. For one thing, he exercised great restraint in his use of power. No emperor, we are told, showed more respect to the Senate than Marcus did. He took care not to waste public money.[37] And although he didn't need to ask the Senate for permission to spend money, he routinely did so, and in one speech reminded them that the imperial palace in which he lived was not his but theirs.[38] To finance wars, he auctioned off imperial possessions, including statues, paintings, gold vases, and some of his wife's jewelry and clothing rather than raise taxes.[39]

Marcus, wrote the historian Edward Gibbon, was the last of the Five Good Emperors (the other four being Nerva, Trajan, Hadrian, and Antoninus) who ruled from 96–180 and brought about "the period in the history of the world during which the condition of the human race was most happy and prosperous."[40] This period, writes the nineteenth-century historian W. E. H. Lecky, "exhibits a uniformity of good government which no other despotic monarchy has equalled. Each of the five emperors who then reigned deserves to be placed among the best rulers who have ever lived."[41] Marcus is, in other words, a rare example of a philosopher king and perhaps the only example of a philosopher whom subjects wanted to have as their king.

LIKE THE OTHER Roman Stoics, Marcus didn't feel compelled to prove that tranquility was worth pursuing. To the contrary, he thought its value was obvious. And if someone had told Marcus that he thought mortal life could offer something better than "peace of mind," Marcus would not have attempted to persuade him otherwise; instead he would have advised this individual to turn to the thing in question "with your whole soul, and rejoice in the prize you have found."[42]

As an adult, Marcus was in great need of the tranquility Stoicism could offer. He was sick, possibly with an ulcer. His family life was a source of distress: His wife appears to have been unfaithful to him, and of the at least fourteen children she bore him, only six survived. Added to this were the stresses that came with ruling an empire. During his reign, there were numerous frontier uprisings, and Marcus often went personally to oversee campaigns against upstart tribes. His own officials—most notably, Avidius Cassius, the governor of Syria—rebelled against him.[43] His subordinates were insolent to him, which insolence he bore with "an unruffled temper."[44] Citizens told jokes at his expense and were not punished for doing so. During his reign, the empire also experienced plague, famine, and natural disasters such as the earthquake at Smyrna.[45] It is therefore with good reason that Marcus observed, in his *Meditations*, that "the art of living is more like wrestling than dancing."[46]

The Roman historian Cassius Dio summarized Marcus's plight as follows: "He did not meet with the good fortune that he deserved, for he was not strong in body and was involved in a multitude of troubles throughout practically his entire reign. But for my part, I admire him all the more for this very reason, that amid unusual and extraordinary difficulties he both survived himself and preserved the empire." Dio adds that from his first days as counselor to Antoninus to his last days as emperor, "he remained the same and did not change in the least."[47]

In 180, Marcus became seriously ill. He refused to eat or drink in an attempt to hurry death.[48] He died on March 17 of that year, at age fifty-eight. His death provoked an outburst of public grief. His soldiers in particular were deeply moved by his passing.[49]

In much the same way as Roman Emperor Constantine's conversion was a boon for Christianity, Marcus's Stoicism could have been a boon for that philosophy. Marcus, however, did not preach Stoicism. He did not lecture his fellow Romans on the benefits of practicing Stoicism; nor did he expose them to his philosophical writings. (The *Meditations* was a private journal—the original title was *To Himself*—and was published only after Marcus's death.) And although Marcus's interest in Stoicism seems to have led many Romans to self-identify as Stoics, presumably to curry favor with him,[50] it did not trigger a widespread interest in the philosophy. In a sense, then, Marcus represents the high-water mark of Stoicism.

That Stoicism has seen better days is obvious. Have you, in the course of your life, encountered even one practicing Stoic? It is tempting to attribute this decline in popularity to some flaw in the Stoic philosophy. I would like to suggest, though, that the unpopularity of Stoicism is due not to a defect in the philosophy but to other factors. For one thing, modern individuals rarely see the need to adopt a philosophy of life. They instead tend to spend their days working hard to be able to afford the latest consumer gadget, in the resolute belief that if only they buy enough stuff, they will have a life that is both meaningful and maximally fulfilling. Furthermore, even if it dawns on these individuals that there is more to life than shopping, they are unlikely, in their pursuit of a philosophy of life, to turn to Stoicism. Either they have no idea at all what they would have to do to practice Stoicism, or—more likely—they have the wrong idea.

Allow me, therefore, as part of my attempt to reanimate Stoicism, to explain, in the chapters that follow, what, exactly, is involved in the practice of this philosophy.

PART TWO

Stoic Psychological Techniques

FOUR

Negative Visualization

What's the Worst That Can Happen?

ANY THOUGHTFUL PERSON will periodically contemplate the bad things that can happen to him. The obvious reason for doing this is to prevent those things from happening. Someone might, for example, spend time thinking about ways people could break into his home so he can prevent them from doing so. Or he might spend time thinking about the diseases that might afflict him so he can take preventive measures.

But no matter how hard we try to prevent bad things from happening to us, some will happen anyway. Seneca therefore points to a second reason for contemplating the bad things that can happen to us. If we think about these things, we will lessen their impact on us when, despite our efforts at prevention, they happen: "He robs present ills of their power who has perceived their coming beforehand."[1] Misfortune weighs most heavily, he says, on those who "expect nothing but good fortune."[2] Epictetus echoes this advice: We should keep in mind that "all things everywhere are perishable." If we fail to recognize this and instead go around assuming that we will always be able to enjoy the things we value, we will likely find ourselves subject to considerable distress when the things we value are taken from us.[3]

Besides these reasons for contemplating the bad things that can happen to us, there is a third and arguably much more important reason. We humans are unhappy in large part because we are insatiable; after working hard to get what we want, we routinely lose interest in the object of our desire. Rather than feeling satisfied, we feel a bit bored, and in response to this boredom, we go on to form new, even grander desires.

The psychologists Shane Frederick and George Loewenstein have studied this phenomenon and given it a name: *hedonic adaptation*. To illustrate the adaptation process, they point to studies of lottery winners. Winning a lottery typically allows someone to live the life of his dreams. It turns out, though, that after an initial period of exhilaration, lottery winners end up about as happy as they previously were.[4] They start taking their new Ferrari and mansion for granted, the way they previously took their rusted-out pickup and cramped apartment for granted.

Another, less dramatic form of hedonic adaptation takes place when we make consumer purchases. Initially, we delight in the wide-screen television or fine leather handbag we bought. After a time, though, we come to despise them and find ourselves longing for an even wider-screen television or an even more extravagant handbag. Likewise, we experience hedonic adaptation in our career. We might once have dreamed of getting a certain job. We might consequently have worked hard in college and maybe graduate school as well to get on the proper career path, and on that path, we might have spent years making slow but steady progress toward our career goal. On finally landing the job of our dreams, we will be delighted, but before long we are likely to grow dissatisfied. We will grumble about our pay, our coworkers, and the failure of our boss to recognize our talents.

We also experience hedonic adaptation in our relationships. We meet the man or woman of our dreams, and after a tumultuous courtship succeed in marrying this person. We start out in a state of wedded bliss, but before long we find ourselves contemplating our spouse's flaws and, not long after that, fantasizing about starting a relationship with someone new.

As a result of the adaptation process, people find themselves on a satisfaction treadmill. They are unhappy when they detect an unfulfilled desire within them. They work hard to fulfill this desire, in the belief that on fulfilling it, they will gain satisfaction. The problem, though, is that once they fulfill a desire for something, they adapt to its presence in their life and as a result stop desiring it—or at any rate, don't find it as desirable as they once did. They end up just as dissatisfied as they were before fulfilling the desire.

One key to happiness, then, is to forestall the adaptation process: We need to take steps to prevent ourselves from taking for granted, once we get them, the things we worked so hard to get. And because we have probably failed to take such steps in the past, there are doubtless many things in our life to which we have adapted, things that we once dreamed of having but that we now take for granted, including, perhaps, our spouse, our children, our house, our car, and our job.

This means that besides finding a way to forestall the adaptation process, we need to find a way to reverse it. In other words, we need a technique for creating in ourselves a desire for the things we already have. Around the world and throughout the millennia, those who have thought carefully about the workings of desire have recognized this—that the easiest way for us to gain happiness is to learn how to want the things we already have. This advice is easy to state and is doubtless true; the trick is in putting it into practice in our life. How, after all, can we convince ourselves to want the things we already have?

THE STOICS THOUGHT they had an answer to this question. They recommended that we spend time imagining that we have lost the things we value—that our wife has left us, our car was stolen, or we lost our job. Doing this, the Stoics thought, will make us value our wife, our car, and our job more than we otherwise would. This technique—let us refer to it as *negative visualization*—was employed by the Stoics at least as far back as Chrysippus.[5] It is, I think, the single most valuable technique in the Stoics' psychological tool kit.

Seneca describes the negative visualization technique in the consolation he wrote to Marcia, a woman who, three years after the death of her son, was as grief-stricken as on the day she buried him. In this consolation, besides telling Marcia how to overcome her current grief, Seneca offers advice on how she can avoid falling victim to such grief in the future: What she needs to do is anticipate the events that can cause her to grieve. In particular, he says, she should remember that all we have is "on loan" from Fortune, which can reclaim it without our permission—indeed, without even advance notice. Thus, "we should love all of our dear ones . . . , but always with the thought that we have no promise that we may keep them forever—nay, no promise even that we may keep them for long."[6] While enjoying the companionship of loved ones, then, we should periodically stop to reflect on the possibility that this enjoyment will come to an end. If nothing else, our own death will end it.

Epictetus also advocates negative visualization. He counsels us, for example, when we kiss our child, to remember that she is mortal and not something we own—that she has been given to us "for the present, not inseparably nor for ever." His advice: In the very act of kissing the child, we should silently reflect on the possibility that she will die tomorrow.[7] In his *Meditations*, by the way, Marcus Aurelius approvingly quotes this advice.[8]

To see how imagining the death of a child can make us appreciate her, consider two fathers. The first takes Epictetus's advice to heart and periodically reflects on his child's mortality. The second refuses to entertain such gloomy thoughts. He instead assumes that his child will outlive him and that she will always be around for him to enjoy. The first father will almost certainly be more attentive and loving than the second. When he sees his daughter first thing in the morning, he will be glad that she is still a part of his life, and during the day he will take full advantage of opportunities to interact with her. The second father, in contrast, will be unlikely to experience a rush of delight on encountering his child in the morning. Indeed, he might not even look up from the newspaper to acknowledge her presence in the room. During the day, he will fail to take advantage of opportunities to interact with her in the belief that such interactions can be postponed until tomorrow. And when he finally does get around to interacting with her, the delight he derives from her company will not be as profound, one supposes, as the delight the first father experiences from such interactions.

Besides contemplating the death of relatives, the Stoics think we should spend time contemplating the loss of friends, to death, perhaps, or to a falling-out. Thus, Epictetus counsels that when we say good-bye to a friend, we should silently remind ourselves that this might be our final parting.[9] If we do this, we will be less likely to take our friends for granted, and as a result, we will probably derive far more pleasure from friendships than we otherwise would.

AMONG THE DEATHS we should contemplate, says Epictetus, is our own.[10] Along similar lines, Seneca advises his friend Lucilius to live each day as if it were his last. Indeed, Seneca takes things even further than this: We should live as if *this very moment* were our last.[11]

What does it mean to live each day as if it were our last? Some people assume that it means living wildly and engaging in all sorts of hedonistic excess. After all, if this day is our last, we will not pay any price for our riotous living. We can use drugs without fear of becoming addicted. We can likewise spend money with reckless abandon without having to worry about how we will pay the bills that will come to us tomorrow.

This, however, is not what the Stoics had in mind when they advise us to live as if today were our last day. To them, living as if each day were our last is simply an extension of the negative visualization technique: As we go about our day, we should periodically pause to reflect on the fact that we will not live forever and therefore that this day could be our last. Such reflection, rather than converting us into hedonists, will make us appreciate how wonderful it is that we are alive and have the opportunity to fill this day with activity. This in turn will make it less likely that we will squander our days. In other words, when the Stoics counsel us to live each day as if it were our last, their goal is not to change our activities but to change our state of mind as we carry out those activities. In particular, they don't want us to stop thinking about or planning for tomorrow; instead they want us, as we think about and plan for tomorrow, to remember to appreciate today.

Why, then, do the Stoics want us to contemplate our own death? Because doing so can dramatically enhance our enjoyment of life.

And besides contemplating the loss of our life, say the Stoics, we should contemplate the loss of our possessions. Most of us spend our idle moments thinking about the things we want but don't have. We would be much better off, Marcus says, to spend this time thinking of all the things we have and reflecting on how much we would miss them if they were not ours.[12] Along these lines, we should think about how we would feel if we lost our material possessions, including our house, car, clothing, pets, and bank balance; how we would feel if we lost our abilities, including our ability to speak, hear, walk, breathe, and swallow; and how we would feel if we lost our freedom.

Most of us are "living the dream"—living, that is, the dream we once had for ourselves. We might be married to the person we once dreamed of marrying, have the children and job we once dreamed of having, and own the car we once dreamed of buying. But thanks to hedonic adaptation, as soon as we find ourselves living the life of our dreams, we start taking that life for granted. Instead of spending our days enjoying our good fortune, we spend them forming and pursuing new, grander dreams for ourselves. As a result, we are never satisfied with our life. Negative visualization can help us avoid this fate.

BUT WHAT ABOUT those individuals who clearly aren't living the dream? What about a homeless person, for example? The important thing to realize is that Stoicism is by no means a rich person's philosophy. Those who enjoy a comfortable and affluent life can benefit from the practice of Stoicism, but so can those who are impoverished. In particular, although their poverty will prevent them from doing many things, it will not preclude them from practicing negative visualization.

Consider the person who has been reduced to possession of only a loincloth. His circumstances could be worse: He could lose the loincloth. He would do well, say the Stoics, to reflect on this possibility. Suppose, then, that he loses his loincloth. As long as he retains his health, his circumstances could again be worse—a point worth considering. And if his health deteriorates? He can be thankful that he is still alive.

It is hard to imagine a person who could not somehow be worse off. It is therefore hard to imagine a person who could not benefit from the practice of negative visualization. The claim is not that practicing it will make life as enjoyable for those who have nothing as it is for those who have much. The claim is merely that the practice of negative visualization—and more generally, the adoption of Stoicism—can take some of the sting out of having nothing and thereby make those who have nothing less miserable than they would otherwise be.

Along these lines, consider the plight of James Stockdale. (If the name rings a bell, it is probably because he was Ross Perot's running mate in the 1992 campaign for president of the United States.) A navy pilot, Stockdale was shot down over Vietnam in 1965 and held as a prisoner of war until 1973. During that time, he experienced poor health, primitive living conditions, and the brutality of his jailers. And yet he not only survived but emerged an unbroken man. How did he manage it? In large part, he says, by practicing Stoicism.[13]

One other thing to realize: Although they offer downtrodden people advice on how to make their existence more tolerable, the Stoics are by no means in favor of keeping these people in their state of subjugation. The Stoics would work to improve their external circumstances, but at the same time, the Stoics would suggest things they could do to alleviate their misery until those circumstances are improved.

One might imagine that the Stoics, because they go around contemplating worst-case scenarios, would tend toward pessimism. What we find, though, is that the regular practice of negative visualization has the effect of transforming Stoics into full-blown optimists. Allow me to explain.

We normally characterize an optimist as someone who sees his glass as being half full rather than half empty. For a Stoic, though, this degree of optimism would only be a starting point. After expressing his appreciation that his glass is half full rather than being completely empty, he will go on to express his delight in even having a glass: It could, after all, have been broken or stolen. And if he is atop his Stoic game, he might go on to comment about what an astonishing thing glass vessels are: They are cheap and fairly durable, impart no taste to what we put in them, and—miracle of miracles!—allow us to see what they contain. This might sound a bit silly, but to someone who has not lost his capacity for joy, the world is a wonderful place. To such a person, glasses are amazing; to everyone else, a glass is just a glass, and it is half empty to boot.

Hedonic adaptation has the power to extinguish our enjoyment of the world. Because of adaptation, we take our life and what we have for granted rather than delighting in them. Negative visualization, though, is a powerful antidote to hedonic adaptation. By consciously thinking about the loss of what we have, we can regain our appreciation of it, and with this regained appreciation we can revitalize our capacity for joy.

One reason children are capable of joy is because they take almost nothing for granted. To them, the world is wonderfully new and surprising. Not only that, but they aren't yet sure how the world works: Perhaps the things they have today will mysteriously vanish tomorrow. It is hard for them to take something for granted when they can't even count on its continued existence.

But as children grow older, they grow jaded. By the time they are teenagers, they are likely to take almost everything and everyone around them for granted. They might grumble about having to live the life they are living, in the home they happen to inhabit, with the parents and siblings they happen to have. And in a frightening number of cases, these children grow up to be adults who are not only unable to take delight in the world around them but seem proud of this inability. They will, at the drop of a hat, provide you with a long list of things about themselves and their life that they dislike and wish they could change, were it possible to do so, including their spouse, their children, their house, their job, their car, their age, their bank balance, their weight, the color of their hair, and the shape of their navel. Ask them what they appreciate about the world—ask them what, if anything, they are satisfied with—and they might, after some thought, reluctantly name a thing or two.

Sometimes a catastrophe blasts these people out of their jadedness. Suppose, for example, a tornado destroys their home. Such events are tragic, of course, but at the same time they potentially have a silver lining: Those who survive them might come to appreciate whatever they still possess. More generally, war, disease, and natural disasters are tragic, inasmuch as they take from us the things we value, but they also havc the power to transform those who experience them. Before, these individuals might have been sleepwalking through life; now they are joyously, thankfully alive—as alive as they have felt in decades. Before, they might have been indifferent to the world around them; now they are alert to the world's beauty.

Catastrophe-induced personal transformations have drawbacks, though. The first is that you can't count on being struck by a catastrophe. Indeed, many people have a catastrophe-free—and as a consequence, joyless—life. (Ironically, it is these people's misfortune to have a life that is blessedly free of misfortune.) A second drawback is that catastrophes that have the power to transform someone can also take his life. Consider, for example, a passenger on an airliner, the engines of which have just burst into flames. This turn of events is likely to cause the passenger to reassess his life, and as a result, he might finally gain some insight into what things in life are truly valuable and what things are not. Unfortunately, moments after this epiphany he might be dead.

The third drawback to catastrophe-induced transformations is that the states of joy they trigger tend to wear off. Those who come close to dying but subsequently revive typically regain their zest for living. They might, for example, feel motivated to contemplate the sunsets they had previously ignored or to engage in heartfelt conversations with the spouse they had previously taken for granted. They do this for a time, but then, in all too many cases, apathy returns: They might ignore the gorgeous sunset that is blazing outside their window in order to complain bitterly to their spouse that there is nothing worth watching on television.

Negative visualization does not have these drawbacks. We don't have to wait to engage in negative visualization the way we have to wait to be struck by a catastrophe. Being struck by a catastrophe can easily kill us; engaging in negative visualization can't. And because negative visualization can be done repeatedly, its beneficial effects, unlike those of a catastrophe, can last indefinitely. Negative visualization is therefore a wonderful way to regain our appreciation of life and with it our capacity for joy.

The Stoics are not alone in harnessing the power of negative visualization. Consider, for example, those individuals who say grace before a meal. Some presumably say it because they are simply in the habit of doing so. Others might say it because they fear that God will punish them if they don't. But understood properly, saying grace—and for that matter, offering any prayer of thanks—is a form of negative visualization. Before eating a meal, those saying grace pause for a moment to reflect on the fact that this food might not have been available to them, in which case they would have gone hungry. And even if the food were available, they might not have been able to share it with the people now at their dinner table. Said with these thoughts in mind, grace has the ability to transform an ordinary meal into a cause for celebration.

Some people don't need the Stoics or a priest to tell them that the key to a cheerful disposition is periodically to entertain negative thoughts; they figured it out on their own. In the course of my life, I have met many such people. They analyze their circumstances not in terms of what they are lacking but in terms of how much they have and how much they would miss it were they to lose it. Many of them have been quite unlucky, objectively speaking, in their life; nevertheless, they will tell you at length how lucky they are—to be alive, to be able to walk, to be living where they live, and so forth. It is instructive to compare these people with those who, objectively speaking, "have it all," but who, because they appreciate none of what they have, are utterly miserable.

Earlier I mentioned that there are people who seem proud of their inability to take delight in the world around them.

They have somehow gotten the idea that by refusing to take delight in the world, they are demonstrating their emotional maturity: To take delight in things, they think, is childish. Or maybe they have decided that it is fashionable to refuse to take delight in the world, the way it is fashionable to refuse to wear white after Labor Day, and they feel compelled to obey the dictates of fashion. To refuse to take delight in the world, in other words, is evidence of sophistication.

If you ask these malcontents for their opinion of the cheerful people just described—or even worse, of those Stoic optimists who go on at length about what a wonderful thing glass is—they are likely to respond with disparaging remarks: "Such people are clearly fools. They shouldn't be satisfied with so little. They should want more and not rest content until they get it." I would argue, though, that what is really foolish is to spend your life in a state of self-induced dissatisfaction when satisfaction lies within your grasp, if only you will change your mental outlook. To be able to be satisfied with little is not a failing, it is a blessing—if, at any rate, what you seek is satisfaction. And if you seek something other than satisfaction, I would inquire (with astonishment) into what it is that you find more desirable than satisfaction. What, I would ask, could possibly be worth sacrificing satisfaction in order to obtain?

If we have an active imagination, it will be easy for us to engage in negative visualization; it will be easy for us to imagine, for example, that our house has burned to the ground, our boss has fired us, or we have gone blind. If we have trouble imagining such things, though, we can practice negative visualization by paying attention to the bad things that happen to other people and reflecting on the fact that these things might instead have happened to us.[14] Alternatively, we can do some historical research to see how our ancestors lived. We will quickly discover that we are living in what to them would have been a dream world—that we tend to take for granted things that our ancestors had to live without, including antibiotics, air conditioning, toilet paper(!), cell phones, television, windows, eyeglasses, and fresh fruit in January. Upon coming to this realization, we can breathe a sigh of relief that we aren't our ancestors, the way our descendants will presumably someday breathe a sigh of relief that they aren't us!

The negative visualization technique, by the way, can also be used in reverse: Besides imagining that the bad things that happened to others happen to us, we can imagine that the bad things that happen to us happened instead to others. In his *Handbook*, Epictetus advocates this sort of "projective visualization." Suppose, he says, that our servant breaks a cup.[15] We are likely to get angry and have our tranquility disrupted by the incident. One way to avert this anger is to think about how we would feel if the incident had happened to someone else instead. If we were at someone's house and his servant broke a cup, we would be unlikely to get angry; indeed, we might try to calm our host by saying "It's just a cup; these things happen." Engaging in projective visualization, Epictetus believes, will make us appreciate the relative insignificance of the bad things that happen to us and will therefore prevent them from disrupting our tranquility.

AT THIS POINT, a non-Stoic might raise the following objection. The Stoics, as we have seen, advise us to pursue tranquility, and as part of their strategy for attaining it they advise us to engage in negative visualization. But isn't this contradictory advice? Suppose, for example, that a Stoic is invited to a picnic. While the other picnickers are enjoying themselves, the Stoic will sit there, quietly contemplating ways the picnic could be ruined: "Maybe the potato salad is spoiled, and people will get food poisoning. Maybe someone will break an ankle playing softball. Maybe there will be a violent thunderstorm that will scatter the picnickers. Maybe I will be struck by lightning and die." This sounds like no fun at all. But more to the point, it seems unlikely that a Stoic will gain tranquility as a result of entertaining such thoughts. To the contrary, he is likely to end up glum and anxiety-ridden.

In response to this objection, let me point out that it is a mistake to think Stoics will spend *all* their time contemplating potential catastrophes. It is instead something they will do periodically: A few times each day or a few times each week a Stoic will pause in his enjoyment of life to think about how all this, all these things he enjoys, could be taken from him.

Furthermore, there is a difference between *contemplating* something bad happening and *worrying about* it. Contemplation is an intellectual exercise, and it is possible for us to conduct such exercises without its affecting our emotions. It is possible, for example, for a meteorologist to spend her days contemplating tornadoes without subsequently living in dread of being killed by one. In similar fashion, it is possible for a Stoic to contemplate bad things that can happen without becoming anxiety-ridden as a result.

Finally, negative visualization, rather than making people glum, will increase the extent to which they enjoy the world around them, inasmuch as it will prevent them from taking that world for granted. Despite—or rather, because of—his (occasional) gloomy thoughts, the Stoic will likely enjoy the picnic far more than the other picnickers who refuse to entertain similarly gloomy thoughts; he will take delight in being part of an event that, he fully realizes, might not have taken place.

THE CRITIC OF STOICISM might now raise another concern. If you don't appreciate something, you won't mind losing it. But thanks to their ongoing practice of negative visualization, the Stoics will be remarkably appreciative of the people and things around them. Haven't they thereby set themselves up for heartache? Won't they be deeply pained when life snatches these people and things away, as it sometimes surely will?

Consider, by way of illustration, the two fathers mentioned earlier. The first father periodically contemplates the loss of his child and therefore does not take her for granted; to the contrary, he appreciates her very much. The second father assumes that his child will always be there for him and therefore takes her for granted. It might be suggested that because the second father does not appreciate his child, he will respond to her death with a shrug of his shoulders, whereas the first father, because he deeply appreciates his child, has set himself up for heartache if she dies.

Stoics, I think, would respond to this criticism by pointing out that the second father almost certainly will grieve the loss of his child: He will be full of regret for having taken her for granted.

In particular, he is likely to be racked with "if only" thoughts: "If only I had spent more time playing with her! If only I had told her more bedtime stories! If only I had gone to her violin recitals instead of going golfing!" The first father, however, will not have similar regrets; because he appreciated his daughter he will have taken full advantage of opportunities to interact with her.

Make no mistake: The first father *will* grieve the death of his child. As we shall see, the Stoics think periodic episodes of grief are part of the human condition. But at least this father can take consolation in the knowledge that he spent well what little time he had with his child. The second father will have no such consolation and as a result might find that his feelings of grief are compounded by feelings of guilt. It is the second father, I think, who has set himself up for heartache.

The Stoics would also respond to the above criticism by observing that at the same time as the practice of negative visualization is helping us appreciate the world, it is preparing us for changes in that world. To practice negative visualization, after all, is to contemplate the impermanence of the world around us. Thus, a father who practices negative visualization, if he does it correctly, will come away with two conclusions: He is lucky to have a child, and because he cannot be certain of her continued presence in his life, he should be prepared to lose her.

This is why Marcus, immediately after advising readers to spend time thinking about how much they would miss their possessions if these possessions were lost, warns them to "beware lest delight in them leads you to cherish them so dearly that their loss would destroy your peace of mind."[16] Along similar lines, Seneca, after advising us to enjoy life, cautions us not to develop "over-much love" for the things we enjoy. To the contrary, we must take care to be "the user, but not the slave, of the gifts of Fortune."[17]

Negative visualization, in other words, teaches us to embrace whatever life we happen to be living and to extract every bit of delight we can from it. But it simultaneously teaches us to prepare ourselves for changes that will deprive us of the things that delight us. It teaches us, in other words, to enjoy what we have without clinging to it. This in turn means that by practicing negative visualization, we can not only increase our chances of experiencing joy but increase the chance that the joy we experience will be durable, that it will survive changes in our circumstances. Thus, by practicing negative visualization, we can hope to gain what Seneca took to be a primary benefit of Stoicism, namely, "a boundless joy that is firm and unalterable."[18]

I MENTIONED IN THE INTRODUCTION that some of the things that attracted me to Buddhism could also be found in Stoicism. Like Buddhists, Stoics advise us to contemplate the world's impermanence. "All things human," Seneca reminds us, "are short-lived and perishable."[19] Marcus likewise reminds us that the things we treasure are like the leaves on a tree, ready to drop when a breeze blows. He also argues that the "flux and change" of the world around us are not an accident but an essential part of our universe.[20]

We need to keep firmly in mind that everything we value and the people we love will someday be lost to us. If nothing else, our own death will deprive us of them. More generally, we should keep in mind that any human activity that cannot be carried on indefinitely must have a final occurrence. There will be—or already has been!—a last time in your life that you brush your teeth, cut your hair, drive a car, mow the lawn, or play hopscotch. There will be a last time you hear the sound of snow falling, watch the moon rise, smell popcorn, feel the warmth of a child falling asleep in your arms, or make love. You will someday eat your last meal, and soon thereafter you will take your last breath.

Sometimes the world gives us advance notice that we are about to do something for the last time. We might, for example, eat at a favorite restaurant the night before it is scheduled to close, orwe might kiss a lover who is forced by circumstances to move to a distant part of the globe, presumably forever. Previously, when we thought we could repeat them at will, a meal at this restaurant or a kiss shared with our lover might have been unremarkable. But now that we know they cannot be repeated, they will likely become extraordinary events: The meal will be the best we ever had at the restaurant, and the parting kiss will be one of the most intensely bittersweet experiences life has to offer.

By contemplating the impermanence of everything in the world, we are forced to recognize that every time we do something could be the last time we do it, and this recognition can invest the things we do with a significance and intensity that would otherwise be absent. We will no longer sleepwalk through our life. Some people, I realize, will find it depressing or even morbid to contemplate impermanence. I am nevertheless convinced that the only way we can be truly alive is if we make it our business periodically to entertain such thoughts.

FIVE

The Dichotomy of Control

On Becoming Invincible

Our most important choice in life, according to Epictetus, is whether to concern ourselves with things external to us or things internal. Most people choose the former because they think harms and benefits come from outside themselves. According to Epictetus, though, a philosopher—by which he means someone who has an understanding of Stoic philosophy—will do just the opposite. He will look "for all benefit and harm to come from himself."[1] In particular, he will give up the rewards the external world has to offer in order to gain "tranquility, freedom, and calm."[2]

In offering this advice, Epictetus is turning the normal logic of desire fulfillment on its head. If you ask most people how to gain contentment, they will tell you that you must work to get it: You must devise strategies by which to fulfill your desires and then implement those strategies. But as Epictetus points out, "It is impossible that happiness, and yearning for what is not present, should ever be united."[3] A better strategy for getting what you want, he says, is to make it your goal to want only those things that are easy to obtain—and ideally to want only those things that you can be certain of obtaining.

While most people seek to gain contentment by changing the world around them, Epictetus advises us to gain contentment by changing ourselves—more precisely, by changing our desires. And he is not alone in giving this advice; indeed, it is the advice offered by virtually every philosopher and religious thinker who has reflected on human desire and the causes of human dissatisfaction.[4] They agree that if what you seek is contentment, it is better and easier to change yourself and what you want than it is to change the world around you.

Your primary desire, says Epictetus, should be your desire not to be frustrated by forming desires you won't be able to fulfill. Your other desires should conform to this desire, and if they don't, you should do your best to extinguish them. If you succeed in doing this, you will no longer experience anxiety about whether or not you will get what you want; nor will you experience disappointment on not getting what you want. Indeed, says Epictetus, you will become invincible: If you refuse to enter contests that you are capable of losing, you will never lose a contest.[5]

EPICTETUS'S *HANDBOOK* OPENS, somewhat famously, with the following assertion: "Some things are up to us and some are not up to us." He offers our opinions, impulses, desires, and aversions as examples of things that are up to us, and our possessions and reputation as examples of things that aren't.[6] From this assertion it follows that we are faced with a choice in the desires we form: We can want things that are up to us, or we can want things that are not up to us.

If we want things that are not up to us, though, we will sometimes fail to get what we want, and when this happens, we will "meet misfortune" and feel "thwarted, miserable, and upset."[7] In particular, Epictetus says, it is foolish for us to want friends and relatives to live forever, since these are things that aren't up to us.[8]

Suppose we get lucky, and after wanting something that is not up to us, we succeed in getting it. In this case, we will not end up feeling "thwarted, miserable, and upset," but during the time we wanted the thing that is not up to us, we probably experienced a degree of anxiety: Since the thing is not up to us, there was a chance that we wouldn't get it, and this probably worried us. Thus, wanting things that are not up to us will disrupt our tranquility, even if we end up getting them. In conclusion, whenever we desire something that is not up to us, our tranquility will likely be disturbed: If we don't get what we want, we will be upset, and if we do get what we want, we will experience anxiety in the process of getting it.

CONSIDER AGAIN Epictetus's "dichotomy of control": He says that some things are up to us and some things aren't up to us. The problem with this statement of the dichotomy is that the phrase "some things aren't up to us" is ambiguous: It can be understood to mean either "There are things over which we have *no control at all*" or to mean "There are things over which we *don't* have *complete* control." If we understand it in the first way, we can restate Epictetus's dichotomy as follows: There are things over which we have complete control and things over which we have no control at all. But stated in this way, the dichotomy is a false dichotomy, since it ignores the existence of things over which we have some but not complete control.

Consider, for example, my winning a tennis match. This is not something over which I have complete control: No matter how much I practice and how hard I try, I might nevertheless lose a match. Nor is it something over which I have no control at all: Practicing a lot and trying hard may not guarantee that I will win, but they will certainly affect my chances of winning. My winning at tennis is therefore an example of something over which I have some control but not complete control.

This suggests that we should understand the phrase "some things aren't up to us" in the second way: We should take it to mean that there are things over which we don't have complete control. If we accept this interpretation, we will want to restate Epictetus's dichotomy of control as follows: There are things over which we have complete control and things over which we don't have complete control. Stated in this way, the dichotomy is a genuine dichotomy. Let us therefore assume that this is what Epictetus meant in saying that "some things are up to us and some things are not up to us."

Now let us turn our attention to the second branch of this dichotomy, to things over which we don't have complete control. There are two ways we can fail to have complete control over something: We might have no control at all over it, or we might have some but not complete control. This means that we can divide the category of things over which we don't have complete control into two subcategories: things over which we have no control at all (such as whether the sun will

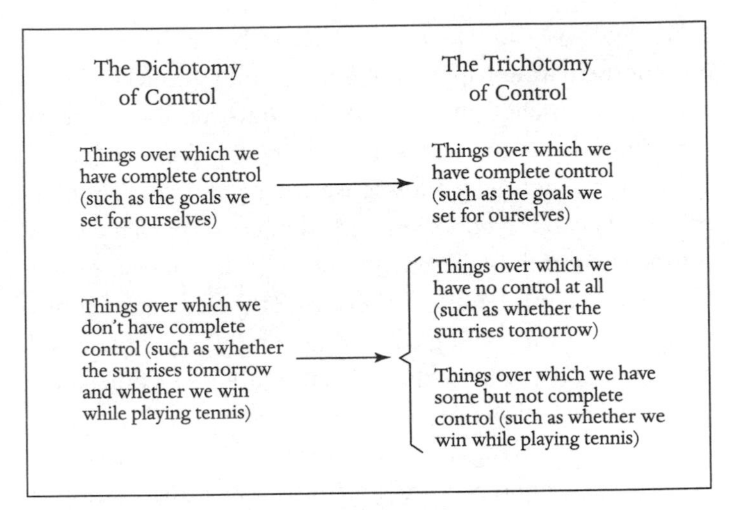

Turning the dichotomy of control into a trichotomy.

rise tomorrow) and things over which we have some but not complete control (such as whether we win at tennis). This in turn suggests the possibility of restating Epictetus's dichotomy of control as a trichotomy: There are things over which we have complete control, things over which we have no control at all, and things over which we have some but not complete control. Each of the "things" we encounter in life will fall into one and only one of these three categories.

In his statement of the dichotomy of control, Epictetus suggests, quite sensibly, that we are behaving foolishly if we spend time worrying about things that are not up to us; because they are not up to us, worrying about them is futile. We should instead concern ourselves with things that are up to us, since we can take steps either to bring them about or prevent them from happening. On restating the dichotomy of control as a trichotomy, though, we must restate his advice regarding what is and isn't sensible to worry about.

To begin with, it makes sense for us to spend time and energy concerning ourselves with things over which we have complete control. In these cases, our efforts will have guaranteed results. Notice, too, that because of the degree of control we have over these things, it will generally require relatively little time and energy for us to make sure they come about. We would be foolish not to concern ourselves with them.

What are the things over which we have complete control? In the passage quoted above, Epictetus says we have complete control over our opinions, impulses, desires, and aversions. I agree with Epictetus that we have complete control over our opinions, as long as we properly construe the meaning of *opinion*—more on this in a moment. I have qualms, though, about including our impulses, desires, and aversions in the category of things over which we have complete control. I would instead place them into the category of things over which we have some but not complete control, or, in some cases, into the category of things over which we have no control at all. Allow me to explain why.

Suppose I am walking through a casino and, on passing a roulette table, detect within me an impulse to place a bet that the number 17 will come up on the next spin of the wheel. I have a degree of control over whether I act on this impulse but no control over whether it arises in me. (If something is truly an impulse, we can't preclude experiencing it.) The same can be said of many (but not all) of my desires. When I am on a diet, for example, I might suddenly find myself craving a bowl of ice cream. I have a degree of control over whether I act on this craving but no control over whether this craving spontaneously arises within me. Likewise, I can't help it that I detect within myself an aversion to spiders. I might, through an act of sheer willpower, pick up and handle a tarantula despite this aversion, but I can't help it that I don't like spiders.

These examples suggest that Epictetus is wrong to include our impulses, desires, and aversions in the category of things over which we have complete control. They belong instead in the category of things over which we have some but not complete control, or, in some instances, in the category of things over which we have no control at all. But having said this, I should add that it is possible that something important has been lost in translation—that in speaking of impulses, desires, and aversions, Epictetus had in mind something different than we do.

WHAT, THEN, ARE the things over which we have complete control? To begin with, I think we have complete control over the goals we set for ourselves. I have complete control, for example, over whether my goal is to become the next pope, a millionaire, or a monk in a Trappist monastery. Having said this, I should add that although I have complete control over which of these goals I set for myself, I obviously don't have complete control over whether I achieve any of them; my achieving the goals I set for myself instead typically falls into the category of things over which I have some but not complete control. Another thing

I think we have complete control over is our values. We have complete control, for example, over whether we value fame and fortune, pleasure, or tranquility. Whether or not we live in accordance with our values is, of course, a different question: It is something over which we have some but not complete control.

Epictetus, as we have seen, thinks we have complete control over our opinions. If by *opinions* he has in mind our opinions on what goals we should set for ourselves or our opinions on the value of things, then I agree with him that our opinions are "up to us."

It will clearly make sense for us to spend time and energy setting goals for ourselves and determining our values. Doing this will take relatively little time and energy. Furthermore, the reward for choosing our goals and values properly can be enormous. Indeed, Marcus thinks the key to having a good life is to value things that are genuinely valuable and be indifferent to things that lack value. He adds that because we have it in our power to assign value to things, we have it in our power to live a good life. More generally, Marcus thinks that by forming opinions properly—by assigning things their correct value—we can avoid much suffering, grief, and anxiety and can thereby achieve the tranquility the Stoics seek.[9]

Besides having complete control over our goals and values, Marcus points out that we have complete control over our character. We are, he says, the only ones who can stop ourselves from attaining goodness and integrity. We have it entirely within our power, for example, to prevent viciousness and cupidity from finding a home in our soul. If we are slow-witted, it might not be in our power to become a scholar, but there is nothing to stop us from cultivating a number of other qualities, including sincerity, dignity, industriousness, and sobriety; nor is there anything to stop us from taking steps to curb our arrogance, to rise above pleasures and pains, to stop lusting after popularity, and to control our temper. Furthermore, we have it in our power to stop grumbling, to be considerate and frank, to be temperate in manner and speech, and to carry ourselves "with authority." These qualities, Marcus observes, can be ours at this very moment—if we choose for them to be.[10]

Now let us turn our attention back to the second branch of the trichotomy of control, to things over which we have no control at all, such as whether the sun will rise tomorrow. It is obviously foolish for us to spend time and energy concerning ourselves with such things. Because we have no control at all over the things in question, any time and energy we spend will have no effect on the outcome of events and will therefore be wasted time and energy, and, as Marcus observes, "Nothing is worth doing pointlessly."[11]

This brings us to the third branch of the trichotomy of control: those things over which we have some but not complete control. Consider, for example, winning a tennis match. As we have seen, although we can't be certain of winning a match, we can hope, through our actions, to affect the outcome; we therefore have some but not complete control. Given that this is so, will a practicing Stoic wish to concern himself with tennis? In particular, should he spend time and energy trying to win matches?

We might think he shouldn't. Because the Stoic doesn't have complete control over the outcome of a tennis match, there is always a chance that he will lose, but if he loses, he will likely be upset, and his tranquility will be disturbed. A safer course of action for a Stoic, then, would seem to be to refrain from playing tennis. By similar reasoning, if he values his tranquility, it seems as though he should not want his wife to love him; there is a chance that, regardless of what he does, she won't, and he will be heartbroken. Likewise, he shouldn't want his boss to give him a raise; there is again a chance that, regardless of what he does, she won't, and he will be disappointed. Indeed, taking this line of thought a step further, the Stoic shouldn't even have asked his wife to marry him or his boss to hire him, since they might have turned him down.

One might conclude, in other words, that Stoics will refuse to concern themselves with things over which they have some but not complete control. But because most of the things that come up in daily living are things over which we have some but not complete control, it would follow that Stoics will not concern themselves with many aspects of everyday life. They will instead be passive, withdrawn underachievers. Indeed, they will resemble depressed individuals who might not even be able to rouse themselves from bed in the morning.

Before we succumb to this line of argument, though, we should recall that the Stoics weren't passive and withdrawn. To the contrary, they were fully engaged in daily life. From this, one of two conclusions follows: Either the Stoics were hypocrites who did not act in accordance with their principles, or we have, in the above argument, somehow misinterpreted Stoic principles. I shall now argue for this second alternative.

REMEMBER THAT AMONG the things over which we have complete control are the goals we set for ourselves. I think that when a Stoic concerns himself with things over which he has some but not complete control, such as winning a tennis match, he will be very careful about the goals he sets for himself. In particular, he will be careful to set *internal* rather than *external* goals. Thus, his goal in playing tennis will not be to win a match (something external, over which he has only partial control) but to play to the best of his ability in the match (something internal, over which he has complete control). By choosing this goal, he will spare himself frustration or disappointment should he lose the match: Since it was not his goal to win the match, he will not have failed to attain his goal, as long as he played his best. His tranquility will not be disrupted.

It is worth noting at this point that playing to the best of your ability in a tennis match and winning that match are causally connected. In particular, what better way is there to win a tennis match than by playing to the best of your ability? The Stoics realized that our internal goals will affect our external performance, but they also realized that the goals we consciously set for ourselves can have a dramatic impact on our subsequent emotional state. In particular, if we consciously set winning a tennis match as our goal, we arguably don't increase our chances of winning that match. In fact, we might even hurt our chances: If it starts looking, early on, as though we are going to lose the match, we might become flustered, and this might negatively affect our playing in the remainder of the game, thereby hurting our chances of winning. Furthermore, by having winning the match as our goal, we dramatically increase our chances of being upset by the outcome of the match. If, on the other hand, we set playing our best in a match as our goal, we arguably don't lessen our chances of winning the match, but we do lessen our chances of being upset by the outcome of the match. Thus, internalizing our goals with respect to tennis would appear to be a no-brainer: To set as our goal playing to the best of our ability has an upside—reduced emotional anguish in the future—with little or no downside.

When it comes to other, more significant aspects of his life, a Stoic will likewise be careful in the goals he sets for himself. Stoics would recommend, for example, that I concern myself with whether my wife loves me, even though this is something over which I have some but not complete control. But when I do concern myself with this, my goal should not be the external goal of making her love me; no matter how hard I try, I could fail to achieve this goal and would as a result be quite upset. Instead, my goal should be an internal goal: to behave, to the best of my ability, in a lovable manner. Similarly, my goal with respect to my boss should be to do my job to the best of my ability. These are goals I can achieve no matter how my wife and my boss subsequently react to my efforts. By internalizing his goals in daily life, the Stoic is able to preserve his tranquility while dealing with things over which he has only partial control.

Categories of Things	Example	Epictetus's Advice
Things over which we have complete control	The goals we set for ourselves, the values we form	We should concern ourselves with these things.
Things over which we have no control at all	Whether the sun will rise tomorrow	We should not concern ourselves with these things.
Things over which we have some but not complete control	Whether we win while playing tennis	We should concern ourselves with these things, but we should be careful to internalize the goals we form with respect to them.

The trichotomy of control.

It is especially important, I think, for us to internalize our goals if we are in a profession in which "external failure" is commonplace. Think, for example, about an aspiring novelist. To succeed in her chosen profession, she must fight and win two battles: She must master her craft, and she must deal with rejection of her work—most novelists hear "No" many, many times before hearing "Yes." Of these two battles, the second is, for most people, the hardest. How many would-be novelists, one wonders, don't submit the manuscript they have written because they dread hearing the word "No"? And how many would-be novelists, on hearing "No" once, are crushed by the experience and never resubmit the manuscript?

How can the aspiring novelist reduce the psychological cost of rejection and thereby increase her chances of success? By internalizing her goals with respect to novel writing. She should have as her goal not something external over which she has little control, such as getting her novel published, but something internal over which she has considerable control, such as how hard she works on the manuscript or how many times she submits it in a given period of time. I don't claim that by internalizing her goals in this manner she can eliminate altogether the sting when she gets a rejection letter (or, as often happens, when she fails to get any response at all to the work she has submitted). It can, however, substantially reduce this sting. Instead of moping for a year before resubmitting her manuscript, she might get her moping period down to a week or even a day, and this change will dramatically increase her chance of getting the manuscript published.

Readers might complain that the process of internalizing our goals is really little more than a mind game. The would-be novelist's *real* goal is obviously to get her novel published—something she knows full well—and in advising her to internalize her goals with respect to the novel, I am doing little more than advising her to pretend as if getting published weren't her goal.

In response to this complaint, I would point out, to begin with, that it might be possible for someone, by spending enough time practicing goal internalization, to develop the ability not to look beyond her internalized goals—in which case they would become her "real" goals. Furthermore, even if the internalization process is a mind game, it is a useful mind game. Fear of failure is a psychological trait, so it is hardly surprising that by altering our psychological attitude toward "failure" (by carefully choosing our goals), we can affect the degree to which we fear it.

The Stoics, as I have explained, were very much interested in human psychology and were not at all averse to using psychological "tricks" to overcome certain aspects of human psychology, such as the presence in us of negative emotions. Indeed, the negative visualization technique described in the previous chapter is really little more than a psychological trick: By thinking about how things could be worse, we forestall or reverse the hedonic adaptation process. It is nevertheless a singularly effective trick, if our goal is to appreciate what we have rather than taking it for granted, and if our goal is to experience joy rather than becoming jaded with respect to the life we happen to be living and the world we happen to inhabit.

Having said all this about the internalization of goals, let me pause here to offer a confession. In my studies of Epictetus and the other Stoics, I found little evidence that they advocate internalizing goals in the manner I have described, which raises questions about whether the Stoics in fact made use of the internalization technique. Nevertheless, I have attributed the technique to them, inasmuch as internalizing one's goals is the obvious thing to do if one wishes, as the Stoics did, to concern oneself only with those things over which one has control and if one wishes to retain one's tranquility while undertaking endeavors that might fail (in the external sense of the word). In talking about the internalization of goals, then, I might be guilty of tampering with or improving on Stoicism. As I shall explain in chapter 20, I have no qualms about doing this.

NOW THAT WE UNDERSTAND the technique of internalizing our goals, we are in a position to explain what would otherwise seem like paradoxical behavior on the part of Stoics. Although they value tranquility, they feel duty-bound to be active participants in the society in which they live. But such participation clearly puts their tranquility in jeopardy. One suspects, for example, that Cato would have enjoyed a far more tranquil life if he did not feel compelled to fight the rise to power of Julius Caesar—if he instead had spent his days, say, in a library, reading the Stoics.

I would like to suggest, though, that Cato and the other Stoics found a way to retain their tranquility despite their involvement with the world around them: They internalized their goals. Their goal was not to change the world, but to do their best to bring about certain changes. Even if their efforts proved to be ineffectual, they could nevertheless rest easy knowing that they had accomplished their goal: They had done what they could do.

A practicing Stoic will keep the trichotomy of control firmly in mind as he goes about his daily affairs. He will perform a kind of triage in which he sorts the elements of his life into three categories: those over which he has complete control, those over which he has no control at all, and those over which he has some but not complete control. The things in the second category—those over which he has no control at all—he will set aside as not worth worrying about. In doing this, he will spare himself a great deal of needless anxiety. He will instead concern himself with things over which he has complete control and things over which he has some but not complete control. And when he concerns himself with things in this last category, he will be careful to set internal rather than external goals for himself and will thereby avoid a considerable amount of frustration and disappointment.

SIX

Fatalism

Letting Go of the Past... and the Present

One way to preserve our tranquility, the Stoics thought, is to take a fatalistic attitude toward the things that happen to us. According to Seneca, we should offer ourselves to fate, inasmuch as "it is a great consolation that it is together with the universe we are swept along."[1] According to Epictetus, we should keep firmly in mind that we are merely actors in a play written by someone else—more precisely, the Fates. We cannot choose our role in this play, but regardless of the role we are assigned, we must play it to the best of our ability. If we are assigned by the Fates to play the role of beggar, we should play the role well; likewise if we are assigned to play the role of king. If we want our life to go well, Epictetus says, we should, rather than wanting events to conform to our desires, make our desires conform to events; we should, in other words, want events "to happen as they do happen."[2]

Marcus also advocates taking a fatalistic attitude toward life. To do otherwise is to rebel against nature, and such rebellions are counterproductive, if what we seek is a good life. In particular, if we reject the decrees of fate, Marcus says, we are likely to experience tranquility-disrupting grief, anger, or fear.

To avoid this, we must learn to adapt ourselves to the environment into which fate has placed us and do our best to love the people with whom fate has surrounded us. We must learn to welcome whatever falls to our lot and persuade ourselves that whatever happens to us is for the best. Indeed, according to Marcus, a good man will welcome "every experience the looms of fate may weave for him."[3]

Like most ancient Romans, the Stoics took it for granted that they had a fate. More precisely, they believed in the existence of three goddesses known as the Fates. Each of these goddesses had a job: Clotho wove life, Lachesis measured it, and Atropos cut it. Try as they might, people could not escape the destiny chosen for them by the Fates.[4]

For ancient Romans, then, life was like a horse race that is fixed: The Fates already knew who would win and who would lose life's contests. A jockey would probably refuse to take part in a race he knew to be fixed; why bother racing when somebody somewhere already knows who will win? One might likewise expect the ancient Romans to refuse to participate in life's contests; why bother, when the future has already been determined? What is interesting is that despite their determinism, despite their belief that whatever happened had to happen, the ancients were not fatalistic about the future. The Stoics, for example, did not sit around apathetically, resigned to whatever the future held in store; to the contrary, they spent their days working to affect the outcome of future events. Likewise, the soldiers of ancient Rome marched bravely off to war and fought valiantly in battles, even though they believed the outcomes of these battles were fated.

THIS LEAVES US, of course, with a puzzle: Although the Stoics advocate fatalism, they seem not to have practiced it. What are we to make, then, of their advice that we take a fatalistic attitude toward the things that happen to us?

To solve this puzzle, we need to distinguish between fatalism with respect to the future and fatalism with respect to the past. When a person is fatalistic with respect to the future, she will keep firmly in mind, when deciding what to do, that her actions can have no effect on future events. Such a person is unlikely to spend time and energy thinking about the future or trying to alter it. When a person is fatalistic with respect to the past, she adopts this same attitude toward past events. She will keep firmly in mind, when deciding what to do, that her actions can have no effect on the past. Such a person is unlikely to spend time and energy thinking about how the past might be different.

When the Stoics advocate fatalism, they are, I think, advocating a restricted form of the doctrine. More precisely, they are advising us to be fatalistic with respect to the past, to keep firmly in mind that the past cannot be changed. Thus, the Stoics would not counsel a mother with a sick child to be fatalistic with respect to the future; she *should* try to nurse the child back to health (even though the Fates have already decided whether the child lives or dies). But if the child dies, they will counsel this woman to be fatalistic with respect to the past. It is only natural, even for a Stoic, to experience grief after the death of a child. But to dwell on that death is a waste of time and emotions, inasmuch as the past cannot be changed. Dwelling on the child's death will therefore cause the woman needless grief.

In saying that we shouldn't dwell on the past, the Stoics are not suggesting that we should never think about it. We sometimes should think about the past to learn lessons that can help us in our efforts to shape the future. The above-mentioned mother, for example, should think about the cause of her child's death so that she may better protect her other children. Thus, if the child died as the result of eating poisonous berries, she should take steps to keep her other children away from those berries and to teach them that they are poisonous. But having done so, she should let go of the past. In particular, she should not spend her days with a head full of "if only" thoughts: "If only I had known she was eating the berries! If only I had taken her to a doctor sooner!"

Fatalism with respect to the past will doubtless be far more palatable to modern individuals than fatalism with respect to the future. Most of us reject the notion that we are fated to live a certain life; we think, to the contrary, that the future is affected by our efforts. At the same time, we readily accept that the past cannot be changed, so when we hear the Stoics counseling us to be fatalistic with respect to the past, we will be unlikely to challenge the advice.

BESIDES RECOMMENDING that we be fatalistic with respect to the past, the Stoics, I think, advocate fatalism with respect to the present. It is clear, after all, that we cannot, through our actions, affect the present, if by *the present* we mean *this very moment.* It may be possible for me to act in a way that affects what happens in a decade, a day, a minute, or even a half-second from now; it is impossible, however, for me to act in a way that alters what is happening *right now*, since as soon as I act to affect what is happening right now, that moment in time will have slipped into the past and therefore cannot be affected.

In their advocacy of fatalism, then, the Stoics were advising us to be fatalistic, not with respect to the future but with respect to the past and present. In support of this interpretation of Stoic fatalism, it is useful to reconsider some of the Stoic advice quoted above. When Epictetus advises us to want events "to happen as they do happen," he is giving us advice regarding events that *do* happen—that either have happened or are happening—not advice regarding events that *will* happen. He is, in other words, advising us to behave fatalistically with respect to the past and present. Likewise, just as you cannot welcome a visitor until he arrives, Marcus's good man cannot welcome the experiences the looms of fate weave for him until those experiences have arrived.

How can fatalism with respect to the present cause our life to go well? The Stoics, as I have said, argued that the best way to gain satisfaction is not by working to satisfy whatever desires we find within us but by learning to be satisfied with our life as it is—by learning to be happy with whatever we've got. We can spend our days wishing our circumstances were different, but if we allow ourselves to do this, we will spend our days in a state of dissatisfaction. Alternatively, if we can learn to want whatever it is we already have, we won't have to work to fulfill our desires in order to gain satisfaction; they will already have been fulfilled.

One of the things we've got, though, is this very moment, and we have an important choice with respect to it: We can either spend this moment wishing it could be different, or we can embrace this moment. If we habitually do the former, we will spend much of our life in a state of dissatisfaction; if we habitually do the latter, we will enjoy our life. This, I think, is why the Stoics recommend that we be fatalistic with respect to the present. It is why Marcus reminds us that all we own is the present moment and why he advises us to live in "this fleeting instant."[5] (This last advice, of course, echoes the Buddhist advice that we should try to live in the moment—another interesting parallel between Stoicism and Buddhism.)

Notice that the advice that we be fatalistic with respect to the past and the present is consistent with the advice, offered in the preceding chapter, that we not concern ourselves with things over which we have no control. We have no control over the past; nor do we have any control over the present, if by *the present* we mean *this very moment*. Therefore, we are wasting our time if we worry about past or present events.

Notice, too, that the advice that we be fatalistic with respect to the past and present is connected, in a curious way, to the advice that we practice negative visualization. In engaging in negative visualization, we think of the ways our situation could be worse, and our goal in doing so is to make us value whatever we have. The fatalism advocated by the Stoics is in a sense the reverse, or one might say the mirror image, of negative visualization: Instead of thinking about how our situation could be worse, *we refuse to think about how it could be better*. In behaving fatalistically with respect to the past and present, we refuse to compare our situation with alternative, preferable situations in which we might have found or might now find ourselves. By doing this, the Stoics think, we will make our current situation, whatever it may be, more tolerable.

My discussion of fatalism in this chapter and of negative visualization in chapter 4 might make readers worry that the practice of Stoicism will lead to complacency. Readers might admit that the Stoics will be unusually satisfied with what they have, whatever it may be—a blessing, to be sure. But won't the Stoics, as a result, be terribly unambitious?

In response to this concern, let me remind readers that the Stoics we have been considering were notably ambitious. Seneca, as we've seen, had an active life as a philosopher, playwright, investor, and political advisor. Musonius Rufus and Epictetus both ran successful schools of philosophy. And Marcus, when he wasn't philosophizing, was hard at work ruling the Roman Empire. These individuals were, if anything, overachievers. It is indeed curious: Although they would have been satisfied with next to nothing, they nevertheless strove for something.

Here is how Stoics would explain this seeming paradox. Stoic philosophy, while teaching us to be satisfied with whatever we've got, also counsels us to seek certain things in life. We should, for example, strive to become better people—to become virtuous in the ancient sense of the word. We should strive to practice Stoicism in our daily life. And we should, as we shall see in chapter 9, strive to do our social duty: This is why Seneca and Marcus felt compelled to participate in Roman government and why Musonius and Epictetus felt compelled to teach Stoicism. Furthermore, the Stoics see nothing wrong with our taking steps to enjoy the circumstances in which we find ourselves; indeed, Seneca advises us to be "attentive to all the advantages that adorn life."[6] We might, as a result, get married and have children. We might also form and enjoy friendships.

And what about worldly success? Will the Stoics seek fame and fortune? They will not. The Stoics thought these things had no real value and consequently thought it foolish to pursue them, particularly if doing so disrupted our tranquility or required us to act in an unvirtuous manner. This indifference to worldly success, I realize, will make them seem unmotivated to modern individuals who spend their days working hard in an attempt to attain (a degree of) fame and fortune. But having said this, I should add that although the Stoics didn't seek worldly success, they often gained it anyway.

Indeed, the Stoics we have been considering would all have counted as successful individuals in their time. Seneca and Marcus were both wealthy and famous, and Musonius and Epictetus, as heads of popular schools, would have enjoyed a degree of renown and would presumably have been financially comfortable. They therefore found themselves in the curious position of people who, though not seeking success, nevertheless gained it. In chapters 14 and 15 we will see how they dealt with this predicament.

SEVEN

Self-Denial

On Dealing with the Dark Side of Pleasure

To ENGAGE IN negative visualization is to contemplate the bad things that can happen to us. Seneca recommends an extension of this technique: Besides *contemplating* bad things happening, we should sometimes *live as if* they had happened. In particular, instead of merely thinking about what it would be like to lose our wealth, we should periodically "practice poverty": We should, that is, content ourselves with "the scantiest and cheapest fare" and with "coarse and rough dress."[1]

According to Seneca, Epicurus, a philosophical rival to the Stoics, also practiced poverty.[2] His goal in doing so, however, appears to have been different from that of Seneca. Whereas Seneca wanted to appreciate what he had, Epicurus wanted to examine the things he thought he needed so he could determine which of them he could in fact live without. He realized that in many cases, we work hard to obtain something because we are convinced that we would be miserable without it. The problem is that we can live perfectly well without some of these things, but we won't know which they are if we don't try living without them.

Musonius takes this technique one step further: He thinks that besides *living as if* bad things had happened to us, we should sometimes *cause* them to happen. In particular, we should periodically cause ourselves to experience discomfort that we could easily have avoided. We might accomplish this by underdressing for cold weather or going shoeless. Or we might periodically allow ourselves to become thirsty or hungry, even though water and food are at hand, and we might sleep on a hard bed, even though a soft one is available.[3]

Many modern readers, on hearing this, will conclude that Stoicism involves an element of masochism. Readers should realize, though, that the Stoics didn't go around flogging themselves. Indeed, the discomforts they inflicted upon themselves were rather minor. Furthermore, they did not inflict these discomforts to punish themselves; rather, they did it to increase their enjoyment of life. And finally, it is misleading to talk about the Stoics *inflicting* discomforts on themselves. This creates the image of someone at odds with himself, of someone forcing himself to do things he doesn't want to do. The Stoics, by way of contrast, *welcomed* a degree of discomfort in their life. What the Stoics were advocating, then, is more appropriately described as a program of voluntary discomfort than as a program of self-inflicted discomfort.

Even this clarification of the Stoics' attitude toward discomfort, though, will leave many modern readers puzzled: "Why should we welcome even minor discomforts when it is possible to enjoy perfect comfort?" they will ask. In response to this question, Musonius would point to three benefits to be derived from acts of voluntary discomfort.

To begin with, by undertaking acts of voluntary discomfort—by, for example, choosing to be cold and hungry when we could be warm and well fed—we harden ourselves against misfortunes that might befall us in the future. If all we know is comfort, we might be traumatized when we are forced to experience pain or discomfort, as we someday almost surely will. In other words, voluntary discomfort can be thought of as a kind of vaccine: By exposing ourselves to a small amount of a weakened virus now, we create in ourselves an immunity that will protect us from a debilitating illness in the future. Alternatively, voluntary discomfort can be thought of as an insurance premium which, if paid, makes us eligible for benefits: Should we later fall victim to a misfortune, the discomfort we experience then will be substantially less than it otherwise would have been.

A second benefit of undertaking acts of voluntary discomfort comes not in the future but immediately. A person who periodically experiences minor discomforts will grow confident that he can withstand major discomforts as well, so the prospect of experiencing such discomforts at some future time will not, at present, be a source of anxiety for him. By experiencing minor discomforts, he is, says Musonius, training himself to be courageous.[4] The person who, in contrast, is a stranger to discomfort, who has never been cold or hungry, might dread the possibility of someday being cold and hungry. Even though he is now physically comfortable, he will likely experience mental discomfort—namely, anxiety with respect to what the future holds in store for him.

A third benefit of undertaking acts of voluntary discomfort is that it helps us appreciate what we already have. In particular, by purposely causing ourselves discomfort, we will better appreciate whatever comfort we experience. It is, of course, nice to be in a warm room when it is cold and blustery outside, but if we really want to enjoy that warmth and sense of shelter, we should go outside in the cold for a while and then come back in. Likewise, we can (as Diogenes observed) greatly enhance our appreciation of any meal by waiting until we are hungry before we eat it and greatly enhance our appreciation of any beverage by waiting until we are thirsty before we drink it.

It is instructive to contrast the advice that we periodically undertake acts of voluntary discomfort with the advice that might be offered by an unenlightened hedonist. Such a person might suggest that the best way to maximize the comfort we experience is to avoid discomfort at all costs. Musonius would argue, to the contrary, that someone who tries to avoid all discomfort is less likely to be comfortable than someone who periodically embraces discomfort. The latter individual is likely to have a much wider "comfort zone" than the former and will therefore feel comfortable under circumstances that would cause the former individual considerable distress. It would be one thing if we could take steps to ensure that we will never experience discomfort, but since we can't, the strategy of avoiding discomfort at all costs is counterproductive.

BESIDES PERIODICALLY ENGAGING in acts of voluntary discomfort, we should, say the Stoics, periodically forgo opportunities to experience pleasure. This is because pleasure has a dark side. Indeed, pursuing pleasure, Seneca warns, is like pursuing a wild beast: On being captured, it can turn on us and tear us to pieces. Or, changing the metaphor a bit, he tells us that intense pleasures, when captured by us, become our captors, meaning that the more pleasures a man captures, "the more masters will he have to serve."[5]

In mistrusting pleasure, the Stoics reveal their Cynic bloodlines. Thus, the Cynic philosopher Diogenes argues that the most important battle any person has to fight is the battle against pleasure. The battle is particularly difficult to win because pleasure "uses no open force but deceives and casts a spell with baneful drugs, just as Homer says Circe drugged the comrades of Odysseus." Pleasure, he cautions, "hatches no single plot but all kinds of plots, and aims to undo men through sight, sound, smell, taste, and touch, with food too, and drink and carnal lust, tempting the waking and the sleeping alike." And pleasure, "with a stroke of her wand . . . cooly drives her victim into a sort of sty and pens him up, and now from that time forth the man goes on living as a pig or a wolf."[6]

There are some pleasures, the Stoics would argue, from which we should always abstain. In particular, we should abstain from those pleasures that can capture us in a single encounter. This would include the pleasure to be derived from certain drugs: Had crystal meth existed in the ancient world, the Stoics would doubtless have counseled against its use.

Significantly, though, the Stoics' mistrust of pleasure doesn't end here. They also counsel us to make a point of sometimes abstaining from other, relatively harmless pleasures. We might, for example, make a point of passing up an opportunity to drink wine—not because we fear becoming an alcoholic but so we can learn self-control. For the Stoics—and, indeed, for anyone attempting to practice a philosophy of life—self-control will be an important trait to acquire. After all, if we lack self-control, we are likely to be distracted by the various pleasures life has to offer, and in this distracted state we are unlikely to attain the goals of our philosophy of life.

More generally, if we cannot resist pleasures, we will end up playing, Marcus says, the role of slave, "twitching puppetwise at every pull of self-interest," and we will spend our life "ever grumbling at today or lamenting over tomorrow." To avoid this fate, we must take care to prevent pains and pleasures from overwhelming our rational capacity. We must learn, as Marcus puts it, to "resist the murmurs of the flesh."[7]

As he goes about his daily business, then, the Stoic, besides sometimes choosing to do things that would make him feel bad (such as underdressing for the weather), will sometimes choose not to do things that would make him feel good (such as having a bowl of ice cream). This makes it sound as if Stoics are antipleasure, but they aren't. The Stoics see nothing wrong, for example, with enjoying the pleasures to be derived from friendship, family life, a meal, or even wealth, but they counsel us to be circumspect in our enjoyment of these things. There is, after all, a fine line between enjoying a meal and lapsing into gluttony. There is also a danger that we will cling to the things we enjoy. Consequently, even as we enjoy pleasant things, we should follow Epictetus's advice and be on guard.[8] Here is how, according to Seneca, a Stoic sage would explain the difference between the Stoic take on pleasure and that of the ordinary person: Whereas the ordinary person embraces pleasure, the sage enchains it; whereas the ordinary person thinks pleasure is the highest good, the sage doesn't think it is even a good; and whereas the ordinary person does everything for the sake of pleasure, the sage does nothing.[9]

Of the Stoic techniques I have discussed in part 2 of this book, the self-denial technique described in this chapter is doubtless the hardest to practice. It won't be fun, for example, for a Stoic, because he is practicing poverty, to ride the bus when he could be driving his car. It won't be fun going out into a winter storm with only a light jacket on just so he can feel uncomfortably cold. And it certainly won't be fun saying no to the ice cream someone has offered him—and saying it not because he is on a diet but so he can practice refusing something he would enjoy. Indeed, a novice Stoic will have to summon up all his willpower to do such things.

What Stoics discover, though, is that willpower is like muscle power: The more they exercise their muscles, the stronger they get, and the more they exercise their will, the stronger it gets. Indeed, by practicing Stoic self-denial techniques over a long period, Stoics can transform themselves into individuals remarkable for their courage and self-control. They will be able to do things that others dread doing, and they will be able to refrain from doing things that others cannot resist doing. They will, as a result, be thoroughly in control of themselves. This self-control makes it far more likely that they will attain the goals of their philosophy of life, and this in turn dramatically increases their chances of living a good life.

The Stoics will be the first to admit that it takes effort to exercise self-control. Having made this admission, though, they will point out that *not* exercising self-control also takes effort: Just think, says Musonius, about all the time and energy people expend in illicit love affairs that they would not have undertaken if they had self-control.[10] Along similar lines, Seneca observes that "chastity comes with time to spare, lechery has never a moment."[11]

The Stoics will then point out that exercising self-control has certain benefits that might not be obvious. In particular, as strange as it may seem, consciously abstaining from pleasure can itself be pleasant. Suppose, for example, that while on a diet, you develop a craving for the ice cream you know to be in your refrigerator. If you eat it, you will experience a certain gastronomic pleasure, along with a certain regret for having eaten it. If you refrain from eating the ice cream, though, you will forgo this gastronomic pleasure but will experience pleasure of a different kind: As Epictetus observes, you will "be pleased and will praise yourself" for not eating it.[12]

This last pleasure, to be sure, is utterly unlike the pleasure that comes from eating ice cream, but it is nevertheless a genuine pleasure. Furthermore, if we paused to do a careful cost-benefit analysis before eating the ice cream—if we weighed the costs and benefits of eating it against the costs and benefits of not eating it—we might find that the sensible thing for us to do, if we wish to maximize our pleasure, is not eat it. It is for just this reason that Epictetus counsels us, when contemplating whether or not to take advantage of opportunities for pleasure, to engage in this sort of analysis.[13]

Along similar lines, suppose we follow Stoic advice to simplify our diet. We might discover that such a diet, although lacking in various gastronomic pleasures, is the source of a pleasure of an entirely different sort: "Water, barley-meal, and crusts of barley-bread," Seneca tells us, "are not a cheerful diet, yet it is the highest kind of pleasure to be able to derive pleasure from this sort of food."[14]

Leave it to the Stoics to realize that the act of forgoing pleasure can itself be pleasant. They were, as I've said, some of the most insightful psychologists of their time.

EIGHT

Meditation

Watching Ourselves Practice Stoicism

To help us advance our practice of Stoicism, Seneca advises that we periodically meditate on the events of daily living, how we responded to these events, and how, in accordance with Stoic principles, we should have responded to them. He attributes this technique to his teacher Sextius, who, at bedtime, would ask himself, "What ailment of yours have you cured today? What failing have you resisted? Where can you show improvement?"[1]

Seneca describes for his readers one of his own bedtime meditations and offers a list of the sorts of events he might reflect on, along with the conclusions he might draw regarding his response to these events:

- Seneca was too aggressive in admonishing someone; consequently, rather than correcting the person, the admonition merely served to annoy him. His advice to himself: When contemplating whether to criticize someone, he should consider not only whether the criticism is valid but also whether the person can stand to be criticized. He adds that the worse a man is, the less likely he is to accept constructive criticism.

- At a party, people made jokes at Seneca's expense, and rather than shrugging them off, he took them to heart. His advice to himself: "Keep away from low company."
- At a banquet, Seneca was not seated in the place of honor he thought he deserved. Consequently, he spent the banquet angry at those who planned the seating and envious of those who had better seats than he did. His assessment of his behavior: "You lunatic, what difference does it make what part of the couch you put your weight on?"
- He has heard that someone has spoken ill of his writing, and he starts treating this critic as an enemy. But then he starts thinking of all the people whose writing he himself has criticized. Would he want all of them to think of him as an enemy? Certainly not. Seneca's conclusion: If you are going to publish, you must be willing to tolerate criticism.[2]

On reading these and the other irritants Seneca lists, one is struck by how little human nature has changed in the past two millennia.

The bedtime meditation Seneca is recommending is, of course, utterly unlike the meditations of, say, a Zen Buddhist. During his meditations, a Zen Buddhist might sit for hours with his mind as empty as he can make it. A Stoic's mind, in contrast, will be quite active during a bedtime meditation. He will think about the events of the day. Did something disrupt his tranquility? Did he experience anger? Envy? Lust? Why did the day's events upset him? Is there something he could have done to avoid getting upset?

Epictetus takes Seneca's bedtime-meditation advice one step further: He suggests that as we go about our daily business, we should simultaneously play the roles of participant and spectator.[3] We should, in other words, create within ourselves a Stoic observer who watches us and comments on our attempts to practice Stoicism. Along similar lines, Marcus advises us to examine each thing we do, determine our motives for doing it, and consider the value of whatever it was we were trying to accomplish. We should continually ask whether we are being governed by our reason or by something else. And when we determine that we are not being governed by our reason, we should ask what it is that governs us. Is it the soul of a child? A tyrant? A dumb ox? A wild beast? We should likewise be careful observers of the actions of other people.[4] We can, after all, learn from their mistakes and their successes.

Besides reflecting on the day's events, we can devote part of our meditations to going through a kind of mental checklist. Are we practicing the psychological techniques recommended by the Stoics? Do we, for example, periodically engage in negative visualization? Do we take time to distinguish between those things over which we have complete control, those things over which we have no control at all, and those things over which we have some but not complete control? Are we careful to internalize our goals? Have we refrained from dwelling on the past and instead focused our attention on the future? Have we consciously practiced acts of self-denial? We can also use our Stoic meditations as an opportunity to ask whether, in our daily affairs, we are following the advice offered by the Stoics. In part 3 of this book I describe this advice in detail.

SOMETHING ELSE we can do during our Stoic meditations is judge our progress as Stoics. There are several indicators by which we can measure this progress. For one thing, as Stoicism takes hold of us, we will notice that our relations with other people have changed. We will discover, says Epictetus, that our feelings aren't hurt when others tell us that we know nothing or that we are "mindless fools" about things external to us. We will shrug off their insults and slights. We will also shrug off any praise they might direct our way. Indeed, Epictetus thinks the admiration of other people is a negative barometer of our progress as Stoics: "If people think you amount to something, distrust yourself."[5]

Other signs of progress, says Epictetus, are the following: We will stop blaming, censuring, and praising others; we will stop boasting about ourselves and how much we know; and we will blame ourselves, not external circumstances, when our desires are thwarted. And because we have gained a degree of mastery over our desires, we will find that we have fewer of them than we did before; we will find, Epictetus says, that our "impulses toward everything are diminished." And quite significantly, if we have made progress as a Stoic, we will come to regard ourselves not as a friend whose every desire must be satisfied but "as an enemy lying in wait."[6]

According to the Stoics, practicing Stoicism, besides affecting the thoughts and desires we have when awake, will affect our dream life. In particular, Zeno suggested that as we make progress in our practice, we will stop having dreams in which we take pleasure in disgraceful things.[7]

Another sign of progress in our practice of Stoicism is that our philosophy will consist of actions rather than words. What matters most, says Epictetus, is not our ability to spout Stoic principles but our ability to live in accordance with them. Thus, at a banquet a Stoic novice might spend her time talking about what a philosophically enlightened individual should eat; a Stoic further along in her practice will simply eat that way. Similarly, a Stoic novice might boast of her simple lifestyle or of giving up wine in favor of water; a more advanced Stoic, having adopted a simple lifestyle and having given up wine in favor of water, will feel no need to comment on the fact. Indeed, Epictetus thinks that in our practice of Stoicism, we should be so inconspicuous that others don't label us Stoics—or even label us philosophers.[8]

The most important sign that we are making progress as Stoics, though, is a change in our emotional life. It isn't, as those ignorant of the true nature of Stoicism commonly believe, that we will stop experiencing emotion. We will instead find ourselves experiencing fewer negative emotions. We will also find that we are spending less time than we used to wishing things could be different and more time enjoying things as they are. We will find, more generally, that we are experiencing a degree of tranquility that our life previously lacked. We might also discover, perhaps to our amazement, that our practice of Stoicism has made us susceptible to little outbursts of joy: We will, out of the blue, feel delighted to be the person we are, living the life we are living, in the universe we happen to inhabit.

For the ultimate proof that we have made progress as Stoics, though, we will have to wait until we are faced with death. It is only then, says Seneca, that we will know whether our Stoicism has been genuine.[9]

When we measure our progress as Stoics, we might find that it is slower than we had hoped or expected. The Stoics, though, would be the first to admit that people can't perfect their Stoicism overnight. Indeed, even if we practice Stoicism all our life, we are unlikely to perfect it; there will always be room for improvement. Along these lines, Seneca tells us that his goal in practicing Stoicism is not to become a sage; instead, he takes his progress to be adequate as long as "every day I reduce the number of my vices, and blame my mistakes."[10]

The Stoics understood that they would encounter setbacks in their practice of Stoicism. Thus, Epictetus, after telling his students what they must do to practice Stoicism, went on to tell them what they should do when they failed to follow his advice.[11] He expected, in other words, that novice Stoics would routinely backslide. Along similar lines, Marcus recommends that when our practice falls short of Stoic precepts, we should not become despondent and certainly should not give up our attempts to practice Stoicism; instead, we should return to the attack and realize that if we can do the right thing, Stoically speaking, most of the time, we are doing pretty well for ourselves.[12]

Let me offer one last thought on making progress as a Stoic. Marcus spent his adult life practicing Stoicism, and even though he had a temperament well suited to it, he found that he would hit low points, during which his Stoicism seemed incapable of providing him the tranquility he sought. In the *Meditations*, he offers advice on what to do at such junctures: Continue to practice Stoicism, "even when success looks hopeless."[13]

PART THREE

Stoic Advice

NINE

Duty

On Loving Mankind

As we have seen, the Stoics advise us to seek tranquility. They realized, however, that this recommendation is not, by itself, very helpful, so they went on to offer guidance on how best to attain tranquility. They advise us, to begin with, to practice the psychological techniques described in part 2 of this book. They also offer advice on specific aspects of daily living. They counsel us, for example, not to seek fame and fortune, since doing so will likely disrupt our tranquility. They warn us to be careful in choosing our associates; other people, after all, have the power to shatter our tranquility—if we let them. They go on to offer advice on how to deal with insults, anger, grief, exile, old age, and even on the circumstances under which we should have sex.

Let us now turn our attention to the Stoics' advice on daily living, beginning, in this chapter and the next, with their advice on forming and maintaining social relations.

On examining our life, we will find that other people are the source of some of the greatest delights life has to offer, including love and friendship. But we will also discover that they are the cause of most of the negative emotions we experience. Strangers upset us when they cut us off in traffic. Relatives trouble us with their problems. Our boss might ruin our day by insulting us, and the incompetence of our coworkers might cause us stress by increasing our workload. Our friends might neglect to invite us to a party and thereby cause us to feel slighted.

Even when other people don't do anything to us, they can disrupt our tranquility. We typically want others—friends, relatives, neighbors, coworkers, and even complete strangers—to think well of us. We therefore spend time and energy trying to wear the right clothes, drive the right car, live in the right house in the right neighborhood, and so forth. These efforts, however, are accompanied by a degree of anxiety: We fear that we will make the wrong choices and that other people will therefore think poorly of us.

Notice, too, that to afford socially desirable clothes, cars, and houses, we have to work for a living and will probably experience anxiety in connection with our job. And even if, through our efforts, we succeed in gaining the admiration of others, our tranquility is likely to be upset by the feelings of envy that other, less successful people direct toward us. Seneca said it well: "To know how many are jealous of you, count your admirers."[1] In addition, we will have to deal with the envy that we feel toward those who have enjoyed even greater success than we have.

Because the Stoics valued tranquility and because they appreciated the power other people have to disrupt our tranquility, we might expect them to have lived as hermits and to advise us to do the same, but the Stoics did no such thing. They thought that man is by nature a social animal and therefore that we have a duty to form and maintain relationships with other people, despite the trouble they might cause us.

In the *Meditations*, Marcus explains the nature of this social duty. The gods, he says, created us for a reason—created us, as he puts it, "for some duty." In the same way that the function of a fig tree is to do a fig tree's work, the function of a dog is to do a dog's work, and the function of a bee is to do a bee's work, the function of a man is to do man's work—to perform, that is, the function for which the gods created us.[2]

What, then, is the function of man? Our primary function, the Stoics thought, is to be rational. To discover our secondary functions, we need only apply our reasoning ability. What we will discover is that we were designed to live among other people and interact with them in a manner that is mutually advantageous; we will discover, says Musonius, that "human nature is very much like that of bees. A bee is not able to live alone: it perishes when isolated."[3] We will likewise discover that, as Marcus puts it, "fellowship is the purpose behind our creation." Thus, a person who performs well the function of man will be both rational and social.[4]

To fulfill my social duty—to do my duty to my kind—I must feel a concern for all mankind. I must remember that we humans were created for one another, that we were born, says Marcus, to work together the way our hands or eyelids do. Therefore, in all I do, I must have as my goal "the service and harmony of all." More precisely, "I am bound to do good to my fellow-creatures and bear with them."[5]

And when I do my social duty, says Marcus, I should do so quietly and efficiently. Ideally, a Stoic will be oblivious to the services he does for others, as oblivious as a grapevine is when it yields a cluster of grapes to a vintner. He will not pause to boast about the service he has performed but will move on to perform his next service, the way the grape vine moves on to bear more grapes. Thus, Marcus advises us to perform with resoluteness the duties we humans were created to perform. Nothing else, he says, should distract us. Indeed, when we awaken in the morning, rather than lazily lying in bed, we should tell ourselves that we must get up to do the proper work of man, the work we were created to perform.[6]

MARCUS, IT SHOULD BE CLEAR, rejects the notion of doing our social duty in a selective manner. In particular, we cannot simply avoid dealing with annoying people, even though doing so would make our own life easier. Nor can we capitulate to these annoying people to avoid discord. Instead, Marcus declares, we should confront them and work for the common welfare. Indeed, we should "show true love" to the people with whom destiny has surrounded us.[7]

It is striking that Marcus would give such advice. Stoics differ in which aspect of the practice of Stoicism they find to be most challenging. Some might find it hardest, for example, to stop dwelling on the past; others might find it hardest to overcome their lust for fame and fortune. The biggest obstacle to Marcus's practice of Stoicism, though, appears to have been his rather intense dislike of humanity.

Indeed, throughout the *Meditations*, Marcus makes it abundantly clear how little he thinks of his fellow man. Earlier, I quoted his advice that we begin each day by reminding ourselves how annoying the people we encounter are going to be—reminding ourselves, that is, of their interference, ingratitude, insolence, disloyalty, ill will, and selfishness. If this assessment of humanity sounds harsh, we don't need to look hard to find even harsher assessments. Even the most agreeable of our associates, Marcus says, is difficult to deal with. He remarks that when someone says he wants to be perfectly straightforward with us, we should be on the lookout for a concealed dagger.[8]

Elsewhere, Marcus suggests that when we know our death is at hand, we can ease our anguish on leaving this world by taking a moment to reflect on all the annoying people we will no longer have to deal with when we are gone. We should also, he says, reflect on the fact that when we die, many of the companions we worked so hard to serve will be delighted by our passing. His disgust for his fellow humans is nicely summarized in the following passage: "Eating, sleeping, copulating, excreting, and the like; what a crew they are!"[9]

What is significant is that despite these feelings of disgust, Marcus did not turn his back on his fellow humans. He could, for example, have had a much easier life if he had delegated his imperial responsibilities to subordinates or if he had simply let things slide, but his sense of duty prevailed; indeed, he gained a reputation for "the unwearied zeal with which he discharged the duties of his great position."[10] And all the while, he worked hard not merely to form and maintain relations with other people but to love them.

Modern readers will naturally wonder how Marcus was able to accomplish this feat, how he was able to overcome his disgust for his fellow humans and work on their behalf. Part of the reason we marvel at Marcus's accomplishment is that we have a different notion of duty than he did. What motivates most of us to do our duty is the fear that we will be punished—perhaps by God, our government, or our employer—if we don't. What motivated Marcus to do his duty, though, was not fear of punishment but the prospect of a reward.

The reward in question is not the thanks of those we help; Marcus says that he no more expects thanks for the services he performs than a horse expects thanks for the races it runs. Nor does he seek the admiration of other people or even their sympathy.[11] To the contrary, the reward for doing one's social duty, Marcus says, is something far better than thanks, admiration, or sympathy.

Marcus, as we have seen, thought the gods created us with a certain function in mind. He also thought that when they created us, they made sure that if we fulfilled this function, we would experience tranquility and have all things to our liking. Indeed, if we do the things we were made for, says Marcus, we will enjoy "a man's true delight."[12] But an important part of our function, as we have seen, is to work with and for our fellow men. Marcus therefore concludes that doing his social duty will give him the best chance at having a good life. This, for Marcus, is the reward for doing one's duty: a good life.

For many readers, I realize, this line of reasoning will fall flat. They will insist that duty is the enemy of happiness and consequently that the best way to have a good life is to escape all forms of duty: Rather than spending our days doing things we *have* to do, we should spend them doing things we *want* to do. In chapter 20 I return to this question. For now, let me say this: Throughout the millennia and across cultures, those who have thought carefully about desire have drawn the conclusion that spending our days working to get whatever it is we find ourselves wanting is unlikely to bring us either happiness or tranquility.

TEN

Social Relations

On Dealing with Other People

THE STOICS, it should by now be clear, are faced with a dilemma. If they associate with other people, they run the risk of having their tranquility disturbed by them; if they preserve their tranquility by shunning other people, they will fail to do their social duty to form and maintain relationships. The question for the Stoics, then, is this: How can they preserve their tranquility while interacting with other people? The Stoics thought long and hard about this question. In the process of answering it, they developed a body of advice on how to deal with other people.

To begin with, the Stoics recommend that we prepare for our dealings with other people before we have to deal with them. Thus, Epictetus advises us to form "a certain character and pattern" for ourselves when we are alone. Then, when we associate with other people, we should remain true to who we are.[1]

The Stoics, as we have seen, think we cannot be selective in doing our social duty: There will be times when we must associate with annoying, misguided, or malicious people in order to work for common interests. We can, however, be selective about whom we befriend. The Stoics therefore recommend that we avoid befriending people whose values have been corrupted, for fear that their values will contaminate ours. We should instead seek, as friends, people who share our (proper Stoic) values and in particular, people who are doing a better job than we are of living in accordance with these values. And while enjoying the companionship of these individuals, we should work hard to learn what we can from them.

Vices, Seneca warns, are contagious: They spread, quickly and unnoticed, from those who have them to those with whom they come into contact.[2] Epictetus echoes this warning: Spend time with an unclean person, and we will become unclean as well.[3] In particular, if we associate with people who have unwholesome desires, there is a very real danger that we will soon discover similar desires in ourselves, and our tranquility will thereby be disrupted. Thus, when it is possible to do so, we should avoid associating with people whose values have been corrupted, the way we would avoid, say, kissing someone who obviously has the flu.

Besides advising us to avoid people with vices, Seneca advises us to avoid people who are simply whiny, "who are melancholy and bewail everything, who find pleasure in every opportunity for complaint." He justifies this avoidance by observing that a companion "who is always upset and bemoans everything is a foe to tranquility."[4] (In his famous dictionary, by the way, Samuel Johnson includes a wonderful term for these individuals: A *seeksorrow*, he explains, is "one who contrives to give himself vexation.")[5]

Besides being selective about the people we befriend, we should be selective, say the Stoics, about which social functions we attend (unless doing our social duty requires us to attend them). Epictetus, for example, advises us to avoid banquets given by nonphilosophers. He also advises us, when we do socialize, to be circumspect in our conversation. People tend to talk about certain things; back in Epictetus's time, he says, they talked about gladiators, horse races, athletes, eating and drinking—and, most of all, about other people. When we find ourselves in a group that is conversing about such things, Epictetus advises us to be silent or to have few words; alternatively, we might subtly attempt to divert the talk to "something appropriate."[6]

This advice, to be sure, is a bit dated; people no longer talk about gladiators (although, significantly, they still do talk about horse races, athletes, eating and drinking—and, of course, about other people). But modern individuals can nevertheless extract the core of Epictetus's social advice. It is permissible—indeed, it is sometimes necessary—for us to socialize with "nonphilosophers," with individuals, that is, who do not share our Stoic values. When we do so, however, we must take care: There is a danger, after all, that their values will contaminate ours and will thereby set us back in our practice of Stoicism.

WHAT ABOUT those occasions on which, in order to do our social duty, we must deal with annoying people? How can we prevent them from disturbing our tranquility?

Marcus recommends that when we interact with an annoying person, we keep in mind that there are doubtless people who find *us* to be annoying. More generally, when we find ourselves irritated by someone's shortcomings, we should pause to reflect on our own shortcomings. Doing this will help us become more empathetic to this individual's faults and therefore become more tolerant of him. When dealing with an annoying person, it also helps to keep in mind that our annoyance at what he does will almost invariably be more detrimental to us than whatever it is he is doing.[7] In other words, by letting ourselves become annoyed, we only make things worse.

We can also, Marcus suggests, lessen the negative impact other people have on our life by controlling our thoughts about them. He counsels us, for example, not to waste time speculating about what our neighbors are doing, saying, thinking, or scheming. Nor should we allow our mind to be filled with "sensual imaginings, jealousies, envies, suspicions, or any other sentiments" about them that we would blush to admit. A good Stoic, Marcus says, will not think about what other people are thinking except when he must do so in order to serve the public interest.[8]

Most important, Marcus thinks it will be easier for us to deal with impudent people if we keep in mind that the world cannot exist without such individuals. People, Marcus reminds us, do not choose to have the faults they do. Consequently, there is a sense in which the people who annoy us cannot help doing so. It is therefore inevitable that some people will be annoying; indeed, to expect otherwise, Marcus says, is like expecting a fig tree not to yield its juice. Thus, if we find ourselves shocked or surprised that a boor behaves boorishly, we have only ourselves to blame: We should have known better.[9]

Marcus, as we have seen, advocates fatalism, as do the other Stoics. What Marcus seems to be advocating in the passages just cited is a special kind of fatalism, what might be called *social fatalism*: In our dealings with others, we should operate on the assumption that they are fated to behave in a certain way. It is therefore pointless to wish they could be less annoying. But having said this, I should add that elsewhere, Marcus suggests not only that other people can be changed but that we should work to change them.[10] Perhaps what Marcus is saying is that even though it is possible to change others, we can take some of the agony out of dealing with them by telling ourselves that they are fated to behave as they do.

Suppose that even though we follow the above advice, someone succeeds in annoying us. In such cases, Marcus says, we should remind ourselves that "this mortal life endures but a moment," meaning that we soon will be dead.[11] Putting annoying incidents into their cosmic context, he thinks, will make their triviality apparent and will therefore alleviate our annoyance.

According to Marcus, the biggest risk to us in our dealings with annoying people is that they will make us hate them, a hatred that will be injurious to us. Therefore, we need to work to make sure men do not succeed in destroying our charitable feelings toward them. (Indeed, if a man is good, Marcus says, the gods will never see him harbor a grudge toward someone.) Thus, when men behave inhumanely, we should not feel toward them as they feel toward others. He adds that if we detect anger and hatred within us and wish to seek revenge, one of the best forms of revenge on another person is to refuse to be like him.[12]

Some of our most important relationships are with members of the opposite sex, and the Stoics had much to say regarding such relationships. A wise man, Musonius says, will not have sex outside of marriage and within marriage will have it only for the purpose of begetting children; to have sex in other circumstances suggests a lack of self-control.[13] Epictetus agrees that we should avoid having sex before marriage, but adds that if we succeed in doing this, we shouldn't boast about our chastity and belittle those who aren't likewise chaste.[14]

Marcus has even more misgivings about sex than Musonius and Epictetus did. In the *Meditations*, he provides us with a technique for discovering the true value of things: If we analyze something into the elements that compose it, we will see the thing for what it really is and thereby value it appropriately. Fine wine, thus analyzed, turns out to be nothing more than fermented grape juice, and the purple robes that Romans valued so highly turn out to be nothing more than the wool of a sheep stained with gore from a shellfish. When Marcus applies this analytical technique to sex, he discovers that it is nothing more than "friction of the members and an ejaculatory discharge."[15] We would therefore be foolish to place a high value on sexual relations and more foolish still to disrupt our life in order to experience such relations.

As it so happens, Buddhists recommend the use of this same analytic technique. When, for example, a man finds himself lusting after a woman, Buddhists might advise him to think not about her as a whole, but about the things that compose her, including her lungs, excrement, phlegm, pus, and spittle. Doing this, Buddhists claim, will help the man extinguish his lustful feelings. If this doesn't do the trick, Buddhists might advise him to imagine her body in the various stages of decomposition.[16]

The Stoics' advocacy of sexual reserve will sound prudish to modern readers, but they had a point. We live in an age of sexual indulgence, and for many people the consequences of this indulgence have been catastrophic in terms of their peace of mind. Think, for example, about the young woman who, because she could not resist sexual temptation, is now faced with the hardship that generally accompanies single parenthood, or the young man who, because he could not resist temptation, is now burdened with responsibilities (or at least child-support payments) that prevent him from pursuing the dreams he once had for himself. It is easy these days to find people who will agree that their life would have gone better if they had shown more sexual reserve; it is hard to find people who think their life would have gone better if they had shown less.

The Stoics, we should note, were not alone among the ancients in pointing to the destructive power of sex. Epicurus may have been the philosophical rival of the Stoics, but he shared their misgivings about sex: "Sexual intercourse has never done a man good, and he is lucky if it has not harmed him."[17]

But having said all this, I should add that despite their misgivings about sex, the Stoics were big advocates of marriage. A wise man, Musonius says, will marry, and having married, he and his wife will work hard to keep each other happy. Indeed, in a good marriage, two people will join in a loving union and will try to outdo each other in the care they show for each other.[18] Such a marriage, one imagines, will be very happy.

And having married, a wise man will bring children into the world. No religious procession, Musonius says, is as beautiful as a group of children guiding their parents through the city, leading them by the hand and taking care of them.[19] Few people, Musonius would have us believe, are happier than the person who has both a loving spouse and devoted children.

ELEVEN

Insults

On Putting Up with Put-Downs

SOME WILL THINK it strange that the Roman Stoics would spend time talking about insults and how best to deal with them. "Is this the proper function of a philosopher?" they will ask. It is, if we think, as the Stoics did, that the proper role of philosophy is to develop a philosophy of life.

The Stoics, as we have seen, counsel us to pursue tranquility. They realized, however, that one thing that prevents people from attaining and maintaining tranquility is the insults of others. As part of the strategy-for-living component of their philosophy of life, the Stoics therefore spent time developing techniques people could use to prevent the insults of others from upsetting them. In this chapter, I examine some of these techniques.

In what follows, I use the word *insult* in a very broad sense, to include not just verbal abuse, such as calling someone a name, but also "insults by omission," such as slighting or snubbing someone, and physical insults, such as slapping someone. People tend to be exquisitely sensitive to insults. As Musonius points out, under some circumstances a mere glance can be construed as an insult.[1] Furthermore, even when they are nonphysical, insults can be quite painful. If someone in a position of authority, a boss or teacher, for example, upbraids you in public, your feelings of anger and humiliation will likely be intense. Not only that, but insults are capable of causing you pain long after they have been delivered. A decade after the upbraiding just described, you might, in an idle moment, recall the incident, and despite the passage of time, you might find yourself again convulsed with anger.

To appreciate the power of insults to upset our tranquility, we need only take a look at the things that upset us in daily living. High on the list will be the insulting behavior of other people, including, most prominently, our friends, relatives, and coworkers. Sometimes these individuals openly and directly insult us: "You are a fool." More commonly, though, their insults are subtle or indirect. They might make us the butt of a joke: "Could you please put on a hat? The sunlight reflecting off the top of your head is blinding me." Or, after congratulating us for some success, they might feel compelled to remind us, for the hundredth time, of some past failure. Or they might offer us backhanded compliments: "That outfit hides your bulges." Or they might slight us by taking us for granted or by failing to give us the respect we feel we deserve. Or they might make a disparaging remark about us to someone else, who subsequently reports the remark to us. Any of these things can, if we let them, ruin our day.

It isn't only in modern times that people have been sensitive to insults. By way of illustration, consider the kinds of things that, according to Seneca, would have counted as insults in ancient Rome: "'So-and-so did not give me an audience to-day, though he gave it to others'; 'he haughtily repulsed or openly laughed at my conversation'; 'he did not give me the seat of honour, but placed me at the foot of the table.' "[2] If any of these things happened today, they would certainly be perceived as insults.

When insulted, people typically become angry. Because anger is a negative emotion that can upset our tranquility, the Stoics thought it worthwhile to develop strategies to prevent insults from angering us—strategies for removing, as it were, the sting of an insult. One of their sting-elimination strategies is to pause, when insulted, to consider whether what the insulter said is true. If it is, there is little reason to be upset. Suppose, for example, that someone mocks us for being bald when we in fact are bald: "Why is it an insult," Seneca asks, "to be told what is self-evident?"[3]

Another sting-elimination strategy, suggested by Epictetus, is to pause to consider how well-informed the insulter is. He might be saying something bad about us not because he wants to hurt our feelings but because he sincerely believes what he is saying, or, at any rate, he might simply be reporting how things seem to him.[4] Rather than getting angry at this person for his honesty, we should calmly set him straight.

One particularly powerful sting-elimination strategy is to consider the source of an insult. If I respect the source, if I value his opinions, then his critical remarks shouldn't upset me. Suppose, for example, that I am learning to play the banjo and that the person who is criticizing my playing is the skilled musician I have hired as my teacher. In this case, I am paying the person to criticize me. It would be utterly foolish, under these circumstances, for me to respond to his criticisms with hurt feelings. To the contrary, if I am serious about learning the banjo, I should thank him for criticizing me.

Suppose, however, that I don't respect the source of an insult; indeed, suppose that I take him to be a thoroughly contemptible individual. Under such circumstances, rather than feeling hurt by his insults, I should feel relieved: If *he* disapproves of what I am doing, then what I am doing is doubtless the right thing to do. What should worry me is if this contemptible person *approved of* what I am doing. If I say anything at all in response to his insults, the most appropriate comment would be, "I'm relieved that you feel that way about me."

When we consider the sources of insults, says Seneca, we will often find that those who insult us can best be described as overgrown children.[5] In the same way that a mother would be foolish to let the "insults" of her toddler upset her, we would be foolish to let the insults of these childish adults upset us. In other cases, we will find that those insulting us have deeply flawed characters. Such people, says Marcus, rather than deserving our anger, deserve our pity.[6]

As we make progress in our practice of Stoicism, we will become increasingly indifferent to other people's opinions of us. We will not go through our life with the goal of gaining their approval or avoiding their disapproval, and because we are indifferent to their opinions, we will feel no sting when they insult us. Indeed, a Stoic sage, were one to exist, would probably take the insults of his fellow humans to be like the barking of a dog. When a dog barks, we might make a mental note that the dog in question appears to dislike us, but we would be utter fools to allow ourselves to become upset by this fact, to go through the rest of the day thinking, "Oh, dear! That dog doesn't like me!"

One other important sting-elimination strategy, say the Stoics, is to keep in mind, when insulted, that we ourselves are the source of any sting that accompanies the insult. "Remember," says Epictetus, "that what is insulting is not the person who abuses you or hits you, but the judgment about them that they *are* insulting." As a result, he says, "another person will not do you harm unless you wish it; you will be harmed at just that time at which you take yourself to be harmed."[7] From this it follows that if we can convince ourselves that a person has done us no harm by insulting us, his insult will carry no sting.

This last advice is really just an application of the broader Stoic belief that, as Epictetus puts it, "what upsets people is not things themselves but their judgments about these things."[8] To better understand this claim, suppose someone deprives me of my property. He has done me harm only if it is my opinion that my property had real value. Suppose, by way of illustration, that someone steals a concrete birdbath from my back yard. If I treasured this birdbath, I will be quite upset by the theft. (And my neighbors, seeing how upset I am, might be puzzled: "Why is he getting all worked up over a stupid birdbath?" they will ask.) If I am indifferent to the birdbath, however, I will not be upset by its loss. To the contrary, I will be philosophical—more precisely, I will be Stoical—about the incident: "There is no point in getting all worked up over a stupid birdbath," I will tell myself. My tranquility will not be disrupted. Suppose, finally, that I abhor the birdbath: I keep it only because it was a gift from a relative who will be upset if I don't display it in my back yard. Under these circumstances, I might be delighted by its disappearance.

Do the things that happen to me help or harm me? It all depends, say the Stoics, on my values. They would go on to remind me that my values are things over which I have complete control. Therefore, if something external harms me, it is my own fault: I should have adopted different values.

EVEN IF WE SUCCEED in removing the sting of an insult, we are left with the question of how best to respond to it. Most people think that the best response is a counterinsult, preferably one that is clever. The Stoics, however, reject this advice. And how are we to respond to an insult, if not with a counterinsult? One wonderful way, say the Stoics, is with humor.

Thus, Seneca points approvingly to Cato's use of humor to deflect a particularly grievous insult. Cato was pleading a case when an adversary named Lentulus spit in his face. Rather than getting angry or returning the insult, Cato calmly wiped off the spit and said, "I will swear to anyone, Lentulus, that people are wrong to say that you cannot use your mouth!"[9] Seneca also approves of Socrates' response to an even more abusive insult. Someone once came up to Socrates and, without warning, boxed his ears. Rather than getting angry, Socrates made a joke about what a nuisance it is, when we go out, that we can never be sure whether or not to wear a helmet.[10]

Of the kinds of humor we might use in response to an insult, self-deprecating humor can be particularly effective. Along these lines, Seneca describes a man, Vatinius, whose neck was covered with wens and whose feet were diseased, who joked about his own deformities so much that others had nothing to add.[11] Epictetus also advocates the use of self-deprecating humor. Suppose, for example, you find out that someone has been saying bad things about you. Epictetus advises you to respond not by behaving defensively but by questioning his competence as an insulter; for example, you can comment that if the insulter knew you well enough to criticize you competently, he wouldn't have pointed to the particular failings that he did but would instead have mentioned other, much worse failings.[12]

By laughing off an insult, we are implying that we don't take the insulter and his insults seriously. To imply this, of course, is to insult the insulter without directly doing so. It is therefore a response that is likely to deeply frustrate the insulter. For this reason, a humorous reply to an insult can be far more effective than a counterinsult would be.

THE PROBLEM WITH replying to insults with humor is that doing so requires both wit and presence of mind. Many of us lack these traits. When insulted, we stand there dumbfounded: We know we have been insulted but don't know what to do next. If a clever response comes to us, it comes hours later, when it is of little use to us. Nothing is more pathetic, after all, than a person who, a day after being insulted, walks up to the person who insulted him, reminds him of what the insult was, and then gives his reply to it.

The Stoics realized this and as a result advocated a second way to respond to insults: with no response at all. Instead of reacting to an insult, says Musonius, we should "calmly and quietly bear what has happened." This is, he reminds us, "appropriate behavior for a person who wants to be magnanimous."[13] The advantage of a nonresponse, of simply carrying on as if the insulter hadn't even spoken, is that it requires no thought on our part. Indeed, even the most slow-witted person on the planet can respond to insults in this manner.

Along these lines, Seneca approvingly points to the response of Cato when someone who did not know who he was struck him at the public baths. When the person subsequently realized who Cato was and apologized to him, Cato, rather than getting angry at the man or punishing him, simply replied, "I don't remember being struck."[14] Cato, says Seneca, showed a finer spirit by not acknowledging the blow than he would have by pardoning it.[15]

Refusing to respond to an insult is, paradoxically, one of the most effective responses possible. For one thing, as Seneca points out, our nonresponse can be quite disconcerting to the insulter, who will wonder whether or not we understood his insult. Furthermore, we are robbing him of the pleasure of having upset us, and he is likely to be upset as a result.[16]

Notice, too, that by not responding to an insulter, we are showing him and anyone who is watching that we simply don't have time for the childish behavior of this person. If a humorous response to an insult shows that we don't take the insulter seriously, a nonresponse to an insult makes it look as if we are indifferent to the existence of the insulter: Not only don't we take him seriously, but we don't take him at all! No one wants to be ignored, though, and the insulter is likely to feel humiliated by our failure to respond to him—not with a counterinsult, not even with humor!

THE ABOVE DISCUSSION makes it sound as if the Stoics are complete pacifists with respect to insults, as if they will never respond to an insult with a counterinsult or by punishing the insulter. This is not the case, though. According to Seneca, there are times when it is appropriate for us to respond vigorously to an insult.

The danger in responding to insults with humor or with no response at all is that some insulters are sufficiently slow-witted that they won't realize that by refusing to respond to their insults with counterinsults, we are displaying disdain for what they think of us. Rather than being humiliated by our response, they might be encouraged by our jokes or silence, and they might start bombarding us with an endless stream of insults. This can be particularly awkward if the person doing the insulting was, in the ancient world, one's slave or if he is, in the modern world, one's employee, student, or child.

The Stoics realized this and offered advice on how to deal with such persons. In the same way that a mother might admonish or punish the child who pulled her hair, we will, in some cases, want to admonish or punish the person who childishly insults us. Thus, if a student insults her teacher in front of the class, the teacher would be unwise to ignore the insult. The insulter and her peers might, after all, interpret the teacher's nonresponse as acquiescence and as a result unleash a barrage of insults against him. This behavior would obviously disrupt the classroom and make it difficult for students to learn.

In such cases, though, the Stoic needs to keep in mind that he is punishing the insulter not because she has wronged him but to correct her improper behavior. It is, says Seneca, like training an animal: If in the course of trying to train a horse, we punish him, it should be because we want him to obey us in the future, not because we are angry about his failure to obey us in the past.[17]

We live in a time, to be sure, in which few people are willing to respond to an insult with humor or with a nonresponse. Indeed, those who advocate politically correct speech think the proper way to deal with some insults is to punish the insulter. What most concerns them are insults directed at the "disadvantaged," including members of minority groups and people with physical, mental, social, or economic handicaps. Disadvantaged individuals, they argue, are psychologically vulnerable, and if we let people insult them, they will suffer grievous psychological harm. Advocates of politically correct speech therefore petition the authorities—government officials, employers, and school administrators—to punish anyone who insults a disadvantaged individual.

Epictetus would reject this manner of dealing with insults as being woefully counterproductive. He would point out, to begin with, that the political correctness movement has some untoward side effects. One is that the process of protecting disadvantaged individuals from insults will tend to make them hypersensitive to insults: They will, as a result, feel the sting not only of direct insults but of implied insults as well. Another is that disadvantaged individuals will come to believe that they are powerless to deal with insults on their own—that unless the authorities intercede on their behalf, they are defenseless.

The best way to deal with insults directed at the disadvantaged, Epictetus would argue, is not to punish those who insult them but to teach members of disadvantaged groups techniques of insult self-defense. They need, in particular, to learn how to remove the sting from whatever insults are directed at them, and until they do this, they will remain hypersensitive to insults and will, as a result, experience considerable distress when insulted.

It is worth noting that Epictetus would, by modern standards, count as doubly disadvantaged: He was both lame and a slave. Despite these disadvantages, he found a way to rise above insults. More important, he found a way to experience joy despite the bad hand fate had dealt him. The modern "disadvantaged," one suspects, could learn a lot from Epictetus.

TWELVE

Grief

On Vanquishing Tears with Reason

Most parents, on learning of the death of a child, will be emotionally devastated. They will weep, perhaps for days on end, and they will be unable to go about their daily routine for a time. Long after the death, they might experience grief flashbacks; their eyes might well up, for example, on seeing a picture of their child. And how will a Stoic respond to the death of a child? One might imagine that he will respond with no response at all, that he will suppress whatever feelings he might be having or, better still, that he will have trained himself not to grieve.

The belief that Stoics never grieve, although widely held, is mistaken. Emotions such as grief, the Stoics understood, are to some extent reflexive. In much the same way that we cannot help being startled when we hear a loud, unexpected noise—it is a physical reflex—we cannot help feeling grief-stricken when we learn of the unexpected loss of a loved one—it is an emotional reflex. Thus, in his consolation to Polybius, who was grieving the death of his brother, Seneca writes, "Nature requires from us some sorrow, while more than this is the result of vanity. But never will I demand of you that you should not grieve at all."[1]

How much should a Stoic grieve? In proper grief, Seneca tells Polybius, our reason "will maintain a mean which will copy neither indifference nor madness, and will keep us in the state that is the mark of an affectionate, and not an unbalanced, mind." Consequently, he advises Polybius to "let your tears flow, but let them also cease, let deepest sighs be drawn from your breast, but let them also find an end."[2]

Although it might not be possible to eliminate grief from our life, it is possible, Seneca thinks, to take steps to minimize the amount of grief we experience over the course of a lifetime. And given that such steps exist, we ought to take them. We live, after all, in a world in which there is potentially much for us to grieve. Consequently, says Seneca, we ought to be parsimonious with our tears, since "nothing must be husbanded more carefully than that of which there is such frequent need."[3] It was with these thoughts in mind that Seneca and the other Stoics developed strategies by which we can prevent ourselves from experiencing excessive grief and overcome quickly whatever grief we might find ourselves experiencing.

The Stoics' primary grief-prevention strategy was to engage in negative visualization. By contemplating the deaths of those we love, we will remove some of the shock we experience if they die; we will in a sense have seen it coming. Furthermore, if we contemplate the deaths of those we love, we will likely take full advantage of our relationships with them and therefore won't, if they die, find ourselves filled with regrets about all the things we could and should have done with and for them.

Besides being used to prevent grief, negative visualization can be used to extinguish it. Consider, for example, the advice Seneca gives to Marcia, a woman who, three years after the death of her son, was as grief-stricken as on the day she buried him. Rather than spending her days thinking bitterly about the happiness she has been deprived of by the death of her son, Marcia should, says Seneca, think about how much worse off she would be today if she had never been able to enjoy his company. In other words, rather than mourning the end of his life, she should be thankful that he lived at all.[4]

This is what might be called *retrospective* negative visualization. In normal, prospective negative visualization, we imagine losing something we currently possess; in retrospective negative visualization, we imagine never having had something that we have lost. By engaging in retrospective negative visualization, Seneca thinks, we can replace our feelings of regret at having lost something with feelings of thanks for once having had it.

In his consolation to Polybius, Seneca offers advice on how to overcome whatever grief we happen to be experiencing. Reason is our best weapon against grief, he maintains, because "unless reason puts an end to our tears, fortune will not do so." More generally, Seneca thinks that although reason might not be able to extinguish our grief, it has the power to remove from it "whatever is excessive and superfluous."[5]

Seneca then sets about using rational persuasion to cure Polybius of his excessive grief. For example, he argues that the brother whose death Polybius is grieving either would or wouldn't want Polybius to be tortured with tears. If he would want Polybius to suffer, then he isn't worthy of tears, so Polybius should stop crying; if he wouldn't want Polybius to suffer, then it is incumbent on Polybius, if he loves and respects his brother, to stop crying. In another argument, Seneca points out that Polybius's brother, because he is dead, is no longer capable of grief and that this is a good thing; it is therefore madness for Polybius to go on grieving.[6]

Another of Seneca's consolations is addressed to Helvia, Seneca's mother. Whereas Polybius had been grieving the death of a loved one, Helvia was grieving the exile of Seneca. In his advice to Helvia, Seneca takes the argument he offered Polybius—that the person whose death Polybius is grieving wouldn't want him to grieve—one step further: Because it is Seneca's circumstances that Helvia is grieving, he argues that inasmuch as he, being a Stoic, doesn't grieve his circumstances, Helvia shouldn't either. (His consolation to Helvia, he observes, is unique: Although he read every consolation he could find, in not one of them did the author console people who were bemoaning the author himself.)[7]

In some cases, such appeals to reason will doubtless help alleviate, if only for a time, the grief someone is experiencing. In cases of extreme grief, though, such appeals are unlikely to succeed for the simple reason that the grieving person's emotions are ruling his intellect. But even in these cases, our attempts to reason with him might be useful, inasmuch as such attempts can make him understand the extent to which his intellect has capitulated to his emotions and thereby induce him, perhaps, to take steps to restore his intellect to its rightful role.

Epictetus also offers advice on grief management. He advises us, in particular, to take care not to "catch" the grief of others. Suppose, for example, we encounter a grief-stricken woman. We should, says Epictetus, sympathize with her and maybe even accompany her moaning with moaning of our own. But in doing so, we should be careful not to "moan inwardly."[8] In other words, we should display signs of grief without allowing ourselves to experience grief.

Some will be offended by this advice. When others are grieving, they will assert, we shouldn't just pretend as if we sympathize with them; we should actually feel their losses and actually grieve ourselves. Epictetus might respond to this criticism by pointing out that the advice that we respond to the grief of friends by grieving ourselves is as foolish as the advice that we help someone who has been poisoned by taking poison ourselves or help someone who has the flu by intentionally catching it from him. Grief is a negative emotion and therefore one that we should, to the extent possible, avoid experiencing. If a friend is grieving, our goal should be to help her overcome her grief (or rather, if we properly internalize our goals, it should be to do our best to help her overcome her grief). If we can accomplish this by moaning insincerely, then let us do so. For us to "catch" her grief, after all, won't help her but will hurt us.

Some readers will at this point become skeptical about the wisdom and efficacy of Stoic techniques for dealing with negative emotions. We live in an age in which the consensus view, held by health professionals and laypersons alike, is that our emotional health requires us to be in touch with our emotions, to share them with others, and to vent them without reservation. The Stoics, on the other hand, advocate that we sometimes feign emotions and that we sometimes take steps to extinguish the genuine emotions we find within us. Some might therefore conclude that it is dangerous to follow Stoic advice regarding our emotions, and because such advice lies at the heart of Stoicism, they might go on to reject Stoicism as a philosophy of life.

Rest assured that in chapter 20 I will respond to this criticism of Stoicism. I will do so, to the amazement of some, by questioning consensus views on what we should do to maintain our emotional health. It is doubtless true that some individuals—those experiencing intense grief, for example—can benefit from psychological counseling. I also think, though, that many people can enjoy robust emotional health without resorting to such counseling. In particular, I think the practice of Stoicism can help us avoid many of the emotional crises that afflict people. I also think that if we do find ourselves in the grip of a negative emotion, following Stoic advice will, in many cases, allow us single-handedly to subdue that emotion.

THIRTEEN

Anger

On Overcoming Anti-Joy

ANGER IS ANOTHER negative emotion that, if we let it, can destroy our tranquility. Indeed, anger can be thought of as anti-joy. The Stoics therefore devised strategies to minimize the amount of anger we experience.

The best single source for Stoic advice on preventing and dealing with anger is Seneca's essay "On Anger." Anger, says Seneca, is "brief insanity," and the damage done by anger is enormous: "No plague has cost the human race more." Because of anger, he says, we see all around us people being killed, poisoned, and sued; we see cities and nations ruined. And besides destroying cities and nations, anger can destroy us individually. We live in a world, after all, in which there is much to be angry about, meaning that unless we can learn to control our anger, we will be perpetually angry. Being angry, Seneca concludes, is a waste of precious time.[1]

SOME MAINTAIN that anger has its uses. They point out that when we are angry, we are motivated. Seneca rejects this claim. It is true, he says, that people sometimes benefit from being angry, but it hardly follows from this that we should welcome anger into our life. Notice, after all, that people also sometimes benefit from being in a shipwreck, yet who in their right mind would therefore take steps to increase their chances of being shipwrecked? What worries Seneca about employing anger as a motivational tool is that after we turn it on, we will be unable to turn it off, and that whatever good it initially does us will (on average) be more than offset by the harm it subsequently does. "Reason," he cautions, "will never enlist the aid of reckless unbridled impulses over which it has no authority."[2]

Is Seneca saying, then, that a person who sees his father killed and his mother raped should not feel angry? That he should stand there and do nothing? Not at all. He should punish the wrongdoer and protect his parents, but to the extent possible he should remain calm as he does so. Indeed, he will probably do a better job of punishing and protecting if he can avoid getting angry. More generally, when someone wrongs us, says Seneca, he should be corrected "by admonition and also by force, gently and also roughly." Such corrections, however, should not be made in anger. We are punishing people not as retribution for what they have done but for their own good, to deter them from doing again whatever they did. Punishment, in other words, should be "an expression not of anger but of caution."[3]

In our discussion of insults, we saw that Seneca makes an exception to his rule to respond to insults with humor or with no response at all: If we are dealing with someone who, despite being an adult, behaves like a child, we might want to punish him for insulting us. It is, after all, the only thing he will understand. Likewise, there are individuals who, when they wrong us, are incapable of changing their behavior in response to our measured, rational entreaties. When dealing with this sort of shallow individual, it does not make sense to become actually angry—doing so will likely spoil our day—but it might make sense, Seneca thinks, to *feign* anger.[4] By doing this, we can get this person to mend his ways with minimal disruption of our own tranquility. In other words, although Seneca rejects the idea of allowing ourselves to become angry in order to motivate ourselves, he is open to the idea of pretending to be angry in order to motivate others.

Seneca offers lots of specific advice on how to prevent anger. We should, he says, fight our tendency to believe the worst about others and our tendency to jump to conclusions about their motivations. We need to keep in mind that just because things don't turn out the way we want them to, it doesn't follow that someone has done us an injustice. In particular, says Seneca, we need to remember that in some cases, the person at whom we are angry in fact helped us; in such cases, what angers us is that he didn't help us even more.[5]

If we are overly sensitive, we will be quick to anger. More generally, says Seneca, if we coddle ourselves, if we allow ourselves to be corrupted by pleasure, nothing will seem bearable to us, and the reason things will seem unbearable is not because they are hard but because we are soft. Seneca therefore recommends that we take steps to ensure that we never get too comfortable. (This, of course, is only one of the reasons Stoics give for eschewing comfort; in chapter 7 we examined some others.) If we harden ourselves in this manner, we are much less likely to be disturbed, he says, by the shouting of a servant or the slamming of a door, and therefore much less likely to be angered by such things. We won't be overly sensitive about what others say or do, and we will be less likely to find ourselves provoked by "vulgar trivialities," such as being served lukewarm water to drink or seeing a couch in a mess.[6]

To avoid becoming angry, says Seneca, we should also keep in mind that the things that anger us generally don't do us any real harm; they are instead mere annoyances. By allowing ourselves to get angry over little things, we take what might have been a barely noticeable disruption of our day and transform it into a tranquility-shattering state of agitation. Furthermore, as Seneca observes, "our anger invariably lasts longer than the damage done to us."[7] What fools we are, therefore, when we allow our tranquility to be disrupted by minor things.

The Stoics, as we have seen, recommend that we use humor to deflect insults: Cato cracked a joke when someone spit in his face, as did Socrates when someone boxed his ears. Seneca suggests that besides being an effective response to an insult, humor can be used to prevent ourselves from becoming angry: "Laughter," he says, "and a lot of it, is the right response to the things which drive us to tears!"[8] The idea is that by choosing to think of the bad things that happen to us as being funny rather than outrageous, an incident that might have angered us can instead become a source of amusement. Indeed, one imagines that Cato and Socrates, by using humor in response to an insult, not only deflected the insult but prevented themselves from getting angry at the person who had insulted them.

Marcus also offers advice on anger avoidance. He recommends, as we have seen, that we contemplate the impermanence of the world around us. If we do this, he says, we will realize that many of the things we think are important in fact aren't, at least not in the grand scheme of things. He reflects on the times, almost a century earlier, of Emperor Vespasian. People everywhere were doing the usual things: marrying, raising children, farming, loving, envying, fighting, and feasting. But, he points out, "of all that life, not a trace survives today."[9] By implication, this will be the fate of our generation: What seems vitally important to us will seem unimportant to our grandchildren. Thus, when we feel ourselves getting angry about something, we should pause to consider its cosmic (in)significance. Doing this might enable us to nip our anger in the bud.

SUPPOSE WE FIND that despite our attempts to prevent anger, the behavior of other people succeeds in angering us. It will help us to overcome our anger, says Seneca, if we remind ourselves that our behavior also angers other people: "We are bad men living among bad men, and only one thing can calm us—we must agree to go easy on one another." He also offers anger-management advice that has a parallel in Buddhism. When angry, says Seneca, we should take steps to "turn all [anger's] indications into their opposites." We should force ourselves to relax our face, soften our voice, and slow our pace of walking. If we do this, our internal state will soon come to resemble our external state, and our anger, says Seneca, will have dissipated.[10] Buddhists practice a similar thought-substitution technique. When they are experiencing an unwholesome thought, Buddhists force themselves to think the opposite, and therefore wholesome, thought. If they are experiencing anger, for example, they force themselves to think about love. The claim is that because two opposite thoughts cannot exist in one mind at one time, the wholesome thought will drive out the unwholesome one.[11]

What if we are unable to control our anger? Indeed, what if we find ourselves lashing out at whoever angered us? We should apologize. Doing this can almost instantly repair the social damage our outburst might have caused. It can also benefit us personally: The act of apologizing, besides having a calming effect on us, can prevent us from subsequently obsessing over the thing that made us angry. Finally, apologizing for the outburst can help us become a better person: By admitting our mistakes, we lessen the chance that we will make them again in the future.

Everyone occasionally experiences anger: Like grief, anger is an emotional reflex. There are also people, though, who seem to be angry pretty much all of the time. These individuals are not only easily provoked to anger, but even when provocation is absent they remain angry. Indeed, during leisure hours, these individuals might spend their time recalling, with a certain degree of relish, past events that made them angry or things in general that make them angry. At the same time that it is consuming them, anger appears to be providing them with sustenance.

Such cases, the Stoics would tell us, are tragic. For one thing, life is too short to spend it in a state of anger. Furthermore, a person who is constantly angry will be a torment to those around her. Why not instead, Seneca asks, "make yourself a person to be loved by all while you live and missed when you have made your departure?"[12] More generally, why experience anti-joy when you have it in your power to experience joy? Why, indeed?

FOURTEEN

Personal Values

On Seeking Fame

PEOPLE ARE UNHAPPY, the Stoics argue, in large part because they are confused about what is valuable. Because of their confusion, they spend their days pursuing things that, rather than making them happy, make them anxious and miserable.

One of the things people mistakenly pursue is fame. The fame in question comes in varying degrees. Some want to be known around the world. Some seek not world fame, but regional or local fame. Those who don't actively pursue even local fame nevertheless seek popularity within their social circle or recognition in their chosen profession. And almost everyone seeks the admiration of friends and neighbors. They are convinced that gaining fame (in some very broad sense of the word) will make them happy. They fail to realize that fame, whether it involves world renown or merely the admiration of their neighbors, comes at a price. Indeed, the Stoics claim that the price of fame is sufficiently high that it far outweighs any benefits fame can confer on us.

TO BETTER APPRECIATE the price of fame, consider the following example, offered by Epictetus. Suppose it is your goal to be a socially prominent individual, to be "famous" within your social circle, and suppose someone within your circle is giving a banquet. If this person fails to invite you, you will pay a price: You will likely be upset by the snub. But even if he does invite you, Epictetus points out, it will be because you paid a price in the past: You went out of your way to pay attention to the banquet giver and to shower him with praise. Epictetus adds that you are both greedy and stupid if you expect a place at the banquet table without having paid this price.[1]

You would have been much better off, Epictetus thinks, if you had been indifferent to social status. For one thing, you would not have had to spend time trying to curry favor with this person. Furthermore, you would have deprived him of the ability to upset you simply by failing to invite you to a banquet.

Stoics value their freedom, and they are therefore reluctant to do anything that will give others power over them. But if we seek social status, we give other people power over us: We have to do things calculated to make them admire us, and we have to refrain from doing things that will trigger their disfavor. Epictetus therefore advises us not to seek social status, since if we make it our goal to please others, we will no longer be free to please ourselves. We will, he says, have enslaved ourselves.[2]

If we wish to retain our freedom, says Epictetus, we must be careful, while dealing with other people, to be indifferent to what they think of us. Furthermore, we should be consistent in our indifference; we should, in other words, be as dismissive of their approval as we are of their disapproval. Indeed, Epictetus says that when others praise us, the proper response is to laugh at them.[3] (But not out loud! Although Epictetus and the other

Stoics think we should be indifferent to people's opinions of us, they would advise us to conceal our indifference. After all, to tell someone else that you don't care what he thinks is quite possibly the worst insult you can inflict.)

Marcus agrees with Epictetus that it is foolish for us to worry about what other people think of us and particularly foolish for us to seek the approval of people whose values we reject. Our goal should therefore be to become indifferent to other people's opinions of us. He adds that if we can succeed in doing this, we will improve the quality of our life.[4]

Notice that the advice that we ignore what other people think of us is consistent with the Stoic advice that we not concern ourselves with things we can't control. I don't have it in my power to stop others from sneering at me, so it is foolish for me to spend time trying to stop them. I should instead, says Marcus, spend this time on something I have complete control over, namely, not doing anything that deserves a sneer.[5]

Marcus also offers some words of advice to those who value what many would take to be the ultimate form of fame: immortal fame. Such fame, Marcus says, is "an empty, hollow thing." After all, think about how foolish it is to want to be remembered after we die. For one thing, since we are dead, we will not be able to enjoy our fame. For another, we are foolish to think that future generations will praise us, without even having met us, when we find it so difficult to praise our contemporaries, even though we meet them routinely. Instead of thinking about future fame, Marcus says, we would do well to concern ourselves with our present situation; we should, he advises, "make the best of today."[6]

Suppose we admit that the Stoics were right: We should ignore what other people think of us. For most people, this will be difficult advice to follow. Most of us, after all, are obsessed with other people's opinions of us: We work hard, first to win the admiration of other people and then to avoid losing it.

One way to overcome this obsession, the Stoics think, is to realize that in order to win the admiration of other people, we will have to adopt their values. More precisely, we will have to live a life that is successful according to their notion of success. (If we are living what they take to be an unsuccessful life, they will have no reason to admire us.) Consequently, before we try to win the admiration of these other people, we should stop to ask whether their notion of success is compatible with ours. More important, we should stop to ask whether these people, by pursuing whatever it is they value, are gaining the tranquility we seek. If they aren't, we should be more than willing to forgo their admiration.

Another way to overcome our obsession with winning the admiration of other people is to go out of our way to do things likely to trigger their disdain. Along these lines, Cato made a point of ignoring the dictates of fashion: When everyone was wearing light purple, he wore dark, and although ancient Romans normally went out in public wearing shoes and a tunic, Cato wore neither. According to Plutarch, Cato did this not because he "sought vainglory"; to the contrary, he dressed differently in order to accustom himself "to be ashamed only of what was really shameful, and to ignore men's low opinion of other things."[7] In other words, Cato consciously did things to trigger the disdain of other people simply so he could practice ignoring their disdain.

Many people are haunted by a fear that in some cases significantly constrains their freedom, namely, the fear of failure. The individuals in question might contemplate doing something that will test their courage, determination, and ability, but then decide against the attempt, with the key factor in their decision being the fear of failure. From their point of view, it is better not even to attempt something than to fail while trying to accomplish it.

There are, to be sure, failures that any sensible person will want to avoid—those failures, for example, that result in death or disfigurement. The failures that many people seek to avoid, though, will not cost them their life or health. The cost of failure is instead having to endure the open mockery, or maybe the silent pity, of those who learn of their failure. It is better, failure-averse people reason, not even to attempt an undertaking than to run the risk of public humiliation.

Realize that many other people, including, quite possibly, your friends and relatives, want you to fail in your undertakings. They may not tell you this to your face, but this doesn't mean that they aren't silently rooting against you. People do this in part because your success makes them look bad and therefore makes them uncomfortable: If you can succeed, why can't they? Consequently, if you attempt something daring they might ridicule you, predict disaster, and try to talk you out of pursuing your goal. If, despite their warnings, you make your attempt and succeed, they might finally congratulate you—or they might not.

Consider again the woman, mentioned in an earlier chapter, whose goal is to write a novel. Suppose she tells her friends, relatives, and coworkers about her literary aspirations. Some of those she confides in will be genuinely encouraging. Others will respond to her announcement, though, with gleeful pessimism. They might predict that she will never finish the novel. (And to annoy her, they might, with clocklike regularity, ask how the novel is coming along.) If she finishes it, they might predict that she will never find a publisher for it. If she finds a publisher, they might predict that the novel will not sell well. And if it sells well, they might hold up her success as evidence of the low standards of the book-buying public.

It is, of course, possible for this woman to win the approval of these naysayers: She need only abandon her dream of becoming a novelist. If she does this, the naysayers will recognize her as a kindred spirit and will welcome her with open arms. They will invite her to sit with them on a comfortable couch somewhere and join them in mocking those individuals who pursue their dreams despite the possibility of failure. But is this really the company she wants to keep? Does she really want to abandon the pursuit of her dream in order to win these individuals' acceptance?

This woman would do well, say the Stoics, to work at becoming indifferent to what others think of her. And the above naysayers, it should be clear, belong at the very top of the list of people whose views she should learn to ignore.

IRONICALLY, BY REFUSING to seek the admiration of other people, Stoics might succeed in gaining their (perhaps grudging) admiration. Many people, for example, will construe the Stoics' indifference to public opinion as a sign of self-confidence: Only someone who really knows who she is—someone who, as they say, feels good about herself—would display this kind of indifference. These people might wish that they, too, could ignore what other people thought of them.

In some cases, people's admiration might be sufficient for them to ask the Stoic how she does it. When she reveals her secret—when she confesses that she is a practicing Stoic—will she thereby trigger a conversion in those who ask? Probably not. They might think she is teasing them. Who, these days, practices Stoicism? Or they might decide that although Stoicism works for her, it won't, because of personality differences, work for them. Or they will, in all too many cases, conclude that although it would be nice to gain the self-confidence enjoyed by the Stoics, there are other things that are even more worth pursuing, things such as fame . . . or a life of luxury.

FIFTEEN

Personal Values

On Luxurious Living

Besides valuing fame, people typically value wealth. These two values may seem independent, but a case can be made that the primary reason we seek wealth is that we seek fame.[1] More precisely, we seek wealth because we realize that the material goods our wealth can buy us will win the admiration of other people and thereby confer on us a degree of fame. But if fame isn't worth pursuing, and if our primary reason for seeking wealth is so we can gain fame, then wealth shouldn't be worth pursuing either. And according to the Stoics, it isn't.

In his consolation to Helvia, for example, Seneca reminds us how small our bodies are and poses this question: "Is it not madness and the wildest lunacy to desire so much when you can hold so little?" Furthermore, he says, it is folly "to think that it is the amount of money and not the state of mind that matters!"[2] Musonius agrees with this assessment. Possessing wealth, he observes, won't enable us to live without sorrow and won't console us in our old age. And although wealth can procure for us physical luxuries and various pleasures of the senses, it can never bring us contentment or banish our grief. In support of this assertion, Musonius points to all the rich men who feel sad and wretched despite their wealth.[3] Along similar lines, Epictetus asserts that "it is better to die of hunger with distress and fear gone than to live upset in the midst of plenty."[4] More generally, he argues that not needing wealth is more valuable than wealth itself is.[5]

It would be bad enough if the acquisition of wealth failed to bring people happiness, but Musonius thinks the situation is even worse than this: Wealth has the power to make people miserable. Indeed, if you wanted to make someone truly miserable, you might consider showering him with wealth. Musonius once gave a sum of money to a man who was posing as a philosopher. When people told him that the man was an imposter, that he was in fact a bad and vicious person, Musonius, rather than taking the money back, let him keep it. He said, with a smile, that if he was in fact a bad person, he deserved the money.[6]

MOST PEOPLE USE their wealth to finance a luxurious lifestyle, one that will win them the admiration of others. But such a lifestyle, the Stoics argued, is counterproductive if our goal is not to live well but to have a good life.

Consider, for example, the extravagant meals associated with luxurious living. Do those who eat such meals experience more pleasure than those whose diets are simple? Musonius doesn't think so. People with extravagant diets, he says, resemble iron that, because it is inferior, must constantly be sharpened; more precisely, these individuals will be unhappy with a meal unless it has been "sharpened" with unmixed wine, vinegar, or a tart sauce.[7]

There is indeed a danger that if we are exposed to a luxurious lifestyle, we will lose our ability to take delight in simple things. At one time, we might have been able to savor a bowl of macaroni and cheese, accompanied by a glass of milk, but after living in luxury for a few months we might find that macaroni no longer appeals to our discriminating palate; we might start rejecting it in favor of fettuccine Alfredo, accompanied by a particular brand of bottled water. And not long after that, we might, if we can afford to do so, reject even this meal in favor of, say, risotto with Maine sweet shrimp and just-picked squash blossoms, accompanied by a bottle of that Riesling the critics have been raving about, and preceded, of course, by a nice salad of baby frisée, topped with braised artichokes, fava beans, Valencay cheese, baby asparagus, and confit cherry tomatoes.[8]

When, as the result of being exposed to luxurious living, people become hard to please, a curious thing happens. Rather than mourning the loss of their ability to enjoy simple things, they take pride in their newly gained inability to enjoy anything but "the best." The Stoics, however, would pity these individuals. They would point out that by undermining their ability to enjoy simple, easily obtainable things—bowls of macaroni and cheese, for example—these individuals have seriously impaired their ability to enjoy life. The Stoics work hard to avoid falling victim to this kind of connoisseurship. Indeed, the Stoics value highly their ability to enjoy ordinary life—and indeed, their ability to find sources of delight even when living in primitive conditions.

It was partly for this reason that Musonius advocated a simple diet. More precisely, he thought it best to eat foods that needed little preparation, including fruits, green vegetables, milk, and cheese. He tried to avoid meat since it was, he thought, a food more appropriate for wild animals. He advised that when someone eats, he should choose food "not for pleasure but for nourishment, not to please his palate but to strengthen his body." Finally, Musonius advises us to follow the example set by Socrates: Rather than living to eat—rather than spending our life pursuing the pleasure to be derived from food—we should eat to live.[9]

Why would Musonius deprive himself of what seem like harmless gastronomic pleasures? Because he thinks they are anything but harmless. He recalls Zeno's observation that we should guard against acquiring a taste for delicacies, because once we start in this direction, it will be difficult to stop. Another thing to keep in mind is that although we may go months or even years between our encounters with other sources of pleasure, we must eat daily, and that the more often we are tempted by a pleasure, the more danger there is that we will succumb to it. It is for this reason, Musonius says, that "the pleasure connected with food is undoubtedly the most difficult of all pleasures to combat."[10]

Besides enjoying extravagant diets, those who live in luxury also wear expensive clothes and live in expensive, finely furnished houses. But according to the Stoics, in the same way that we should favor a simple diet, we should favor simple clothing, housing, and furnishings. Musonius, for example, advises us to dress to protect our bodies, not to impress other people. Likewise, our housing should be functional: It should do little more than keep out extreme heat and cold, and shelter us from the sun and wind. A cave would be fine, if one were available. He reminds us that houses with courtyards, fancy color schemes, and gilded ceilings are hard to maintain. Furthermore, our simple house should be furnished simply. Its kitchen should be supplied with earthenware and iron vessels rather than those made of silver and gold; besides being cheaper, Musonius observes, such vessels are easier to cook with and less likely to be stolen.[11]

People who achieve luxurious lifestyles are rarely satisfied: Experiencing luxury only whets their appetite for even more luxury. In defense of this claim, Seneca asks his friend Lucilius to imagine that he has become magnificently wealthy, that his house has marble floors and is decked with gold, and that his clothing is royal purple. Having all this, he observes, will not make Lucilius happy: "You will only learn from such things to crave still greater." This is because the desire for luxuries is not a natural desire. Natural desires, such as a desire for water when we are thirsty, can be satisfied; unnatural desires cannot.[12] Therefore, when we find ourselves wanting something, we should pause to ask whether the desire is natural or unnatural, and if it is unnatural, we should think twice about trying to satisfy it.

Luxury, Seneca warns, uses her wit to promote vices: First she makes us want things that are inessential, then she makes us want things that are injurious. Before long, the mind becomes slave to the body's whims and pleasures.[13] Along similar lines, Musonius tells us that he would rather be sick than live in luxury. Sickness, he argues, may harm the body, but a life of luxury harms the soul as well by making it "undisciplined and cowardly." Therefore, he concludes, "luxurious living must be completely avoided."[14]

If we take to heart the advice of the Stoics and forgo luxurious living, we will find that our needs are easily met, for as Seneca reminds us, life's necessities are cheap and easily obtainable.[15] Those who crave luxury typically have to spend considerable time and energy to attain it; those who eschew luxury can devote this same time and energy to other, more worthwhile undertakings.

HOW MUCH WEALTH should we acquire? According to Seneca, our financial goal should be to acquire "an amount that does not descend to poverty, and yet is not far removed from poverty." We should, he says, learn to restrain luxury, cultivate frugality, and "view poverty with unprejudiced eyes."[16] The lifestyle of a Stoic, he adds, should be somewhere in between that of a sage and that of an ordinary person.[17]

Epictetus is more austere in the advice he offers: We should, he said, "take what has to do with the body to the point of bare need." And what is it that we need? Food enough to nourish our body, clothing enough to cover it, and a house big enough to enclose it.[18] It is worth noting that despite living a spartan lifestyle, the Stoic, because he practices negative visualization, might be more content with what he has than someone living in the lap of luxury.

Epictetus encourages us to keep in mind that self-respect, trustworthiness, and high-mindedness are more valuable than wealth, meaning that if the only way to gain wealth is to give up these personal characteristics, we would be foolish to seek wealth. Furthermore, we should remember that one person's being richer than another does not mean that the first person is better than the other.[19] Likewise, we should keep in mind Seneca's comment to Lucilius that "the man who adapts himself to his slender means and makes himself wealthy on a little sum, is the truly rich man."[20] (The Stoics, by the way, are not alone in making this observation. On the other side of the globe, for example, Lao Tzu observed that "he who knows contentment is rich.")[21]

EVEN THOUGH SHE DOESN'T pursue wealth, a Stoic might nevertheless acquire it. A Stoic will, after all, do what she can to make herself useful to her fellow humans. And thanks to her practice of Stoicism, she will be self-disciplined and single-minded, traits that will help her accomplish the tasks she sets for herself. As a result, she might be quite effective in helping others, and they might reward her for doing so. It is possible, in other words, for the practice of Stoicism to be financially rewarding.

Suppose that this Stoic—thanks, once again, to her practice of Stoicism—has also lost interest in luxurious living and, more generally, has overcome her craving for consumer goods. As a result, she is likely to retain a large portion of her income and might thereby become wealthy. It is indeed ironic: A Stoic who disparages wealth might become wealthier than those individuals whose principal goal is its acquisition. The Roman Stoics we have been considering appear to have experienced this prosperity paradox. Seneca and Marcus were beyond wealthy, and

Musonius and Epictetus, as heads of successful Stoic schools, would presumably have been financially comfortable. (Indeed, Musonius's income was sufficient, as we have seen, for him to be able to give money to a philosophical imposter.)

What will a Stoic do if, despite not pursuing wealth, she finds herself well off? Stoicism does not require her to renounce wealth; it allows her to enjoy it and use it to the benefit of herself and those around her. It does, however, require her enjoyment to be thoughtful. She must keep firmly in mind that her wealth can be snatched from her; indeed, she should spend time preparing herself for the loss of it—by, for example, periodically practicing poverty. She must also keep in mind that unless she is careful, enjoyment of her wealth can undermine her character and her capacity to enjoy life. She will, for this reason, steer clear of a luxurious lifestyle. Thus, the Stoic's enjoyment of wealth will be strikingly different from that of, say, the typical person who has just won the lottery.

We need to keep in mind the difference between the Cynics and the Stoics. Cynicism requires its adherents to live in abject poverty; Stoicism does not. As Seneca reminds us, Stoic philosophy "calls for plain living, but not for penance."[22] More generally, it is perfectly acceptable, says Seneca, for a Stoic to acquire wealth, as long as he does not harm others to obtain it. It is also acceptable for a Stoic to enjoy wealth, as long as he is careful not to cling to it. The idea is that it is possible to enjoy something and at the same time be indifferent to it. Thus, Seneca claims, "I shall despise riches alike when I have them and when I have them not, being neither cast down if they shall lie elsewhere, nor puffed up if they shall glitter around me." Indeed, a wise man "never reflects so much upon poverty as when he abides in the midst of riches," and he will be careful to regard his riches as his slave, not as his master.[23]

(And having said this, I should add that different Stoics had different ideas about just how heartily a Stoic should enjoy his wealth. Musonius and Epictetus appear to have thought that even a minimal exposure to luxurious living would corrupt us, while Seneca and Marcus thought it possible to live in a palace without being corrupted.)

The Buddhist viewpoint regarding wealth, by the way, is very much like the view I have ascribed to the Stoics: It is permissible to be a wealthy Buddhist, as long as you don't cling to your wealth. This, at any rate, is the advice Buddha gave to Anathapindika, a man of "unmeasurable wealth": "He that cleaves to wealth had better cast it away than allow his heart to be poisoned by it; but he who does not cleave to wealth, and possessing riches, uses them rightly, will be a blessing unto his fellows."[24]

THE PRECEDING COMMENTS about wealth, by the way, also apply to fame. The Stoics, as we have seen, will not seek fame; to the contrary, they will strive to be indifferent to what others think of them. It is nevertheless possible for them to become famous. Indeed, the four Roman Stoics we have been considering all enjoyed fame. (Musonius and Epictetus obviously weren't as famous as Seneca and Marcus, but they were recognized in their chosen profession, and even those Romans who didn't attend their schools were likely to have heard of them.)

So what should a Stoic do if, despite not seeking it, she finds herself famous? Should she enjoy this fame, the way she might enjoy the wealth she acquired, despite not having pursued it? I think the Stoics would have been more wary of enjoying fame than enjoying fortune. There is a danger, as we have seen, that wealth will corrupt us, particularly if we use it to finance luxurious living. The danger that fame will corrupt us, however, is even greater. In particular, the glow that comes from being famous might trigger in us a desire for even more fame, and the obvious way to accomplish this is by saying things and living in a manner calculated to gain the admiration of other people. To do this, though, we will probably have to betray our Stoic principles.

It is therefore unlikely that a Stoic will bask in any fame that comes her way. At the same time, she will not hesitate to use this fame as a tool in the performance of what she takes to be her social duty. Thus, Musonius and Epictetus presumably did not mind that their names were known to many, inasmuch as this increased their chances of drawing students to their schools and thereby enabled them to disseminate their Stoic views in a more effective manner

SIXTEEN

Exile

On Surviving a Change of Place

In ancient Rome, people were sentenced to exile for a variety of crimes, both real and imagined, and it would appear that being a philosopher increased one's chances of being punished in this manner. Indeed, philosophers were expelled from Rome at least three times: in 161 BC, again during the reign of Emperor Vespasian, and yet again during the reign of Domitian.

If being a philosopher made one susceptible to banishment, being a Stoic philosopher made one particularly susceptible. By stubbornly doing what they took to be their social duty, even though it meant defying the powers that be, the Stoics made lots of political enemies. Of the four great Roman Stoics, only Marcus escaped banishment—but then again, he was the emperor. Seneca and Epictetus were each banished once, and Musonius was banished twice. Other noteworthy banished Stoics include Rutilius Rufus, Posidonius, Helvidius Priscus, and Paconius Agrippinus. And these were arguably the Stoics who got lucky. Other Stoics managed to offend those in power sufficiently that, rather than being exiled, they were sentenced to death; this was the fate of Thrasea Paetus and Barea Soranus. (According to Tacitus, Emperor Nero's desire to kill these two Stoics can best be understood as an attempt "to extirpate virtue herself.")[1]

Paconius's response to banishment, by the way, is a wonderful example of a Stoical response to what most people would take to be a personal calamity. When someone reported to him that he was being tried in the Senate, Paconius was uninterested; he merely set off for his daily exercise and bath. When he was informed that he had been condemned, he asked whether it was to banishment or death. "To banishment," came the reply. He then asked whether his property at Aricia had also been confiscated, and when he was told that it hadn't, he replied, "Let us go to Aricia then and dine." Epictetus holds this up as a model of Stoic behavior: "This is what it means to have rehearsed the lessons one ought to rehearse, to have set desire and aversion free from every hindrance and made them proof against chance. I must die. If forthwith, I die; and if a little later, I will take lunch now, since the hour for lunch has come, and afterwards I will die at the appointed time."[2]

Philosophers, to be sure, no longer fear banishment. This is in part because governments are more enlightened than they used to be and in part because philosophers have succeeded in making themselves invisible to both politicians and the public at large. Sometimes, in idle moments, I find myself wishing that the government of my country would consider banishing philosophers—or, if not banishing us, at least locking us up for a few days to teach us a lesson. Not that I want to be banished or want my colleagues to be banished, but the fact that a government would consider banishing a group is evidence that the group *matters,* that it somehow makes a difference in a culture, a difference that might worry the authorities. What I am really wishing, I suppose, is that philosophy mattered in my culture the way it mattered to ancient Romans.

In chapter 12, I mentioned Seneca's consolation to his mother Helvia, who was upset at his being exiled. In the consolation, Seneca comforts her by telling her that exile isn't really that bad not as bad, at any rate, as people make it out to be. Exile, he explains, is nothing but a change of place. Furthermore, even in the worst places of exile, the exiled person will find people who are there of their own free will.[3]

It may be true, says Seneca, that by being exiled he has been deprived of his country, his friends and family, and his property, but he has taken with him into exile the things that matter most: his place in Nature and his virtue. He adds, "It is the mind that makes us rich; this goes with us into exile, and in the wildest wilderness, having found there all that the body needs for its sustenance, it itself overflows in the enjoyment of its own goods."[4] Seneca apparently spent his time in exile reading, writing, and studying nature.

Musonius's exile, as we have seen, was one of the worst exiles possible, to the "worthless" island of Gyara. Nevertheless, he says, those who visited him during his exile never heard him complain or saw him disheartened. Being exiled may have deprived him of his country, but it didn't deprive him, he says, of his ability to endure exile. Indeed, Musonius thinks exile deprives a person of nothing that is truly valuable. Exile cannot prevent us, for example, from being courageous or just. If we are virtuous—if we have the proper values—exile cannot harm or degrade us. If we are not virtuous, though, exile will deprive us of much of what we (mistakenly) think is valuable, and we will therefore be miserable.[5]

To endure and even thrive in exile, Musonius says, a person must keep in mind that his happiness depends more on his values than on where he resides. Indeed, Musonius views himself as a citizen not of Rome but of "the city of Zeus which is populated by human beings and gods."[6] He points out that even in exile we can associate with others and that our true friends will not refuse to associate with us just because we have been exiled. If those in exile find themselves lacking things, he asserts, it is because they seek to live in luxury. Furthermore, those in exile have something that those in Rome lack—namely, freedom to speak their mind.

Musonius also reminds us that exile has changed people for the better. It has, for example, forced people to curtail their luxurious living and has thereby improved their health. It has also transformed ordinary people, such as Diogenes of Sinope, into philosophers.[7] (Before becoming a Cynic, Diogenes had been forced to flee Sinope because either he or his banker father had adulterated the coinage there; when someone later brought up this incident in an attempt to shame him, Diogenes, with typical Cynic wit, responded that although it was true that the people of Sinope had sentenced him to exile, he in turn had sentenced them to remain in Sinope.)[8]

It is clear why the Stoics had an interest in exile: As we have seen, they ran an interesting chance of being sentenced to it. People no longer live in fear of being exiled by their government, so it might seem as if the Stoic advice on exile is of theoretical and historical interest only. But this is not so.

Even though readers of this book are unlikely to be exiled by their government, they run a considerable risk, if current social trends continue, of being exiled by their children—exiled, that is, to a nursing home. It is a transition that, if they let it, can severely disrupt their tranquility. Indeed, there is a very real danger that this exile will cause them to spend their final, precious days on earth complaining about their life rather than enjoying it. In the next chapter, we will turn our attention to this special kind of exile and to other problems associated with aging.

SEVENTEEN

Old Age

On Being Banished to a Nursing Home

As a college professor, I spend my days around twenty-year-olds. Many of them, I have found, are convinced that the world will be their oyster. They think they will be rock stars, either literally or figuratively speaking. (It is understandable that they would think this. What perplexes me is their belief that, as rock stars, they will find profound and lasting happiness. They need, perhaps, to follow the entertainment news more closely.) These twentysomethings aren't willing to settle for "mere tranquility" when there is so much else to be had: a perfect boyfriend, girlfriend, or spouse, a perfect job, and the love and admiration of all those around them. For them, Stoicism sounds like a philosophy for losers, and they aren't losers.

In extreme cases, these young people harbor a profound sense of entitlement. They think it is life's job to unroll a red carpet ahead of them, down whatever path they choose to take. When life fails to do this—when the path they have chosen gets bumpy and rutted, or even becomes impassible—they are astonished. This isn't how things are supposed to be! Surely someone, somewhere, has made a terrible mistake!

As the years go by, though, these twentysomethings come to realize that life will present them with obstacles, and they start developing skill at overcoming those obstacles. In particular, when the world does not hand them fame and fortune on a silver platter, they realize that they must work to get it, and so they do. Often, the world rewards their efforts, and as a result, they find that when they are in their thirties, their external circumstances, although not quite what they had hoped they would be when they were twenty, are nevertheless tolerable. At this point, they often redouble their efforts to improve their external circumstances in the belief that this will somehow gain them the perfect life they dream of having.

After trying this strategy for another decade, though, it might dawn on them that they aren't gaining any ground. They are getting paid twenty times more than they once were, they are living in a four-bedroom house instead of a studio apartment, and they are the subject of adulatory articles in the newspaper, but they are no closer to happiness than they used to be. Indeed, thanks to the complexity of their schemes for gaining happiness, they find themselves experiencing anxiety, anger, and frustration. They also discover that their success has a downside: They have become the target of other people's envy. It is at this stage that many people who were formerly oblivious to philosophy start getting philosophical. "Is this all life has to offer?" they wonder. "Is this the life I want to live?"

Sometimes this period of philosophical speculation triggers what, in our culture, we call a midlife crisis. The person experiencing the crisis might sensibly conclude that his unhappiness is the result of wanting the wrong things. In all too many cases, though, he doesn't draw this conclusion; instead, he concludes that he is unhappy as the result of making certain short-term sacrifices to attain various long-term goals. He therefore decides to stop making these short-term sacrifices: He buys a new car, or abandons his wife and takes on a lover. After a time, though, it becomes apparent to him that this strategy for gaining happiness is no better and is in many ways worse than his previous strategy.

He might, at this point, turn his attention back to meaning-of-life questions. And if this isn't sufficient to make him take up such questions, the aging process—and along with it, the prospect of death drawing ever nearer—probably will. As a result of contemplating these questions, he might find that Stoicism, which held no appeal whatsoever for him when he was young, now seems plausible as a philosophy of life.

WHEN WE WERE YOUNG, we might have wondered what it would be like to be old. And if we are Stoics, we might, in our practice of negative visualization, have imagined what it would be like. Unless death intervenes, though, a day will come when we won't need to wonder or imagine what it would be like to be old; we will know full well. The abilities we once took for granted will have departed. We used to run for miles; now we get winded walking down the hallway. We used to handle the finances of a corporation; now we can't even balance our checkbook. We used to be the person who knew when everyone's birthday was; now we can't even remember our own.

The loss of these abilities means we can no longer fend for ourselves, and as a result we might find ourselves banished to a nursing home. The home in question will not, to be sure, be a desolate island like the one to which Musonius was banished. Indeed, it will be physically quite comfortable, with regular meals and someone to do our laundry, clean our room, and maybe even help us bathe. But although our new environment is physically comfortable, it is likely to be quite challenging socially. We will find ourselves surrounded by people not of our choosing. We might, as a result, have to interact, each and every day, over breakfast and before we have had our coffee, with the same ornery individuals. We might find that despite having enjoyed a high degree of social status in our prime, we are now low man on the nursing home's status totem pole; it might turn out, for example, that there is a "cool table" in the nursing home's dining room, and we have not been invited to sit there.

Living in a nursing home resembles, in many respects, being in high school. Cliques form, and their members spend considerable amounts of time talking down the members of rival cliques. In other respects, it resembles living in a college dorm: You are in a single room that opens onto a communal corridor; you can either stay in your room and stare at the four walls, or venture out of your room into an environment you might find socially challenging.

Living in a nursing home also resembles living in a time of plague: You watch as the ambulance pulls up a few times each month—or, in a large home, a few times each week—to haul away the bodies of those who did not survive the night. If you don't live in a nursing home, you will be spared these recurring ambulances, but you probably won't be spared learning of the deaths of long-time friends, brothers and sisters, and perhaps even your own children.

A twenty-year-old might reject Stoicism in the belief that the world is going to be her oyster; an eighty-year-old knows full well that the world isn't her oyster and that her situation is only going to worsen with the passing years. Although she may have believed she was immortal when she was twenty, her own mortality is now painfully obvious to her. Faced with death, she might finally be willing to settle for "mere tranquility," and she might, as a result, be ripe for Stoicism.

Having said this, I should add that it is entirely possible to grow old without becoming ripe for Stoicism or any other philosophy of life. Indeed, many people go through life repeatedly making the same mistakes and are no closer to happiness in their eighties than they were in their twenties. These individuals, rather than enjoying their life, will have been embittered by it, and now, near the end of their life, they live to complain—about their circumstances, their relatives, the food, the weather, in short, about absolutely everything.

Such cases are tragic inasmuch as these people had it in their power—and, indeed, still have it in their power—to experience joy, but they either chose the wrong goals in living, or chose the right goals but adopted a defective strategy to attain those goals. This is the downside of failing to develop an effective philosophy of life: You end up wasting the one life you have.

OLD AGE, Seneca argues, has its benefits: "Let us cherish and love old age; for it is full of pleasure if one knows how to use it." Indeed, he claims that the most delightful time of life is "when it is on the downward slope, but has not yet reached the abrupt decline." He adds that even the time of "abrupt decline" has pleasures of its own. Most significantly, as one loses the ability to experience certain pleasures, one loses the desire to experience them: "How comforting it is," he says, "to have tired out one's appetites, and to have done with them!"[1]

Consider lust, the desire for sexual gratification. Lust is, for many people—and for males in particular, I think—a major distraction in daily living. We might be able to control whether or not we act on lustful feelings, but the feelings themselves seem to be hardwired into us. (If we lacked such feelings or could easily extinguish them, it is unlikely that we would have survived as a species.) Because they distract us, feelings of lust have a significant impact on how we spend our days.

As we age, though, our feelings of lust and the state of distraction that accompanies them diminish. Some would argue that this is a bad thing, that it is yet another example of one of the pleasures of youth that is lost to us. But the Greek dramatist Sophocles offered another viewpoint. When he had grown old and someone asked whether, despite his years, he could still make love to a woman, he replied, "I am very glad to have escaped from this, like a slave who has escaped from a mad and cruel master."[2]

Seneca points out that by causing our bodies to deteriorate, old age causes our vices and their accessories to decay. The same aging process, though, needn't cause our mind to decay; indeed, Seneca remarks that despite his age, his mind "is strong and rejoices that it has but slight connexion with the body." He is also thankful that his mind has thereby "laid aside the greater part of its load."[3]

One downside of being old is that we live in the knowledge that our death is in some sense imminent. In our youth, we delude ourselves into thinking death is for other people. By our middle years, we understand that we are going to die, but we also expect to live for decades before we do. When we are old, we know full well that we will die—maybe not tomorrow but soon. For many people, this knowledge makes old age a depressing stage of life.

The Stoics, however, thought the prospect of death, rather than depressing us, could make our days far more enjoyable than would otherwise be the case. We examined this seeming paradox back in chapter 4. We saw that by imagining how our days could go worse—and in particular, by contemplating our own death—we could increase our chance of experiencing joy. In our youth, it takes effort to contemplate our own death; in our later years, it takes effort to *avoid* contemplating it. Old age therefore has a way of making us do something that, according to the Stoics, we should have been doing all along.

Thus, the proximity of death, rather than depressing us, can be turned to our advantage. In our youth, because we assumed that we would live forever, we took our days for granted and as a result wasted many of them. In our old age, however, waking up each morning can be a cause for celebration. As Seneca notes, "If God is pleased to add another day, we should welcome it with glad hearts."[4] And after celebrating having been given another day to live, we can fill that day with appreciative living. It is entirely possible for an octogenarian to be more joyful than her twenty-year-old grandchild, particularly if the octogenarian, in part because of her failing health, takes nothing for granted, while the grandchild, in part because of her perfect health, takes everything for granted and has therefore decided that life is a bore.

AMONG THE VARIOUS philosophies of life, Stoicism is particularly well suited to our later years. For most people, old age will be the most challenging time of life. A primary objective of Stoicism, though, is to teach us not only to meet life's challenges but to retain our tranquility as we do. In addition, old people are more likely than young people to value the tranquility offered by the Stoics. A young person might find it baffling that someone would be willing to settle for "mere tranquility"; an octogenarian will probably not only appreciate how precious a thing tranquility is but will realize how few people manage, over the course of a lifetime, to attain it.

It is in part for this reason that Musonius counsels us to take up Stoicism while we are young: It is, he thinks, the best way to prepare for old age. Someone who has acted on this advice will be unlikely, as he gets older, to complain about the loss of youth and its pleasures, his body growing weak, his failing health, or being neglected by his relatives, since he would have "an effective antidote against all these things in his own intelligence and in the education he possesses."[5]

If someone neglected to study Stoicism in his youth, though, he can always take it up later in life. The aging process might prevent us from, say, boxing or solving differential equations, but only rarely will it prevent us from practicing Stoicism. Even those who are old and feeble can read the Stoics and reflect on their writings. They can also engage in negative visualization and refuse to worry about things that are beyond their control. And perhaps most important, they can take a fatalistic attitude toward their life and refuse to spend their final years wishing, pointlessly, that it could have been different than it was.

EIGHTEEN

Dying

On a Good End to a Good Life

WHAT MAKES OLD AGE a miserable thing, Musonius says, usually isn't the frailty or sickness that accompanies it; rather, it is the prospect of dying.[1] And why are people, both young and old, disturbed by the prospect of dying? Some are disturbed because they fear what might come after death. Many more, though, are disturbed because they fear that they have mislived—that they have, that is, lived without having attained the things in life that are truly valuable. Death, of course, will make it impossible for them ever to attain these things.

It may seem paradoxical, but having a coherent philosophy of life, whether it be Stoicism or some other philosophy, can make us more accepting of death. Someone with a coherent philosophy of life will know what in life is worth attaining, and because this person has spent time trying to attain the thing in life he believed to be worth attaining, he has probably attained it, to the extent that it was possible for him to do so. Consequently, when it comes time for him to die, he will not feel cheated. To the contrary, he will, in the words of Musonius, "be set free from the fear of death."[2]

Consider, by way of illustration, the last days of the Stoic philosopher Julius Canus. When Caligula, whom Canus had angered, ordered his death, Canus retained his composure: "Most excellent prince," he said, "I tender you my thanks." Ten days later, when a centurion came to take him to be executed, Canus was playing a board game. Rather than complaining bitterly about his fate or begging the centurion to spare his life, Canus simply pointed out to the centurion that he, Canus, was one piece ahead in the game—meaning that his opponent would be lying if he subsequently claimed to have won. On the way to his execution, when someone asked about his state of mind, Canus replied that he was preparing himself to observe the moment of death in order to learn whether, in that moment, the spirit is aware that it is leaving the body. "Here," says Seneca approvingly, "is tranquility in the very midst of the storm." He adds that "no one has ever played the philosopher longer."[3]

Those who have lived without a coherent philosophy of life, though, will desperately want to delay death. They might want the delay so that they can get the thing that—at last!—they have discovered to be of value. (It is unfortunate that this dawned on them so late in life, but, as Seneca observes, "what you have done in the past will be manifest only at the time when you draw your last breath.")[4] Or they might want the delay because their improvised philosophy of life has convinced them that what is worth having in life is more of everything, and they cannot get more of everything if they die.

At this point, readers might conclude that the Stoics were obsessed with death. They counsel us, as we have seen, to contemplate our own death. They tell us to live each day as if it were our last. They tell us to practice Stoicism in part so we will not fear death.

Besides being seemingly fixated on death while alive, the Stoics had an unfortunate tendency to die in an unnatural manner. The Greek Stoics Zeno and Cleanthes apparently committed suicide,[5] and Cato unquestionably did so. It isn't clear how Musonius died, but while alive, he was an advocate of suicide. In particular, he advised old people to "choose to die well while you can; wait too long, and it might become impossible to do so." He added, "It is better to die with distinction than to live long."[6]

Furthermore, many of those Stoics who did not commit suicide outright did things that hastened their death. When it seemed that death was near, Marcus refused to eat. Seneca behaved in a manner that brought on a death sentence when he could have avoided doing so, as did the Stoics Thrasea Paetus and Barea Soranus. After hearing about how these Stoics met their end, readers might conclude that anyone who loves life and wants to die a natural death would do well to avoid Stoicism.

In response to this concern, let me point out, to begin with, that it is unclear that the rate of unnatural deaths among the Stoics was unusually high for ancient times. Furthermore, in many of the cases in which the Stoics did things to hasten their death, it is understandable why they did so. In particular, it is possible that Zeno and Cleanthes, who lived to an advanced age, didn't so much "commit suicide" as self-euthanize: They might have been incurably ill and might therefore have taken steps to hasten death. (This is what Marcus had done.) And although it is true that Cato committed suicide while in his prime, he did so not because he was indifferent to life but because he knew that his staying alive would have been politically advantageous to Julius Caesar, the dictator he was trying to overthrow. What we don't find, when we examine the lives of the Stoics, is individuals who committed suicide on a whim or out of boredom with life, the way a nihilist might.

Furthermore, when Stoics contemplate their own death, it is not because they long for death but because they want to get the most out of life. As we have seen, someone who thinks he will live forever is far more likely to waste his days than someone who fully understands that his days are numbered, and one way to gain this understanding is periodically to contemplate his own death. Likewise, when the Stoics live each day as if it were their last, it is not because they plan to take steps to make that day their last; rather, it is so they can extract the full value of that day—and, hopefully, the days that follow it. And when the Stoics teach us not to fear death, they are simply giving us advice on how to avoid a negative emotion. We are all going to die, after all, and it is better that our death not be marred by fear.

It is also important to keep in mind that the Stoics thought suicide was permissible only under certain circumstances. Musonius tells us, for example, that it is wrong for us to choose to die if our living "is helpful to many."[7] Inasmuch as Stoics, in doing what they take to be their social duty, will be helpful to many, they will rarely find themselves in these circumstances.

Along these lines, let us reconsider Musonius's comment that old people who know death to be near should consider suicide. This is a case that seems to meet the condition just described: It is unlikely, after all, that others would depend for their well-being on an old and sickly individual. Furthermore, in such cases the question isn't whether the person will soon die; the question is whether hers will be a good death at her own hands or a pointlessly painful death through natural processes. Besides counseling us to live a good life, Musonius counsels us to end that good life with a good death, when it is possible to do so.

LET ME MAKE one last comment about the Stoics' views regarding death. We have seen that the Stoics were inclined to take principled stands against powerful people and thereby get themselves into trouble. Why take such stands? For one thing, the Stoics thought they had a social duty to take them. Furthermore, because they feared neither death nor exile, the prospect of being punished for taking such stands—a prospect that would have deterred ordinary people—didn't deter them.

To many modern individuals, such behavior is inexplicable. They feel this way in part because to them, nothing is worth dying for. Indeed, they focus their energy not on doing their duty regardless of the consequences and not on taking principled stands that could get them into trouble, but on doing whatever it takes to go on enjoying the pleasures life has to offer. The Stoics, I am convinced, would respond to such thinking by asking whether a life in which nothing is worth dying for can possibly be worth living.

NINETEEN

On Becoming a Stoic

Start Now and Prepare to Be Mocked

PRACTICING STOICISM won't be easy. It will take effort, for example, to practice negative visualization, and practicing self-denial will take more effort still. It will take both effort and willpower to abandon our old goals, such as the attainment of fame and fortune, and replace them with a new goal, namely, the attainment of tranquility.

Some people, on hearing that it would take effort on their part to practice a philosophy of life, will immediately dismiss the idea. The Stoics would respond to this rejection by pointing out that although it indeed takes effort to practice Stoicism, it will require considerably more effort *not* to practice it. Along these lines, Musonius observes, as we have seen, that the time and energy people expend on illicit love affairs far outweighs the time and energy it would take them, as practicing Stoics, to develop the self-control required to avoid such affairs. Musonius goes on to suggest that we would also be better off if, instead of working hard to become wealthy, we trained ourselves to be satisfied with what we have; if, instead of seeking fame, we overcame our craving for the admiration of others; if, instead of spending time scheming to harm someone we envy, we spent that time overcoming our feelings of envy; and if, instead of knocking ourselves out trying to become popular, we worked to maintain and improve our relationships with those we knew to be true friends.[1]

More generally, having a philosophy of life, whether it be Stoicism or some other philosophy, can dramatically simplify everyday living. If you have a philosophy of life, decision making is relatively straightforward: When choosing between the options life offers, you simply choose the one most likely to help you attain the goals set forth by your philosophy of life. In the absence of a philosophy of life, though, even relatively simple choices can degenerate into meaning-of-life crises. It is, after all, hard to know what to choose when you aren't really sure what you want.

The most important reason for adopting a philosophy of life, though, is that if we lack one, there is a danger that we will mislive—that we will spend our life pursuing goals that aren't worth attaining or will pursue worthwhile goals in a foolish manner and will therefore fail to attain them.

ANYONE WISHING to become a Stoic should do so unobtrusively. This is because those who hear of your "conversion" to Stoicism will likely mock you.[2] You can avoid this sort of harassment, though, by keeping a low philosophical profile and practicing what might be called *stealth Stoicism*. You should have as your model Socrates, who kept such a low profile that people would come to him, not realizing that he himself was a philosopher, and ask whether he could introduce them to any philosophers. Socrates was, Epictetus reminds us, "tolerant of being overlooked,"[3] and those practicing Stoicism should likewise be tolerant.

Why do people behave this way? Why do they mock someone for adopting a philosophy of life? In part because by adopting one, whether it be Stoicism or some rival philosophy, a person is demonstrating that he has different values than they do. They might therefore infer that he thinks their values are somehow mistaken, which is something people don't want to hear. Furthermore, by adopting a philosophy of life, he is, in effect, challenging them to do something they are probably reluctant to do: reflect on their life and how they are living it. If these people can get the convert to abandon his philosophy of life, the implied challenge will vanish, and so they set about mocking him in an attempt to make him rejoin the unreflecting masses.

WHAT WILL BE our reward for practicing Stoicism? According to the Stoics, we can hope to become more virtuous, in the ancient sense of the word. We will also, they say, experience fewer negative emotions, such as anger, grief, disappointment, and anxiety, and because of this we will enjoy a degree of tranquility that previously would have been unattainable. Along with avoiding negative emotions, we will increase our chances of experiencing one particularly significant positive emotion: delight in the world around us.

For most people, experiencing delight requires a change in circumstances; they might, for example, have to acquire a new consumer gadget. Stoics, in contrast, can experience delight without any such change; because they practice negative visualization, they will deeply appreciate the things they already have. Furthermore, for most people, the delight they experience will be somewhat clouded by the fear that they will lose the source of their delight. Stoics, however, have a three-part strategy for minimizing this fear or avoiding it altogether.

To begin with, they will do their best to enjoy things that can't be taken from them, most notably their character. Along these lines, consider Marcus's comment that if we fall victim to a catastrophe, we can still take delight in the fact that it has not, because of the character we possess, made us bitter.[4]

Furthermore, as they are enjoying things that *can* be taken from them—the Stoics, as we have seen, are not averse to doing this—they will simultaneously be preparing for the loss of those things. In particular, as part of our practice of negative visualization, say the Stoics, we need to keep in mind that it is a lucky accident that we are enjoying whatever it is we are enjoying, that our enjoyment of it might end abruptly, and that we might never be able to enjoy it again. We need, in other words, to learn how to enjoy things without feeling entitled to them and without clinging to them.

Finally, the Stoics are careful to avoid becoming connoisseurs in the worst sense of the word—becoming, that is, individuals who are incapable of taking delight in anything but "the best." As a result, they will be capable of enjoying a wide range of easily obtainable things. They will keep firmly in mind Seneca's comment that although "to have whatsoever he wishes is in no man's power," it is in every man's power "not to wish for what he has not, but cheerfully to employ what comes to him."[5] Thus, if life should snatch one source of delight from them, Stoics will quickly find another to take its place: Stoic enjoyment, unlike that of a connoisseur, is eminently transferable. Along these lines, remember that when Seneca and Musonius were banished to islands, rather than succumbing to depression, they set about studying their new environment.

Because they have learned to enjoy things that are easily obtainable or that can't be taken from them, Stoics will find much in life to enjoy. They might, as a result, discover that they enjoy being the person they are, living the life they are living, in the universe they happen to inhabit. This, I should add, is no small accomplishment.

Stoics might also find that besides enjoying things in life, they enjoy the mere fact of being alive; they experience, in other words, joy itself. The Stoic sage will apparently be able to experience this joy all the time.[6] Those of us whose practice of Stoicism is less than perfect will not; instead, the joy we experience can best be described as intermittent. It will nevertheless be significantly greater than the joy we had previously known—again, no small accomplishment.

WHEN SHOULD WE begin our practice of Stoicism? Epictetus makes the case for starting immediately. We are no longer children, he says, and yet we procrastinate. Keep this up and we will one day realize that we have grown old without having acquired a philosophy of life—and that, as a result, we have wasted our life. Practicing Stoicism, he adds, is like training for the Olympics but with one important difference: Whereas the Olympic contests for which we might train will be held at some future date, the contest that is our life has already begun. Consequently, we do not have the luxury of postponing our training; we must start it this very day.[7]

PART FOUR

Stoicism for Modern Lives

TWENTY

The Decline of Stoicism

MARCUS AURELIUS WAS SIMULTANEOUSLY a Stoic philosopher and, as Roman emperor, the most powerful man in the Western world. This confluence of philosophy and politics could have been quite beneficial to Stoicism, but as we have seen, he did not try to convert his fellow Romans to the philosophy. As a result, Marcus became, in the words of the nineteenth-century historian W. E. H. Lecky, "the last and most perfect representative of Roman Stoicism."[1] After his death, Stoicism fell into a slump from which it has yet to recover.

As is the case with any complex social phenomenon, several factors lay behind this decline. For example, Lecky (whose views, I have been told, have fallen out of favor) argued that the increasing corruption and depravity of Roman society made Stoicism—which, as we have seen, calls for considerable self-control—unattractive to many Romans.[2] The classicist M. L. Clarke offers a different explanation: Stoicism, he suggests, declined in part because of a lack of charismatic teachers of Stoicism after the death of Epictetus.[3] Many people are capable of describing the principles of a philosophy in a coherent fashion, but one of the things that made Stoicism a vital force was that teachers such as Musonius and Epictetus, besides being able to explain Stoicism, were in a sense embodiments of the doctrine. They were living proof that Stoicism, if practiced, would yield the benefits the Stoics promised. When Stoicism was taught by mere mortals, potential pupils were much less likely to be swept away by it.

Stoicism was also undermined by the rise of Christianity, in part because the claims made by Christianity were similar to those made by Stoicism. The Stoics claimed, for example, that the gods created man, care about man's well-being, and gave him a divine element (the ability to reason); the Christians claimed that God created man, cares about him in a very personal way, and gave him a divine element (a soul). Stoicism and Christianity both enjoined people to overcome unwholesome desires and to pursue virtue. And Marcus's advice that we "love mankind" was certainly echoed in Christianity.[4]

Because of these similarities, Stoics and Christians found themselves competing for the same potential adherents. In this competition, however, Christianity had one big advantage over Stoicism: It promised not just life after death but an afterlife in which one would be infinitely satisfied for an eternity. The Stoics, on the other hand, thought it possible that there was life after death but were not certain of it, and if there was indeed life after death, the Stoics were uncertain what it would be like.

SINCE THE DEATH of Marcus, Stoicism has led an underground existence, only occasionally emerging into the light of day. In the seventeenth century, for example, René Descartes revealed his Stoic leanings in his *Discourse on Method.* At one point he describes the maxims that, if followed, would enable him to live as happily as was possible. The third of these maxims could have been—indeed, probably was—lifted straight out of Epictetus: "Always to seek to conquer myself rather than fortune, to change my desires rather than the established order, and generally to believe that nothing except our thoughts is wholly under our control, so that after we have done our best in external matters, what remains to be done is absolutely impossible, at least as far as we are concerned."[5] (Notice, by the way, the internalization of goals implied in Descartes' comment about doing our best.)

In the nineteenth century, the influence of Stoicism could be found in the writings of the German philosopher Arthur Schopenhauer; his essays "Wisdom of Life" and "Counsels and Maxims," although not explicitly Stoical, have a distinctly Stoical tone. At this same time, across the Atlantic, the influence of Stoicism could be found in the writings of the New England Transcendentalists. Henry David Thoreau, for example, doesn't directly mention Stoicism or any of the great Stoics in *Walden*, his masterpiece, but to those who know what to look for, the Stoic influence is present. In his *Journal*, Thoreau is more forthcoming. He writes, for example, that "Zeno the Stoic stood in precisely the same relation to the world that I do now."[6]

Like the Stoics, Thoreau was interested in developing a philosophy of life. According to the Thoreau scholar Robert D. Richardson, "His was always the practical question, how best can I live my daily life?," and his life itself can best be understood, says Richardson, as "one long uninterrupted attempt to work out the practical concrete meaning of the stoic idea that the laws which rule nature rule men as well."[7] Thoreau went to Walden Pond to conduct his famous two-year experiment in simple living in large part so that he could refine his philosophy of life and thereby avoid misliving: A primary motive in going to Walden, he tells us, was his fear that he would, "when I came to die, discover that I had not lived."[8]

Some of his friends and neighbors, who might or might not have been aware of his attraction to Stoicism, accused Thoreau of being stoical—of being, that is, grim and unfeeling. The accusation, Richardson argues, is unfounded. Although it may not have been obvious to those around him, Thoreau appears to have experienced the joy the Stoics sought. Thus, we find Thoreau declaring that "surely joy is the condition of life."[9] And Thoreau's *Journal*, says Richardson, "is filled with comments reflecting his gusto, his appetite for experience, the keenness of his senses, the sheer joy of being alive."[10]

During most of the twentieth century, Stoicism was a neglected doctrine. Indeed, according to the philosopher Martha Nussbaum, twentieth-century philosophers, in both Europe and North America, made less use of Stoicism and the other Hellenistic philosophies—namely, Epicureanism and Skepticism—than "almost any other philosophical culture in the West since the fourth century B.C.E."[11] By the turn of the millennium, Stoicism was, for most people, a nonstarter as a philosophy of life. For one thing, they saw no need to live in accordance with a philosophy. And those enlightened individuals who did seek a philosophy of life rarely regarded Stoicism as a viable candidate. They were convinced that they knew what Stoicism was: a doctrine whose adherents are humorless, grim, and unfeeling. Who would voluntarily join such a crowd?

If this book has done its job, readers will appreciate how woefully mistaken this characterization of Stoicism is. The Stoics were not stoical! Nor did they live joyless lives! Indeed, they were probably more likely to experience joy than most non-Stoics.

This realization, though, is rarely sufficient to overcome people's aversion toward Stoicism. Even after they acknowledge that the Stoics were fully functional individuals, capable of joy and worthy of our admiration, they retain a degree of hostility toward the doctrine. Let us now explore some of the reasons for the modern aversion to Stoicism, beginning with the argument that if modern psychology is right, Stoicism is a misguided philosophy of life.

THE STOICS HAD many important psychological insights. They realized, for example, that what makes insults painful is our interpretation of the insults rather than the insults themselves. They also realized that by engaging in negative visualization we can convince ourselves to be happy with what we already have and thereby counteract our tendency toward insatiability.

Anti-Stoics might concede that these are important insights but go on to point out that a lot has happened in the two millennia since the Roman Stoics pondered the human psyche. In particular, the twentieth century witnessed the transformation of psychology into a proper scientific discipline.

Anti-Stoics might add that among the most significant psychological discoveries made in the past hundred years was the realization of the danger we pose to ourselves if we try to conquer our emotions, the way the Stoics did. Indeed, the consensus view among psychological therapists is that we should stay in touch with our emotions: Rather than trying to deny their existence, we should contemplate them, and rather than trying to bottle them up, we should vent them. And if we find ourselves disturbed by negative emotions, we should not attempt to deal with them on our own but should instead share them with a psychological counselor who has made it her business to understand how the human mind works.

By way of illustration, consider grief. Modern psychology has shown (anti-Stoics will explain) that grief is a perfectly natural response to a personal tragedy. A grief-stricken person should vent his grief, not suppress it. If he feels like crying, he should cry. He should share his feelings with friends and relatives and should probably even seek the assistance of a professional grief counselor who will periodically meet with him, talk to him about his grief, and help him work through it. If he instead follows the advice of the Stoics and tries to suppress his grief, he may spare himself anguish in the short term, but he sets himself up for a debilitating episode of "delayed grief" months or even years later.

It is doubtless true that some people, under some circumstances, can benefit greatly from grief counseling. The consensus view among psychologists, though, is that nearly everyone can benefit, and this belief has transformed the way authorities respond to natural and manmade disasters. These days, after doing what they can to save lives, authorities are quick to call in grief counselors to help those who survived the disaster, those who lost loved ones in it, and those who witnessed it. When, for example, the Alfred P. Murrah Federal Building in Oklahoma City was bombed in 1995, killing 168, a horde of grief counselors descended on the city to help people work through their grief. Likewise, in 1999, when three dozen people were shot by two rampaging students at Columbine High School in Littleton, Colorado, a team of grief counselors was brought in to help the surviving students, their parents, and members of the community deal with their grief.[12]

It is instructive to contrast these responses to disaster with the way authorities responded to disasters in the middle of the twentieth century. When, for example, a landslide of coal-mine waste buried a village school in Aberfan, South Wales, in 1966, the parents of the 116 children who died were left to deal with their grief on their own.[13] As a result, many of them simply bore the disaster with, as the British say, a stiff upper lip. By the end of the century, one would have been hard-pressed to find a psychological therapist who would recommend a stiff upper lip as an appropriate response to disaster.

In reply to this criticism of Stoic psychology, let me remind readers that despite widespread belief to the contrary, the Stoics did not advocate that we "bottle up" our emotions. They did advise us to take steps to prevent negative emotions and to overcome them when our attempts at prevention fail, but this is different from keeping them bottled up: If we prevent or overcome an emotion, there will be nothing to bottle.

Suppose, in particular, that a Stoic finds himself grieving the loss of a loved one. This Stoic, it should be noted, will *not* react by trying to stifle the grief within him—by pretending, for example, that he is not grieving or by grimacing to block the flow of tears. He will instead recall Seneca's comment to Polybius that when people experience personal catastrophes, it is perfectly natural to experience grief. After this bout of reflexive grief, though, a Stoic will try to dispel whatever grief remains in him by trying to reason it out of existence. He will, in particular, invoke the kinds of arguments Seneca used in his consolations: "Is this what the person who died would want me to do? Of course not! She would want me to be happy! The best way to honor her memory is to leave off grieving and get on with life."

Because grief is a negative emotion, the Stoics opposed it. At the same time, they realized that because we are mere mortals, some grief is inevitable in the course of a lifetime, as are some fear, some anxiety, some anger, some hatred, some humiliation, and some envy. The goal of the Stoics was therefore not to eliminate grief but to minimize it.

An anti-Stoic might at this point suggest that the goal of minimizing grief, although less misguided than the goal of suppressing it, remains misguided. According to psychological counselors, we should work through our grief. It is true that trying to reason our way out of grieving is one way to work through it, but a better way is to try to elicit from ourselves various grief-related behaviors; we might, for example, make a point of having a good cry even though we don't particularly feel like doing so. We might also make a point of talking to others about our grief, even though this kind of sharing of emotions doesn't come naturally to us. Most important, if our grief is significant, we will seek the assistance of a grief counselor to assist us in the working-through process.

In response to this suggestion, I would challenge current psychological thinking on the best way to deal with our emotions. I would, in particular, question the claim, made by many psychological therapists, that people are not well equipped to deal with grief on their own. I think people are less brittle and more resilient, emotionally speaking, than therapists give them credit for.

To see why I say this, let us turn our attention back to the Aberfan disaster. Parents whose children were buried alive in the Aberfan landslide experienced a profound personal tragedy but received no professional help thereafter. According to the current psychological consensus, the lack of grief counseling should have turned these parents into emotional wrecks. The truth of the matter, though, is that they did remarkably well dealing with their grief on their own.[14] In other words, the technique of keeping a stiff upper lip seems to have served them admirably.

For another example of the consequences of dealing with negative emotions on one's own, consider the plight of the British during World War II. When the war broke out, psychologists worried that mental hospitals would swell with civilians unable to cope with the horrors of war. As it turned out, though, the Brits were quite capable of fending for themselves, emotionally speaking: There was no change in the incidence of mental illness.[15] In the absence of professional grief counselors, the Brits had little choice but to deal with their hardships with Stoic resolve, and for them, Stoic self-therapy proved to be remarkably successful.

It would be bad enough if grief counseling were simply ineffective. In some cases, though, such counseling seems to intensify and prolong people's grief; in other words, it only makes things worse. One study on the efficacy of grief counseling examined parents whose children had died of Sudden Infant Death Syndrome. It compared the parents who consciously tried to work through their loss, in accordance with the principles of grief therapy, with the parents who did not. Three weeks after the death of their child, the parents in the first group were experiencing more distress than the parents in the second group, and even after eighteen months the parents in the first group were worse off, emotionally speaking, than the parents in the second group. The obvious conclusion to draw from this research is that "forced grieving" in accordance with the principles of grief therapy, rather than curing grief, can delay the natural healing process; it is the psychological equivalent of picking at the scab on a wound. Similar research, by the way, has focused on Holocaust survivors, abused young women, and the partners of men who died of AIDS, and has obtained similar results.[16]

But what about delayed grief? If we cut short the grieving process, aren't we setting ourselves up for a much more debilitating bout of grief later on? The consensus among experts is that the delayed grief phenomenon is genuine.[17] Am I suggesting that they are wrong?

Indeed I am. The concept of delayed grief apparently made its debut in a paper titled "The Absence of Grief," written in 1937 by the psychiatrist Helene Deutsch. She claimed that failing to grieve after a personal loss would subsequently trigger a delayed bout of grief that would be "as fresh and intense as if the loss just occurred."[18] Unfortunately, Deutsch did not attempt to verify her theory empirically. Researchers who subsequently have tried to verify it have been disappointed: Cases of delayed grief seem to be quite rare.[19]

More generally, the psychiatrist Sally Satel and the philosopher Christina Hoff Sommers, in a book that challenges certain aspects of modern psychological therapy, write, "Recent findings suggest that reticence and suppression of feelings, far from compromising one's psychological well-being, can be healthy and adaptive. For many temperaments, an excessive focus on introspection and self-disclosure is depressing. Victims of loss and tragedy differ widely in their reactions: Some benefit from therapeutic intervention; most do not and should not be coerced by mental health professionals into emotionally correct responses. Trauma and grief counselors have erred massively in this direction." These authors add that they reject the doctrine, now commonly accepted, that "uninhibited emotional openness is essential to mental health."[20]

In conclusion, although the Stoics' advice on how best to deal with negative emotions is old-fashioned, it would nevertheless appear to be good advice. According to Seneca, "A man is as wretched as he has convinced himself that he is." He therefore recommends that we "do away with complaint about past sufferings and with all language like this: 'None has ever been worse off than I. What sufferings, what evils have I endured!' " After all, what point is there in "being unhappy, just because once you were unhappy?"[21]

Modern politics presents another obstacle to the acceptance of Stoicism. The world is full of politicians who tell us that if we are unhappy it isn't our fault. To the contrary, our unhappiness is caused by something the government did to us or is failing to do for us. We citizens are encouraged, in our pursuit of happiness, to resort to politics rather than philosophy. We are encouraged to march in the streets or write to our congressman rather than read Seneca or Epictetus. More significantly, we are encouraged to vote for the candidate who claims to possess the ability, by skillfully using the powers of government, to make us happy.

The Stoics, of course, rejected such thinking. They were convinced that what stands between most of us and happiness is not our government or the society in which we live, but defects in our philosophy of life—or our failing to have a philosophy at all. It is true that our government and our society determine, to a considerable extent, our external circumstances, but the Stoics understood that there is at best a loose connection between our external circumstances and how happy we are. In particular, it is entirely possible for someone banished to a desolate island to be happier than someone living a life of luxury.

The Stoics understood that governments can wrong their citizens; indeed, the Roman Stoics, as we have seen, had an unfortunate tendency to be unjustly punished by the powers that be. The Stoics also agree with modern social reformers that we have a duty to fight against social injustice. Where they differ from modern reformers is in their understanding of human psychology. In particular, the Stoics don't think it is helpful for people to consider themselves victims of society—or victims of anything else, for that matter. If you consider yourself a victim, you are not going to have a good life; if, however, you refuse to think of yourself as a victim—if you refuse to let your inner self be conquered by your external circumstances—you are likely to have a good life, no matter what turn your external circumstances take. (In particular, the Stoics thought it possible for a person to retain his tranquility despite being punished for attempting to reform the society in which he lived.)

Others may have it in their power to affect how and even whether you live, but they do not, say the Stoics, have it in their power to ruin your life. Only you can ruin it, by failing to live in accordance with the correct values.

The Stoics believed in social reform, but they also believed in personal transformation. More precisely, they thought the first step in transforming a society into one in which people live a good life is to teach people how to make their happiness depend as little as possible on their external circumstances. The second step in transforming a society is to change people's external circumstances. The Stoics would add that if we fail to transform ourselves, then no matter how much we transform the society in which we live, we are unlikely to have a good life.

Many of us have been persuaded that happiness is something that someone else, a therapist or a politician, must confer on us. Stoicism rejects this notion. It teaches us that we are very much responsible for our happiness as well as our unhappiness. It also teaches us that it is only when we assume responsibility for our happiness that we will have a reasonable chance of gaining it. This, to be sure, is a message that many people, having been indoctrinated by therapists and politicians, don't want to hear.

If modern psychology and politics have been unkind to Stoicism, so has modern philosophy. Before the twentieth century, those who were exposed to philosophy would likely have read the Stoics. In the twentieth century, though, philosophers not only lost interest in Stoicism but lost interest, more generally, in philosophies of life. It was possible, as my own experience demonstrates, to spend a decade taking philosophy classes without having read the Stoics and without having spent time considering philosophies of life, much less adopting one.

One reason philosophers lost interest in Stoicism was their insight, in the first decades of the twentieth century, that many traditional philosophical puzzles arise because of our sloppy use of language. From this it followed that anyone wishing to solve philosophical puzzles should do so not by observing humanity (as the Stoics were likely to do) but by thinking very carefully about language and how we use it. And along with the increasing emphasis on linguistic analysis came a growing belief, on the part of professional philosophers, that it simply was not the business of philosophy to tell people how to live their life.

If you had gone to Epictetus and said, "I want to live a good life. What should I do?" he would have had an answer for you:

"Live in accordance with nature." He would then have told you, in great detail, how to do this. If, by way of contrast, you went to a twentieth-century analytic philosopher and asked the same question, he probably would have responded not by answering the question you asked but by analyzing the question itself: "The answer to your question depends on what you mean by 'a good life,' which in turn depends on what you mean by 'good' and 'a life.'" He might then walk you through all the things you could conceivably mean in asking how to live a good life and explain why each of these meanings is logically muddled. His conclusion: It makes no sense to ask how to live a good life. When this philosopher had finished speaking, you might be impressed with his flair for philosophical analysis, but you might also conclude, with good reason, that he himself lacked a coherent philosophy of life.

One final but quite significant obstacle to modern acceptance of Stoicism is the degree of self-control it requires. Do we detect in ourselves a lust for fame? According to the Stoics, we should extinguish this desire. Do we find ourselves longing for a mansion filled with fine furniture? We would do well, say the Stoics, to content ourselves with a simple lifestyle. And besides overcoming our longing for fame and fortune, the Stoics want us to set many of our other personal desires aside so we can do our duty to serve our fellow humans. They were, as we have seen, a duty-bound group; unlike many modern individuals, the Stoics were convinced that there was something in life bigger than themselves.

Many people, on hearing about the self-control Stoicism requires, will reject the philosophy. If you don't have something you want, they reason, you will obviously be unhappy. Therefore, the best way to gain happiness is to get what you want, and the best way to get what you want is with a three-stage strategy: First, you take an inventory of the desires that lurk in your mind; second, you devise a plan for satisfying those desires; and third, you implement that plan. The Stoics, however, are suggesting that we do just the opposite of this. In some cases, they advise us to extinguish rather than fulfill our desires, and in other cases, they advise us to do things we don't want to do, because it is our duty to do them. Stoicism, in other words, sounds like a sure-fire recipe for unhappiness.

Although the strategy of gaining happiness by working to get whatever it is we find ourselves wanting is obvious and has been used by most people throughout recorded history and across cultures, it has an important defect, as thoughtful people throughout recorded history and across cultures have realized: For each desire we fulfill in accordance with this strategy, a new desire will pop into our head to take its place. This means that no matter how hard we work to satisfy our desires, we will be no closer to satisfaction than if we had fulfilled none of them. We will, in other words, remain dissatisfied.

A much better, albeit less obvious way to gain satisfaction is not by working to satisfy our desires but by working to master them. In particular, we need to take steps to slow down the desire-formation process within us. Rather than working to fulfill whatever desires we find in our head, we need to work at preventing certain desires from forming and eliminating many of the desires that have formed. And rather than wanting new things, we need to work at wanting the things we already have.

This is what the Stoics advise us to do. It may be true that being a Stoic requires self-control and requires that we sacrifice in order to do our duty, but the Stoics would argue that we are more likely to achieve happiness—indeed, joy—by following this path than by spending our life, as most people do, working to fulfill whatever desires pop into our head.

Having said this, I should add that the word *sacrifice*, as I have just used it, is a bit misleading. The Stoics, while doing their social duty, will not think in terms of sacrifice. Ideally, they will, as a result of practicing Stoicism, *want* to do what their social duty requires them to do. If this sounds strange, think about the duties involved in parenting. Parents do lots of things for their children, but Stoic parents—and, I suspect, good parents in general—don't think of parenting as a burdensome task requiring endless sacrifice; instead, they think about how wonderful it is that they have children and can make a positive difference in the lives of these children.

The Stoics, as I have suggested, are not alone in claiming that our best hope at gaining happiness is to live not a life of self-indulgence but a life of self-discipline and, to a degree, self-sacrifice. Similar claims have been made in other philosophies, including Epicureanism and Skepticism, as well as in numerous religions, including Buddhism, Hinduism, Christianity, Islam, and Taoism. The question isn't, I think, whether self-disciplined and duty-bound people can have a happy, meaningful life; it is whether those who lack self-control and who are convinced that nothing is bigger than they are can have such a life.

TWENTY-ONE

Stoicism Reconsidered

In the previous chapter, I described the decline of Stoicism and tried to fathom the reason for its current moribund state. In this chapter, I will attempt to reanimate the doctrine. My goal in doing so is to make Stoicism more attractive to individuals who seek a philosophy of life.

In the introduction to this book, I explained that philosophies of life have two components: They tell us what things in life are and aren't worth pursuing, and they tell us how to gain the things that are worth having. The Stoics, as we have seen, thought tranquility was worth pursuing, and the tranquility they sought, it will be remembered, is a psychological state in which we experience few negative emotions, such as anxiety, grief, and fear, but an abundance of positive emotions, especially joy. The Stoics did not argue that tranquility was valuable; rather, they assumed that in the lives of most people its value would at some point become apparent.

To develop and refine their strategy for attaining tranquility, the Stoics became keen observers of humanity. They sought to determine what sorts of things disrupt people's tranquility, how people can avoid having their tranquility disrupted by these things, and how they can quickly restore their tranquility when, despite their efforts, it is disrupted. On the basis of these investigations, the Stoics produced a body of advice for anyone seeking tranquility. Among their recommendations were the following:

- We should become self-aware: We should observe ourselves as we go about our daily business, and we should periodically reflect on how we responded to the day's events. How did we respond to an insult? To the loss of a possession? To a stressful situation? Did we, in our responses, put Stoic psychological strategies to work?
- We should use our reasoning ability to overcome negative emotions. We should also use our reasoning ability to master our desires, to the extent that it is possible to do so. In particular, we should use reason to convince ourselves that things such as fame and fortune aren't worth having—not, at any rate, if what we seek is tranquility—and therefore aren't worth pursuing. Likewise, we should use our reasoning ability to convince ourselves that even though certain activities are pleasurable, engaging in those activities will disrupt our tranquility, and the tranquility lost will outweigh the pleasure gained.
- If, despite not having pursued wealth, we find ourselves wealthy, we should enjoy our affluence; it was the Cynics, not the Stoics, who advocated asceticism. But although we should enjoy wealth, we should not cling to it; indeed, even as we enjoy it, we should contemplate its loss.

- We are social creatures; we will be miserable if we try to cut off contact with other people. Therefore, if what we seek is tranquility, we should form and maintain relations with others. In doing so, though, we should be careful about whom we befriend. We should also, to the extent possible, avoid people whose values are corrupt, for fear that their values will contaminate ours.
- Other people are invariably annoying, though, so if we maintain relations with them, they will periodically upset our tranquility—if we let them. The Stoics spent a considerable amount of time devising techniques for taking the pain out of our relationships with other people. In particular, they came up with techniques for dealing with the insults of others and preventing them from angering us.
- The Stoics pointed to two principal sources of human unhappiness—our insatiability and our tendency to worry about things beyond our control—and they developed techniques for removing these sources of unhappiness from our life.
- To conquer our insatiability, the Stoics advise us to engage in negative visualization. We should contemplate the impermanence of all things. We should imagine ourselves losing the things we most value, including possessions and loved ones. We should also imagine the loss of our own life. If we do this, we will come to appreciate the things we now have, and because we appreciate them, we will be less likely to form desires for other things. And besides simply imagining that things could be worse than they are, we should sometimes cause things to be worse than they would otherwise be; Seneca

advises us to "practice poverty," and Musonius advises us voluntarily to forgo opportunities for pleasure and comfort.

- To curb our tendency to worry about things beyond our control, the Stoics advise us to perform a kind of triage with respect to the elements of our life and sort them into those we have no control over, those we have complete control over, and those we have some but not complete control over. Having done this, we should not bother about things over which we have no control. Instead, we should spend some of our time dealing with things over which we have complete control, such as our goals and values, and spend most of our time dealing with things over which we have some but not complete control. If we do this, we will avoid experiencing much needless anxiety.
- When we spend time dealing with things over which we have some but not complete control, we should be careful to internalize our goals. My goal in playing tennis, for example, should be not to win the match but to play the best match possible.
- We should be fatalistic with respect to the external world: We should realize that what has happened to us in the past and what is happening to us at this very moment are beyond our control, so it is foolish to get upset about these things.

THE STOICS COULD HAVE given us a philosophy of life without explaining why it is a good philosophy. They could, in other words, have left adoption of their philosophy of life as a leap of faith, the way Zen Buddhists do with theirs. But being philosophers, they felt the need to prove that theirs was the "correct" philosophy of life and that rival philosophies were somehow mistaken.

In their proof of Stoicism, the Stoics first observe that Zeus created us and in doing so made us different from the other animals by giving us reason. Because he cares about us, Zeus wanted to design us so that we would always be happy, but he lacked the power to do so. Instead, he did for us what he could: He gave us the means to make life not just endurable but enjoyable. More precisely, he designed for us a pattern of living that, if followed, would enable us to flourish. The Stoics used their reasoning ability to discover this pattern of living. They then designed a philosophy of life that, if followed, would enable us to live in accordance with this pattern—in accordance, as they put it, with nature—and thereby to flourish. In conclusion, if we live in accordance with Stoic principles, we will have the best life it is possible for a human to have. QED.

Adherents of most religions will, of course, reject this proof of Stoicism, inasmuch as they will reject the claim that it was Zeus who created us. Nevertheless, they might be willing to accept a slightly altered version of the proof, one that substitutes God for Zeus. They might thereby transform the Stoics' proof into a proof that is compatible with their religion.

Consider, however, the predicament of modern Stoics who deny the existence of both Zeus and God, and therefore reject the claim that Zeus or God created man. Suppose these individuals believe instead that man came to exist through a process of evolution. In this case, man wouldn't have been created for any purpose, meaning that it is impossible for us to discover the purpose of a human being so that we can, by performing that purpose well, flourish. These individuals can, I think, resolve their predicament by abandoning the Stoic justification of Stoicism in favor of a justification that makes use of scientific discoveries that were unavailable to the Stoics. Let me explain how this can be done.

IF SOMEONE ASKED ME why Stoicism works, I would not tell a story about Zeus (or God). Instead, I would talk about evolutionary theory, according to which we humans came to exist as the result of an interesting series of biological accidents. I would then start talking about evolutionary psychology, according to which we humans, besides gaining a certain anatomy and physiology through evolutionary processes, gained certain psychological traits, such as a tendency to experience fear or anxiety under certain circumstances and a tendency to experience pleasure under other circumstances. I would explain that we evolved these tendencies not so that we could have a good life but so that we would be likely to survive and reproduce. I would add that unlike Zeus (or God), evolutionary processes are indifferent to whether we flourish; they are concerned only that we survive and reproduce. Indeed, an individual who is utterly miserable but manages, despite his misery, to survive and reproduce will play a greater role in evolutionary processes than a joyful individual who chooses not to reproduce.

I would, at this point, pause to make sure my listener understands how our evolutionary past contributes to our current psychological makeup. Why, for example, do we experience pain? Not because the gods or God wanted us to experience it or thought we could somehow benefit from experiencing it, but because our evolutionary ancestors for whom (thanks to an evolutionary "experiment") injuries were painful were much more likely to avoid such injuries—and therefore much more likely to survive and reproduce—than ancestors who were incapable of experiencing pain. Those who could experience pain were therefore more effective at transmitting their genes than those who couldn't, and as a result we humans have inherited the ability to experience pain.

It is also because of evolutionary processes that we possess the ability to experience fear: Our evolutionary ancestors who feared lions were less likely to be eaten by one than those who were indifferent to them. Likewise, our tendency to experience anxiety and insatiability is a consequence of our evolutionary past. Our evolutionary ancestors who felt anxious about whether they had enough food were less likely to starve than those who didn't worry about where their next meal was coming from. Similarly, our evolutionary ancestors who were never satisfied with what they had, who always wanted more food or better shelter, were more likely to survive and reproduce than those who were easily satisfied.

Our ability to experience pleasure also has an evolutionary explanation. Why, for example, does sex feel good? Because our evolutionary ancestors who found sex to be pleasurable were far more likely to reproduce than those who were indifferent to sex or, even worse, found it to be unpleasant. We inherited the genes of those ancestors for whom sex felt good, and as a result we also find it to be pleasurable.

The Stoics, as we have seen, thought Zeus designed us to be gregarious. I agree with the Stoics that we are "by nature" gregarious. I reject the claim, though, that Zeus (or God) made us this way. Rather, we are gregarious because our evolutionary ancestors who felt drawn to other people, and who therefore joined groups of individuals, were more likely to survive and reproduce than those who didn't.

Besides being evolutionarily "programmed" to seek relationships with other people, I think we are programmed to seek social status among them. Presumably, the groups our evolutionary ancestors formed had social hierarchies within them, the way troops of monkeys do. A group member who had low status ran the risk of being deprived of resources or even of being driven from the group, events that could threaten his survival. Furthermore, the low-status males of a group were unlikely to reproduce. Therefore, those ancestors who felt motivated to seek social status—those ancestors for whom gaining social status felt good and losing it felt bad—were more likely to survive and reproduce than those who were indifferent to social status. Thanks to our evolutionary past, today's humans find it pleasant to gain social status and unpleasant to lose it. This is why it is delightful when others praise us and painful when they insult us.

According to the Stoics, Zeus gave us the ability to reason so we could be godlike. I, however, think we gained the ability to reason in the same way that we gained our other abilities: through evolutionary processes. Our evolutionary ancestors who had reasoning ability were more likely to survive and reproduce than those who didn't. It is also important to realize that we did not gain the ability to reason so that we could transcend our evolutionarily programmed desires, such as our desire for sex and social status. To the contrary, we gained the ability to reason so that we could more effectively satisfy those desires—so that we could, for example, devise complex strategies by which to satisfy our desire for sex and social status.

We have the abilities we do because possessing them enabled our evolutionary ancestors to survive and reproduce. From this it does not follow, though, that we must use these abilities to survive and reproduce. Indeed, thanks to our reasoning ability, we have it in our power to "misuse" our evolutionary inheritance. Allow me to explain.

Consider our ability to hear. We gained this ability through evolutionary processes: Those ancestors who had the ability to hear approaching predators had a better chance of surviving and reproducing than those who didn't. And yet modern humans rarely use their hearing ability for this purpose. Instead we might use it to listen to Beethoven, an activity that in no way increases our chances of surviving and reproducing. Besides misusing our ability to hear, we also misuse the ears that evolved in conjunction with this ability; we might use them, for example, to hold on eyeglasses or earrings. Likewise, we gained the ability to walk because our ancestors who had this ability were more likely to survive and reproduce than those who didn't, and yet some people use this ability to climb Mount Everest, an activity that distinctly reduces their chances of surviving.

Just as we can "misuse" our ability to hear or walk—use these abilities, that is, in a way that has nothing to do with the survival and reproduction of our species—we can misuse our ability to reason. In particular, we can use it to circumvent the behavioral tendencies that have been programmed into us by evolution. Thanks to our evolutionary past, for example, we are rewarded for having sex. But thanks to our reasoning ability, we can decide to forgo opportunities for sex because taking advantage of these opportunities will lead us away from various goals we have set for ourselves, goals that have nothing to do with our surviving and reproducing. (Most dramatically, we can decide to remain celibate, a decision that will reduce to zero our chance of reproducing.) More important, we can use our reasoning ability to conclude that many of the things that our evolutionary programming encourages us to seek, such as social status and more of anything we already have, may be valuable if our goal is simply to survive and reproduce, but aren't at all valuable if our goal is instead to experience tranquility while we are alive.

The Stoics, as we have seen, thought that although Zeus made us susceptible to suffering, he also gave us a tool—our reasoning ability—that, if used properly, could prevent much suffering. A parallel claim, I think, can be made about evolution: Evolutionary processes made us susceptible to suffering but also gave us—accidentally—a tool by which we can prevent much of this suffering. The tool, once again, is our reasoning ability. Because we can reason, we can not only understand our evolutionary predicament but take conscious steps to escape it, to the extent possible.

Although our evolutionary programming helped us flourish as a species, it has in many respects outlived its usefulness.

Consider, for example, the pain we might experience when someone publicly insults us. I have given an evolutionary explanation for this pain: We experience it because our evolutionary ancestors who cared deeply about gaining and retaining social status were more likely to survive and reproduce than our ancestors who were indifferent to social status and who, therefore, didn't experience pain on being insulted. But the world has changed dramatically since our ancestors roamed the savannas of Africa. Today it is quite possible to survive despite having low social status; even if others despise us, the law prevents them from taking our food from us or driving us from our home. Furthermore, low social status is no longer an impediment to reproduction; indeed, in many parts of the world, men and women with low social status have higher rates of reproduction than men and women with high social status.

If our goal is not merely to survive and reproduce but to enjoy a tranquil existence, the pain associated with a loss of social status isn't just useless, it is counterproductive. As we go about our daily affairs, other people, because of their evolutionary programming, will work, often unconsciously, to gain social status. As a result, they will be inclined to snub us, insult us, or, more generally, do things to put us in our place, socially speaking. Their actions can have the effect of disrupting our tranquility—if we let them. What we must do, in these cases, is use—more precisely, "misuse"—our intellect to override the evolutionary programming that makes insults painful to us. We must, in other words, use our reasoning ability to remove the emotional sting of insults and thereby make them less disruptive to our tranquility.

Along similar lines, consider our insatiability. As we have seen, our evolutionary ancestors benefited from wanting more of everything, which is why we today have this tendency. But our insatiability, if we do not take steps to bridle it, will disrupt our tranquility; instead of enjoying what we already have, we will spend our life working hard to gain things we don't have, in the sadly mistaken belief that once we have them, we will enjoy them and search no further. What we must do, again, is misuse our intellect. Instead of using it to devise clever strategies to get more of everything, we must use it to overcome our tendency toward insatiability. And one excellent way for us to do this is to use our intellect to engage in negative visualization.

Consider, finally, anxiety. We are evolutionarily programmed, as we have seen, to be worriers: Our evolutionary ancestors who, instead of worrying about where their next meal was coming from and about the source of that growling noise in the trees, sat around blissfully enjoying the sunset probably didn't live to a ripe old age. But most modern individuals—in developed countries, at any rate—live in a remarkably safe and predictable environment; there are no growling noises in the trees, and we can be reasonably certain that our next meal is forthcoming. There is simply much less for us to worry about. Nevertheless, we retain our ancestors' tendency to worry. What we must do, if we wish to gain tranquility, is "misuse" our intellect to overcome this tendency. In particular, we can, in accordance with Stoic advice, determine which are the things we cannot control. We can then use our reasoning ability to eradicate our anxieties with respect to these things. Doing this will improve our chances of gaining tranquility.

Allow me to recapitulate. The Stoics thought they could prove that Stoicism was the one correct philosophy of life, and in their proof, they assumed that Zeus exists and created us for a certain purpose. I think it is possible, though, for someone to reject the Stoic proof of Stoicism without rejecting Stoicism itself. In particular, someone who thinks that the Stoics were mistaken in their assertion that we were created for a purpose might nevertheless think that the Stoics, in their philosophy of life, chose the correct goal (tranquility) and discovered a number of useful techniques for attaining this goal.

Thus, if someone asked me, "Why should I practice Stoicism?" my answer would not invoke the name of Zeus (or God) and would not talk about the function that humans were designed to fulfill. Instead, I would talk about our evolutionary past; about how, because of this past, we are evolutionarily programmed to want certain things and to experience certain emotions under certain circumstances; about how living in accordance with our evolutionary programming, although it may have allowed our evolutionary ancestors to survive and reproduce, can result in modern humans living miserable lives; and about how, by "misusing" our reasoning ability, we can overcome our evolutionary programming. I would go on to point out that the Stoics, although they didn't understand evolution, nevertheless discovered psychological techniques that, if practiced, can help us overcome those aspects of our evolutionary programming that might otherwise disrupt our tranquility.

Stoicism, understood properly, is a cure for a disease. The disease in question is the anxiety, grief, fear, and various other negative emotions that plague humans and prevent them from experiencing a joyful existence. By practicing Stoic techniques, we can cure the disease and thereby gain tranquility. What I am suggesting is that although the ancient Stoics found a "cure" for negative emotions, they were mistaken about why the cure works.

To BETTER UNDERSTAND the point I am making, consider aspirin. That aspirin works is indisputable; people have known this and used it as a medicine for thousands of years. The question is, how and why does it work?

Ancient Egyptians, who made medicinal use of willow bark, which contains the same active ingredient as aspirin does, had a theory. They thought four elements flow in us: blood, air, water, and a substance called *wekhudu*. They theorized that an overabundance of wekhudu caused pain and inflammation and that chewing on willow bark or drinking willow tea reduced the amount of wekhudu in someone experiencing pain or inflammation and thereby restored his health.[1] This theory, of course, was wrong: There is no such thing as wekhudu. What is significant is that even though their theory about how aspirin works was mistaken, aspirin nevertheless worked for them.

In the early centuries of the first millennium, the use of willow bark as a medicine was widespread, but then Europeans appear to have forgotten about its medicinal power. It was rediscovered in the eighteenth century by an Englishman, the Reverend Edward Stone. He knew that willow bark was an effective analgesic and antipyretic, but was as much in the dark about how it worked as the ancient Egyptians were. In the nineteenth century, chemists determined that the active ingredient in willow bark is salicylic acid but remained ignorant of how and why salicylic acid works. Indeed, it wasn't until the 1970s that researchers finally figured out how aspirin works: Damaged cells produce arachidonic acid, which triggers the creation of prostaglandins, which in turn cause fever, inflammation, and pain. By preventing the formation of prostaglandins, aspirin short-circuits this process.[2]

The thing to realize is that people's ignorance about how and why aspirin works did not stop it from working. I would like to make a parallel claim about Stoicism. The Stoics were like the ancient Egyptians who stumbled across a cure for a common ailment and exploited it without knowing why it works. Whereas the Egyptians stumbled across a cure for headaches and fever, the Stoics stumbled across a cure for negative emotions; more precisely, they developed a group of psychological techniques that, if practiced, could promote tranquility. Both the Egyptians and the Stoics were mistaken about why their cure works but not about its efficacy.

The early Stoics, it will be remembered, had an active interest in science. The problem is that their science was primitive and could not answer many of the questions they asked. As a result, they resorted to *a priori* explanations for the efficacy of Stoicism and the techniques it provides—explanations based not on observations of the world but on philosophical first principles. Would they, one wonders, have offered different explanations if they had known about evolution and, more important, evolutionary psychology?

Someone might, at this point, take the aspirin analogy one step further and turn it against Stoicism. In the same way that we have a better understanding of science than the Stoics did, we have (in part, because of this improved understanding) medicines that they lacked. In particular, we have tranquilizers such as Xanax that can relieve feelings of anxiety that would otherwise be an obstacle to our tranquility. This suggests the existence of a "royal road" to the tranquility the Stoics sought: Rather than going to our bookstore to buy a copy of Seneca, we should go to our doctor for a Xanax prescription. According to this line of thinking, the Stoic strategy for attaining tranquility can best be described as old-fashioned. Stoicism might have made sense for people who lived two thousand years ago; medical science was in its infancy, and Xanax didn't exist. But for someone today to resort to Stoicism to deal with anxiety is like someone going to a witch doctor to deal with an ulcer.

In response to this suggestion, let me point out that even though it is true that taking Xanax can alleviate our anxieties, there are nevertheless reasons to reject Xanax in favor of Stoicism. To better understand this point, let us turn our attention to a related debate. Given the state of modern medicine, an obese person has two alternatives available to him. He can change his lifestyle: In particular, he can eat less and differently and exercise more. Or he can resort to science to deal with his obesity: He can take a weight-loss drug or undergo, say, gastric bypass surgery.

Almost all doctors would recommend the first alternative, an old-fashioned change of lifestyle, even though modern, high-tech alternatives exist. Only if a lifestyle change fails to reduce the obese person's weight would these doctors recommend medication or surgery. In defense of this recommendation, doctors would point out that surgery is dangerous and that weight-loss medications can have serious side effects. Exercise, done properly, not only isn't dangerous but promotes our health. Furthermore, the benefits of exercise will probably spill over into other areas of our life. We are likely, for example, to find that we have more energy than we used to. Our self-esteem is also likely to rise.

Much the same can be said of resorting to Stoicism to prevent and deal with feelings of anxiety. It is safer than the medical alternatives, as any number of Xanax addicts will attest. Furthermore, Stoicism has benefits that spill over into other areas of our life. Practicing Stoicism might not cause us to gain energy, the way exercising will, but practicing it will cause us to gain self-confidence; we will become confident, in particular, of our ability to handle whatever life throws our way. The person who takes Xanax, in contrast, will gain no such confidence; indeed, he knows full well what a mess he would be if his supply of Xanax was cut off. Another benefit of practicing Stoicism is that it will help us appreciate our life and circumstances and may, as a consequence, enable us to experience joy. This is a benefit, one supposes, that taking Xanax is unlikely to deliver.

NOT EVERYONE, I REALIZE, will be happy with my "modernization" of Stoicism. My fellow philosophers, for example, might complain that in moving from a philosophical justification of Stoicism to a scientific justification, I have, in essence, ripped the head (advice and psychological techniques) off Stoicism and grafted it onto the body (justification) of an entirely different animal. They might add that the resulting doctrine is not an elegant chimera but a ghastly and unnatural monster—indeed, a Frankenstein.

My fellow philosophers might go on to complain that my scientific justification of Stoicism is distinctly anti-Stoical. The Stoics, as we have seen, advise us to live in accordance with nature. I am suggesting, though, that we use our reasoning ability to override our evolutionary programming—and therefore live, in a sense, in discordance with nature!

Stoic purists might also complain that in my treatment of Stoicism I have ignored differences in opinion among the Stoics I quote. Marcus, for example, seems to have been more duty-bound than the other Stoics. And Musonius and Seneca, while agreeing that Stoics needn't be ascetics—that their philosophy should not prevent them from enjoying life—disagreed on just how heartily Stoics should enjoy it. Some will complain about the way I have swept these and other disagreements under the rug.

In response to such criticisms, let me say this. What I have done in the preceding pages is play the role of philosophical detective: I have tried to determine what modern individuals must do if they wish to adopt the philosophy of life advocated by the Roman Stoics. What I discovered is that these Stoics did not provide us with a handbook on how to become a Stoic; indeed, not even Epictetus's *Handbook* is such a handbook. (Or if they did write treatises on how to practice Stoicism, these treatises have subsequently been lost.)[3] And it is understandable that they wouldn't provide a handbook: In their time, those wishing to learn how to practice Stoicism didn't need to learn it from a book; they could instead attend a Stoic school.

As a result, I had to cobble together a brand of Stoicism from clues scattered throughout the writings of the Roman Stoics. The resulting version of Stoicism, although derived from the ancient Stoics, is therefore unlike the Stoicism advocated by any particular Stoic. It is also likely that the version of Stoicism I have developed is in various respects unlike the Stoicism one would have been taught to practice in an ancient Stoic school.

What I have attempted to do is develop a brand of Stoicism that is useful to myself and, possibly, to those around me, and to accomplish this goal I have tailored the philosophy to our circumstances. If someone told me that she sought tranquility, I would advise her to try the Stoic psychological techniques described in this book. I would also encourage her to explore the writings of the ancient Stoics. I would warn her, though, that on doing this, she would discover differences between my version of Stoicism and the version favored by, say, Epictetus. I would add that if she found Epictetus's version more suited to her needs than my version is, she should by all means choose his version.

I am not, to be sure, the first Stoic to tamper with Stoicism. The Romans, as we have seen, adapted Greek Stoicism to suit their needs. Furthermore, individual Stoics were unafraid to "customize" Stoicism; as Seneca put it, "I do not bind myself to some particular one of the Stoic masters; I, too, have the right to form an opinion."[4] The Stoics regarded the principles of Stoicism not as being chiseled into stone but as being molded into clay that could, within limits, be remolded into a form of Stoicism that people would find useful.

I have presented Stoicism as I think the Stoics intended it to be used. They did not invent Stoicism for the amusement of future philosophers. To the contrary, they can best be understood as toolmakers, and Stoicism is the tool they invented. It is a tool that, if used properly, they thought would enable a person to live a good life. I came across this tool, dusty and disused, lying on a library shelf. I have taken it up, dusted it off, replaced a few parts, and put it to work to see if it can still do the job the Stoics designed it to do. I have discovered, to my surprise and delight, that it can. In fact, I have discovered that despite all the similar tools that have been invented since this one fell into disuse, it does the job better than they do.

NONPHILOSOPHERS—the people, as I have explained, who are the primary audience for this book—won't be concerned with preserving the purity of Stoicism. For them the question is, Does it work? And even if Stoicism can in some sense be said to work, they will go on to ask whether there is an alternative philosophy of life that works better still—whether, that is, there is an alternative philosophy that delivers the same (or greater) benefits at a lower cost. If Stoicism doesn't work better than the alternatives, a thoughtful individual will refuse to adopt it as his philosophy of life and will instead favor, say, Epicureanism or Zen Buddhism.

Even though I have adopted Stoicism as my philosophy of life, I do not claim that it is the only philosophy that "works" or even that, for every person, in all circumstances, it works better than alternative philosophies of life. All I am claiming is that for some people in some circumstances—I seem to be one of those people—Stoicism is a wonderfully effective way to gain tranquility.

Who, then, should give Stoicism a try? Someone who, to begin with, seeks tranquility; it is, after all, the thing Stoicism promises to deliver. Someone who thinks something is more valuable than tranquility would therefore be foolish to practice Stoicism.

Having the attainment of tranquility as a goal in living will eliminate some potential philosophies of life. It will, for example, eliminate hedonism, which has as its goal not tranquility but maximization of pleasure. But even after we settle on tranquility as a primary goal of our philosophy of life, we will have to choose among the philosophies of life that share this goal; we will have to choose, for starters, among Stoicism, Epicureanism, Skepticism, and Zen Buddhism. Which of these philosophies of life is best for us? Which will best enable us to gain the tranquility we seek? It depends, I think, on our personality and circumstances: What works for one person might not work for another whose personality and circumstances are different. When it comes to philosophies of life, in other words, there is no one size that fits all.

There are people, I think, whose personality is uniquely well-suited to Stoicism. Even if no one formally introduces these individuals to Stoicism, they will figure it out on their own. These "congenital Stoics" are perpetually optimistic, and they are appreciative of the world they find themselves in. If they were to pick up Seneca and start reading, they would instantly recognize him as a kindred spirit.

There are other people who, because of their personality, would find it psychologically challenging to practice Stoicism.

These individuals simply refuse to consider the possibility that they are the source of their own discontent. They spend their days waiting, often impatiently, for the one thing to happen that will make them feel good about themselves and their lives. The missing ingredient, they are convinced, is something external to them: It is something that someone must hand to them or do for them. The thing in question might be a certain job, a certain sum of money, or a certain form of cosmetic surgery. They are also convinced that when this missing ingredient is provided, their dissatisfaction with life will be remedied and they will live happily ever after. If you suggest to one of these chronic malcontents that she try Stoicism, she will likely dig in her heels and refuse the suggestion: "It can't work!" Such cases are tragic; the innate pessimism of these individuals prevents them from taking steps to overcome their pessimism and thereby dramatically reduces their chances of experiencing joy.

Most people have personalities that fall somewhere between these two extremes. They are not congenital Stoics, nor are they chronic malcontents. But although they might benefit from the practice of Stoicism, many of the individuals in this group see no need to give it—or, for that matter, any other philosophy of life—a try. They instead spend their days on evolutionary autopilot: They go around seeking the rewards their evolutionary programming has to offer, such as the pleasure to be derived from having sex or consuming a big meal, and avoiding the punishments their programming can inflict, such as the pain of being publicly insulted.

The day might come, though, when something happens to take them off autopilot. It might be a personal tragedy or maybe a flash of insight. At first, they will be rather disoriented. They might then set out in search of a philosophy of life. The first step in such a search, I would maintain, is to assess their personality and circumstances. Thereafter, their goal should not be to find the one, true philosophy of life but to find the philosophy that best suits them.

As I explained in the introduction to this book, there was a time when I was attracted to Zen Buddhism as a philosophy of life, but the more I learned about Zen, the less attractive it became. In particular, I came to realize that Zen is incompatible with my personality. I am a relentlessly analytical person. For Zen to work for me, I would have to abandon my analytical nature. Stoicism, though, expects me to put my analytical nature to work. As a result, for me the cost of practicing Stoicism is considerably less than the cost of practicing Zen. I would probably be miserable trying to solve *koans* or trying to sit for hours with an empty mind, but for other people, this won't be the case.

THE PREVIOUS COMMENTS make it sound as if I am a relativist with respect to philosophies of life, as if I take them all to be equally valid. Rest assured that this is not the case. Although I will not try to talk anyone into thinking that tranquility is the thing to be most valued in life, I will try to talk people out of certain other life goals. If, for example, you tell me that in your philosophy of life your primary goal is to experience pain, I will not take your philosophy to be as valid as Zen Buddhism or Stoicism; I will instead take you to be quite misguided. Why, I will ask, do you seek pain?

Suppose, on the other hand, that you tell me your goal in living is the same as that of the Zen Buddhists and Stoics—namely, the attainment of tranquility—but that you have a different strategy for attaining this goal than they do: You are convinced that the best way to attain it is to get your name mentioned in *People* magazine. In this case, I will praise the insight you have demonstrated in your choice of a goal, but I will express serious reservations about your strategy for attaining this goal. Do you honestly think that getting mentioned in *People* will induce a state of tranquility? And if so, how long will it last?

In summary, my advice to those seeking a philosophy of life parallels my advice to those seeking a mate. They should realize that which mate is best for them depends on their personality and circumstances. This means that no one is the ideal mate for everyone and that some people are a suitable mate for no one at all. Furthermore, they should realize that for the vast majority of people, life with a less than perfect mate is better than life with no mate at all.

In much the same way, there is no one philosophy of life that is ideal for everyone, and there are some philosophies of life that no one should adopt. Furthermore, in almost all cases, a person is better off to adopt a less than ideal philosophy of life than to try to live with no philosophy at all. Indeed, if this book converts not a single soul to Stoicism but encourages people to think actively about their philosophy of life, I will feel that I have, in accordance with Stoic principles, done a service for my fellow humans.

TWENTY-TWO

Practicing Stoicism

I WILL END THIS BOOK by sharing some of the insights I have gained in my practice of Stoicism. In particular, I will offer advice on how individuals wishing to try Stoicism as their philosophy of life can derive the maximum benefit from the trial with the minimum effort and frustration. I will also describe some of the surprises, as well as some of the delights, that lie in store for would-be Stoics.

The first tip I would offer to those wishing to give Stoicism a try is to practice what I have referred to as *stealth Stoicism*: You would do well, I think, to keep it a secret that you are a practicing Stoic. (This would have been my own strategy, had I not taken it upon myself to become a teacher of Stoicism.) By practicing Stoicism stealthily, you can gain its benefits while avoiding one significant cost: the teasing and outright mockery of your friends, relatives, neighbors, and coworkers.

It is, I should add, quite easy to practice Stoicism on the sly: You can, for example, engage in negative visualization without anyone being the wiser. If your practice of Stoicism is successful, friends, relatives, neighbors, and coworkers might notice a difference in you—a change for the better—but they will probably be hard-pressed to explain the transformation. If they come to you, perplexed, and ask what your secret is, you might choose to reveal the sordid truth to them: that you are a closet Stoic.

My next piece of advice for would-be Stoics is not to try to master all the Stoic techniques at once but to start with one technique and, having become proficient in it, go on to another. And a good technique to start with, I think, is negative visualization. At spare moments in the day, make it a point to contemplate the loss of whatever you value in life. Engaging in such contemplation can produce a dramatic transformation in your outlook on life. It can make you realize, if only for a time, how lucky you are—how much you have to be thankful for, almost regardless of your circumstances.

It is my experience that negative visualization is to daily living as salt is to cooking. Although it requires minimal time, energy, and talent for a cook to add salt to food, the taste of almost any food he adds it to will be enhanced as a result. In much the same way, although practicing negative visualization requires minimal time, energy, and talent, those who practice it will find that their capacity to enjoy life is significantly enhanced. You might find yourself, after engaging in negative visualization, embracing the very life that, a short time before, you had complained wasn't worth living.

One thing I have discovered, though, in my practice of Stoicism is that it is easy to forget to engage in negative visualization and as a result to go for days or even weeks without having visualized. I think I know why this happens. By engaging in negative visualization, we increase our satisfaction with our circumstances, but on gaining this sense of satisfaction, the natural thing to do is simply enjoy life. Indeed, it is decidedly unnatural for someone who is satisfied with life to spend time thinking about the bad things that can happen. The Stoics, however, would remind us that negative visualization, besides making us appreciate what we have, can help us avoid clinging to the things we appreciate. Consequently, it is as important to engage in negative visualization when times are good as it is when times are bad.

I tried making it my practice to engage in negative visualization each night at bedtime, as part of the "bedtime meditation" described back in chapter 8, but the experiment failed. My problem is that I tend to fall asleep remarkably fast after my head hits the pillow; there simply isn't time to visualize. I have instead made it my practice to engage in negative visualization (and more generally to assess my progress as a Stoic) while driving to work. By doing this, I transform idle time into time well spent.

AFTER MASTERING negative visualization, a novice Stoic should move on to become proficient in applying the trichotomy of control, described in chapter 5. According to the Stoics, we should perform a kind of triage in which we distinguish between things we have no control over, things we have complete control over, and things we have some but not complete control over; and having made this distinction, we should focus our attention on the last two categories. In particular, we waste our time and cause ourselves needless anxiety if we concern ourselves with things over which we have no control.

I have discovered, by the way, that applying the trichotomy of control, besides helping me manage my own anxieties, is an effective technique for allaying the anxieties of the non-Stoics around me, which anxieties might otherwise disrupt my tranquility. When relatives and friends share with me the sources of anxiety in their lives, it often turns out that the things they are worried about are beyond their control. My response to such cases is to point this out to them: "What can you do about this situation? Nothing! Then why are you worrying about it? It is out of your hands, so it is pointless to worry." (And if I am in the mood, I follow this last comment with a quotation from Marcus Aurelius: "Nothing is worth doing pointlessly.") It is interesting that even though some of the people I have tried this on can charitably be described as anxiety-prone, they almost always respond to the logic of the trichotomy of control: Their anxiety is dispelled, if only for a time.

As a Stoic novice, you will want, as part of becoming proficient in applying the trichotomy of control, to practice internalizing your goals. Instead of having winning a tennis match as your goal, for example, make it your goal to prepare for the match as best you can and to try your hardest in the match. By routinely internalizing your goals, you can reduce (but probably not eliminate) what would otherwise be a significant source of distress in your life: the feeling that you have failed to accomplish some goal.

In your practice of Stoicism, you will also want, in conjunction with applying the trichotomy of control, to become a psychological fatalist about the past and the present—but not about the future. Although you will be willing to think about the past and present in order to learn things that can help you better deal with the obstacles to tranquility thrown your way in the future, you will refuse to spend time engaging in "if only" thoughts about the past and present. You will realize that inasmuch as the past and present cannot be changed, it is pointless to wish they could be different. You will do your best to accept the past, whatever it might have been, and to embrace the present, whatever it might be.

OTHER PEOPLE, as we have seen, are the enemy in our battle for tranquility. It was for this reason that the Stoics spent time developing strategies for dealing with this enemy and, in particular, strategies for dealing with the insults of those with whom we associate. One of the most interesting developments in my practice of Stoicism has been my transformation from someone who dreaded insults into an insult connoisseur. For one thing, I have become a collector of insults: On being insulted, I analyze and categorize the insult. For another thing, I look forward to being insulted inasmuch as it affords me the opportunity to perfect my "insult game." I know this sounds strange, but one consequence of the practice of Stoicism is that one seeks opportunities to put Stoic techniques to work. I will have more to say about this phenomenon below.

One of the things that makes insults difficult to deal with is that they generally come as surprises. You are calmly chatting with someone when—wham!—he says something that, although it might not have been intended as an insult, can easily be construed as one. Recently, for example, I was talking to a colleague about a book he was writing. He said that in this book, he was going to comment on some political material I had published. I was delighted that he was aware of my work and was going to mention it, but then came the put-down: "I'm trying to decide," he said, "whether, in my response to what you have written, I should characterize you as evil or merely misguided."

Realize that such comments are to be expected from academics. We are a pathetically contentious lot. We want others not only to be aware of our work but to admire it and, better still, to defer to the conclusions we have drawn. The problem is that our colleagues seek the same admiration and deference from us. Something has to give, and as a result, on campuses everywhere, academics routinely engage in verbal fisticuffs. Put-downs are commonplace, and insults fly.

In my pre-Stoic days, I would have felt the sting of this insult and probably would have gotten angry. I would have vigorously defended my work and would have done my best to unleash a counterinsult. But on that particular day, having fallen under the influence of the Stoics, I had the presence of mind to respond to this insult in a Stoically acceptable manner, with self-deprecating humor: "Why can't you portray me as being *both* evil *and* misguided?" I asked.

Self-deprecating humor has become my standard response to insults. When someone criticizes me, I reply that matters are even worse than he is suggesting. If, for example, someone suggests that I am lazy, I reply that it is a miracle that I get any work done at all. If someone accuses me of having a big ego,

I reply that on most days it is noon before I become aware that anyone else inhabits the planet. Such responses may seem counterproductive since in offering them, I am in a sense validating the insulter's criticisms of me. But by offering such responses, I make it clear to the insulter that I have enough confidence in who I am to be impervious to his insults; for me, they are a laughing matter. Furthermore, by refusing to play the insult game—by refusing to respond to an insult with a counterinsult—I make it clear that I regard myself as being above such behavior. My refusal to play the insult game will likely irritate the insulter more than a counterinsult would.

ONE OF THE WORST THINGS we can do when other people annoy us is get angry. The anger will, after all, be a major obstacle to our tranquility. The Stoics realized that anger is anti-joy and that it can ruin our life if we let it. In the course of observing my emotions, I have paid careful attention to anger and as a result have discovered a few things about it.

To begin with, I have become fully aware of the extent to which anger has a life of its own within me. It can lie dormant, like a virus, only to revive and make me miserable when I least expect it. I might, for example, be in yoga class trying to empty my head of thoughts, when out of nowhere I find myself filled with anger about some incident that took place years before.

Furthermore, I have drawn the conclusion that Seneca was mistaken in suggesting that there is no pleasure in expressing anger.[1] This is the problem with anger: It feels good to vent it and feels bad to suppress it. Indeed, when our anger is righteous anger—when we are confident that we are right and whomever we are angry at is wrong—it feels quite wonderful to vent it and let the person who wronged us know of our anger. Anger, in other words, resembles a mosquito bite: It feels bad not to scratch a bite and feels good to scratch it. The problem with mosquito bites, of course, is that after you scratch one, you typically wish you hadn't done so: The itch returns, intensified, and by scratching the bite, you increase the chance that it will become infected. Much the same can be said of anger: Although it feels good to vent it, you will probably subsequently regret having done so.

It is one thing to vent anger (or better still, feign anger) with the goal of modifying someone's behavior: People do respond to anger. What I have discovered, though, is that a significant portion of the anger I vent can't be explained in these terms. When I am driving my car, for example, I periodically get angry—righteously, I think—at other drivers who drive incompetently, and sometimes I even yell at them. Since my windows and theirs are rolled up, the other drivers can't hear me and therefore can't respond to my anger by not doing again in the future whatever it was that made me mad. This anger, although righteous, is utterly pointless. By venting it, I accomplish nothing other than to disturb my own tranquility.

In other cases, although I am (righteously) angry at someone, I cannot, because of my circumstances, express my anger directly to him, so instead I find myself having black thoughts about him. Again, these feelings of anger are pointless: They disturb me but have no impact at all on the person at whom I am angry. Indeed, if anything, they serve to compound the harm he does me. What a waste!

I have found, by the way, that practicing Stoicism has helped me reduce the frequency with which I get angry at other drivers: I yell perhaps a tenth as often as I used to. It has also helped me reduce the number of black thoughts I have about people who wronged me long ago. And when black thoughts do infect me, they don't last as long as they used to.

Because anger has these characteristics—because it can lie dormant within us and because venting it feels good—our anger will be difficult to overcome, and learning to overcome it is one of the biggest challenges a Stoic practitioner faces. But one thing I have found is that the more you think about and understand anger, the easier it is to control it. As it so happens, I read Seneca's essay on anger while waiting at a doctor's office. The doctor was woefully behind schedule, and as a result I was left sitting in the waiting room for nearly an hour. I had every right to be angry, and in my pre-Stoic days I almost certainly would have been angry. But because I was thinking about anger during that hour, I found it impossible to get angry.

I have also found that it is quite useful to use humor as a defense against anger. In particular, I have found that one wonderful way to avoid getting angry is to imagine myself as a character in an absurdist play: Things aren't supposed to make sense, people aren't supposed to be competent, and justice, when it happens at all, happens by accident. Instead of letting myself be angered by events, I persuade myself to laugh at them. Indeed, I try to think of ways the imaginary absurdist playwright could have made things still more absurd.

Seneca, I am certain, was right when he pointed to laughter as the proper response to "the things which drive us to tears."[2]

Seneca also observes that "he shows a greater mind who does not restrain his laughter than he who does not restrain his tears, since the laughter gives expression to the mildest of the emotions, and deems that there is nothing important, nothing serious, nor wretched either, in the whole outfit of life."[3]

Besides advising us to imagine bad things happening to us, the Stoics, as we have seen, advise us to cause bad things to happen as the result of our undertaking a program of voluntary discomfort. Seneca, for example, advises us periodically to live as if we were poor, and Musonius advises us to do things to cause ourselves discomfort. Following this advice requires a greater degree of self-discipline than practicing the other Stoic techniques does. Programs of voluntary discomfort are therefore best left to "advanced Stoics."

I have experimented with a program of voluntary discomfort. I have not attempted to go barefoot, as Musonius suggested, but I have tried less radical behavior, such as underdressing for winter weather, not heating my car in the winter, and not air conditioning it in the summer.

I have also started taking yoga classes. Yoga has improved my balance and flexibility, reminded me of the importance of play, and made me acutely aware of how little control I have over the contents of my mind. But besides conferring these and other benefits on me, yoga has been a wonderful source of voluntary discomfort. While doing yoga, I twist myself into poses that are uncomfortable or that in some cases border on being painful. I will, for example, bend my legs until they are at the very edge of a cramp and then back off a bit. My yoga teacher, though, never talks about pain; instead, she talks about poses giving rise to "too much sensation." She has taught me how to "breathe into" the place that hurts, which of course is physiologically impossible if what I am experiencing is, say, a leg cramp. And yet, the technique undeniably works.

Another source of discomfort—and admittedly, of entertainment and delight as well—is rowing. Shortly after I began practicing Stoicism, I learned to row a racing shell and have since started racing competitively. We rowers are exposed to heat and humidity in the summer and to cold, wind, and sometimes even snow in the spring and fall. We are periodically splashed, unceremoniously, with water. We develop blisters and then calluses. (Whittling down calluses is a favorite off-water activity of serious rowers.)

Besides being a source of physical discomfort, rowing is a wonderful source of emotional discomfort. In particular, rowing has provided me with a list of fears to overcome. The racing shells I row are quite unstable; indeed, given half a chance, they will gleefully dump a rower into the water. It took me considerable effort to overcome my fear of flipping (by successfully surviving three flips). From there, I went on to work through other fears, including a fear of rowing in the predawn darkness, a fear of pushing off from the dock while standing up in the boat, and a fear of being out in the middle of a lake, hundreds of yards from the nearest shore, in a tiny boat (that has thrice betrayed me).

WHENEVER YOU UNDERTAKE an activity in which public failure is a possibility, you are likely to experience butterflies in your stomach. I mentioned above that since becoming a Stoic, I have become a collector of insults. I have also become a collector of butterflies. I like to engage in activities, such as competitive rowing, that give me butterflies simply so I can practice dealing with them. These feelings are, after all, an important component of the fear of failure, so that by dealing with them I am working to overcome my fear of failure. In the hours before a race, I experience some truly magnificent butterflies. I do my best to turn them to my advantage: They make me focus on the race that lies ahead. Once a race has begun, I have the pleasure of watching the butterflies depart.

I have also turned elsewhere in my pursuit of butterflies. After I began practicing Stoicism, for example, I decided to learn how to play a musical instrument, something I had never done before. The instrument I chose was the banjo. After several months of lessons, my teacher asked if I wanted to participate in the recital his students give. I initially rejected the offer; it sounded like no fun at all to risk public humiliation trying to play banjo in front of a bunch of strangers. But then it occurred to me that this was a wonderful opportunity to cause myself psychological discomfort and to confront—and hopefully vanquish—my fear of failing. I agreed to take part.

The recital was the most stress-inducing event I had experienced in a long time. It isn't that I have a fear of crowds; I can, with zero anxiety, walk into a classroom of sixty students I have never met and start lecturing them. But this was different. Before my performance, I experienced butterflies the size of small bats. Not only that, but I also slipped into an altered state of consciousness in which time was distorted and the laws of physics seemed to stop working. But to make a long story short, I survived the recital.

The butterflies I experience racing in a regatta or giving a banjo recital are, of course, a symptom of anxiety, and it might seem contrary to Stoic principles to go out of my way to cause myself anxiety. Indeed, if a goal of Stoicism is the attainment of tranquility, shouldn't I go out of my way to avoid anxiety-inducing activities? Shouldn't I, rather than collecting butterflies, flee from them?

Not at all. In causing myself anxiety by, for example, giving a banjo recital, I have precluded much future anxiety in my life. Now, when faced with a new challenge, I have a wonderful bit of reasoning I can use: "Compared to the banjo recital, this new challenge is *nothing*. I survived that challenge, so surely I will survive this one." By taking part in the recital, in other words, I immunized myself against a fair amount of future anxiety. It is an immunization, though, that will wear off with the passage of time, and I will need to be reimmunized with another dose of butterflies.

When doing things to cause myself physical and mental discomfort, I view myself—or at any rate, a part of me—as an opponent in a kind of game. This opponent—my "other self," as it were—is on evolutionary autopilot: He wants nothing more than to be comfortable and to take advantage of whatever opportunities for pleasure present themselves. My other self lacks self-discipline; left to his own devices, he will always take the path of least resistance through life and as a result will be little more than a simple-minded pleasure seeker. He is also a coward. My other self is not my friend; to the contrary, he is best regarded, in the words of Epictetus, "as an enemy lying in wait."[4]

To win points in the contest with my other self, I must establish my dominance over him. To do this, I must cause him to experience discomfort he could easily have avoided, and I must prevent him from experiencing pleasures he might otherwise have enjoyed. When he is scared of doing something, I must force him to confront his fears and overcome them.

Why play this game against my other self? In part to gain self-discipline. And why is self-discipline worth possessing? Because those who possess it have the ability to determine what they do with their life. Those who lack self-discipline will have the path they take through life determined by someone or something else, and as a result, there is a very real danger that they will mislive.

Playing the game against my other self also helps me build character. These days, I realize, people smirk at talk of building character, but it is an activity that the Stoics would heartily have endorsed and would have recommended to anyone wishing to have a good life.

One other reason for playing the game against my other self is that it is, somewhat surprisingly, fun to do. It is quite enjoyable to "win a point" in this game by, for example, successfully overcoming a fear. The Stoics realized as much. Epictetus, as we saw in chapter 7, talks about the pleasure to be derived from denying ourselves various pleasures.[5] Along similar lines, Seneca reminds us that even though it may be unpleasant to endure something, we will, on successfully enduring it, be pleased with ourselves.[6]

When I row competitively, it may look as though I am trying to beat the other rowers, but I am in fact engaged in a much more significant competition: the one against my other self. He didn't want to learn to row. He didn't want to do workouts, preferring instead to spend the predawn hours asleep in a warm bed. He didn't want to row to the starting line of the race. (Indeed, on the way there, he repeatedly whined about how tired he felt.) And during the race, he wanted to quit rowing and simply let the other rowers win. ("If you just quit rowing," he would say in his most seductive voice, "all this pain would come to an end. Why not just quit? Think of how good it would feel!")

It is curious, but my competitors in a race are simultaneously my teammates in the much more important competition against my other self. By racing against each other, we are all simultaneously racing against ourselves, although not all of us are consciously aware of doing so. To race against each other, we must individually overcome ourselves—our fears, our laziness, our lack of self-discipline. And it is entirely possible for someone to lose the competition against the other rowers—indeed, to come in last—but in the process of doing so to have triumphed in the competition against his other self.

THE STOICS, as we have seen, recommend simplifying one's lifestyle. Like programs of voluntary discomfort, lifestyle simplification is a process best left to advanced Stoics. As I have explained, a novice Stoic will probably want to keep a low philosophical profile. If you start dressing down, people will notice. Likewise, people will notice if you keep driving the same old car or—horrors!—give up the car to take the bus or ride a bike. People will assume the worst: impending bankruptcy, perhaps, or even the early stages of mental illness. And if you explain to them that you have overcome your desire to impress those who are impressed by a person's external trappings, you will only make matters worse.

When I started experimenting with a simplified lifestyle, it took some getting used to. When, for example, someone asked me where I had gotten the T-shirt I was wearing and I answered that I had bought it at a thrift store, I found myself feeling a bit ashamed. This incident made me appreciate Cato's manner of dealing with such feelings. Cato, as we have seen, dressed differently as a kind of training exercise: He wanted to teach himself "to be ashamed only of what was really shameful." He therefore went out of his way to do things that would trigger inappropriate feelings of shame in himself, simply so he could practice overcoming such feelings. I have lately been trying to emulate Cato in this respect.

SINCE BECOMING A STOIC, my desires have changed dramatically: I no longer want many of the things I once took to be essential for proper living. I used to dress nattily, but my wardrobe has lately become what can best be described as utilitarian: I have one tie and one sport coat that I can don if required; fortunately, they are rarely required. I used to long for a new car, but when my sixteen-year-old car recently died, I replaced it with a nine-year-old car, something that a decade ago I could not have imagined myself doing. (The "new" car, by the way, has two things that my old car lacked: a cup holder and a working radio. What joy!) There was a time when I would have understood why someone would want to own a Rolex watch; now such behavior puzzles me. I used to have less money than I knew what to do with; this is no longer the case, in large part because I want so few of the things that money can buy.

I read that many of my fellow Americans are in deep financial trouble. They have an unfortunate tendency to use up all the credit that is available to them and, when this doesn't satisfy their craving for consumer goods, to keep spending anyway. Many of these individuals, one suspects, would be affluent rather than bankrupt—and far happier as well—if only they had developed their capacity to enjoy life's simple pleasures.

I have become dysfunctional as a consumer. When I go to a mall, for example, I don't buy things; instead, I look around me and am astonished by all the things for sale that I not only don't need but can't imagine myself wanting. My only entertainment at a mall is to watch the other mall-goers. Most of them, I suspect, come to the mall not because there is something specific that they need to buy. Rather, they come in the hope that doing so will trigger a desire for something that, before going to the mall, they didn't want. It might be a desire for a cashmere sweater, a set of socket wrenches, or the latest cell phone.

Why go out of their way to trigger a desire? Because if they trigger one, they can enjoy the rush that comes when they extinguish that desire by buying its object. It is a rush, of course, that has as little to do with their long-term happiness as taking a hit of heroin has to do with the long-term happiness of a heroin addict.

Having said this, I should add that the reason I have so few consumer desires is not because I consciously fight their formation. To the contrary, such desires have simply stopped popping into my head—or at any rate, they don't pop nearly as often as they used to. In other words, my ability to form desires for consumer goods seems to have atrophied.

What brought about this state of affairs? The profound realization, thanks to the practice of Stoicism, that acquiring the things that those in my social circle typically crave and work hard to afford will, in the long run, make zero difference in how happy I am and will in no way contribute to my having a good life. In particular, were I to acquire a new car, a fine wardrobe, a Rolex watch, and a bigger house, I am convinced that I would experience no more joy than I presently do—and might even experience less.

As a consumer, I seem to have crossed some kind of great divide. It seems unlikely that, having crossed it, I will ever be able to return to the mindless consumerism that I once found to be so entertaining.

LET ME NOW DESCRIBE a surprising side effect of the practice of Stoicism. As a Stoic, you will constantly be preparing yourself for hardship by, for example, engaging in negative visualization or voluntarily causing yourself discomfort. If hardship doesn't follow, it is possible for a curious kind of disappointment to set in. You might find yourself wishing that your Stoicism would be put to the test so you can see whether you in fact possess the skills at hardship management that you have worked to acquire. You are, in other words, like a firefighter who has practiced his firefighting skills for years but has never been called on to put out an actual fire or like a football player who, despite diligently practicing all season long, has never been put in a game.

Along these lines, the historian Paul Veyne has commented that if we attempt to practice Stoicism, "a calm life is actually disquieting because we are unaware of whether we would remain strong in the case of a tempest."[7] Likewise, according to Seneca, when someone attempts to harm a wise man, he might actually welcome the attempt, since the injuries can't hurt him but can help him: "So far . . . is he from shrinking from the buffetings of circumstances or of men, that he counts even injury profitable, for through it he finds a means of putting himself to the proof and makes trial of his virtue."[8] Seneca also suggests that a Stoic might welcome death, inasmuch as it represents the ultimate test of his Stoicism.[9]

Although I have not been practicing Stoicism for very long, I have discovered in myself a desire to have my Stoicism tested. I already mentioned my desire to be insulted: I want to see whether I will respond to insults in a Stoically appropriate manner. I have likewise gone out of my way to put myself into situations that test my courage and willpower, in part to see whether I can pass such tests. And while I was writing this book, an incident took place that gave me a deeper understanding of the Stoics' desire to have their Stoicism tested.

The incident in question began when I noticed flashes of light along the periphery of my visual field whenever I blinked my eyes in a dark room. I went to my eye doctor and was informed that I had a torn retina and that, to prevent my retina from detaching, I should undergo laser surgery. The nurse who prepared me for the surgery explained that the doctor would repeatedly zap my retina with a high-powered laser beam. She asked whether I had ever seen a light show and said that what I was about to witness was a spectacle far more splendid than that. The doctor then entered the room and started zapping me. The first pops of light were indeed intense and beautiful, but then something unexpected happened: I stopped seeing the bursts of light. I could still hear the laser popping but saw nothing. Indeed, when the laser was finally turned off, all I could see through the eye that had been operated on was a purple blob that covered my entire visual field. It occurred to me that something might have gone wrong during the surgery—perhaps the laser had malfunctioned—and that I might as a result now be blind in one eye.

This thought was unsettling, to be sure, but after having it, I detected in myself another, wholly unexpected thought: I found myself reflecting on how I would respond to being blind in one eye. In particular, would I be able to deal with it in proper Stoic fashion? I was, in other words, responding to the possible loss of sight in an eye by sizing up the Stoic test potential of such a loss! This response probably seems strange to you; it seemed and still seems strange to me as well. Nevertheless, this was my response, and in responding this way, I was apparently experiencing a predictable (and some would say perverse) side effect of the practice of Stoicism.

I informed the nurse that I could not see in the eye that had been operated on. She told me—at last! why didn't she tell me before?—that this was normal and that my vision would come back within an hour. It did, and as a result I was deprived—thankfully, I think—of this opportunity to have my Stoicism tested.

UNLESS AN UNTIMELY DEATH prevents it, I will, in about a decade, be confronted with a major test of my Stoicism. I will be in my mid-sixties; I will, in other words, be on the threshold of old age.

Throughout my life, I have sought role models, people who were in the next stage of life and who, I thought, were handling that stage successfully. On reaching my fifties, I started examining the seventy- and eighty-year-olds I knew in an attempt to find a role model. It was easy, I discovered, to find people in that age group who could serve as *negative* role models; my goal, I thought, should be to *avoid* ending up like them. Positive role models, however, proved to be in short supply.

When I went to the seventy- and eighty-year-olds I knew and asked for advice on dealing with the onset of old age, they had an annoying tendency to offer the same nugget of wisdom: "Don't get old!" Barring the discovery of a "fountain of youth" drug, though, the only way I can act on this advice is to commit suicide. (It has subsequently occurred to me that this is precisely what they were advising me to do, albeit in an oblique manner. It has also occurred to me that their advice not to get old echoes Musonius's observation that "he is blessed who dies not late but well.")

It is possible that when I am in my seventies or eighties I will conclude, as the elderly people I know seem to have concluded, that nonexistence is preferable to old age. It is also possible, though, that many of those who find old age to be so burdensome have themselves to blame for their predicament:

They neglected, while young, to prepare for old age. Had they taken the time to properly prepare themselves—had they, in particular, started practicing Stoicism—it is conceivable that they would not have found old age to be burdensome; instead, they might have found it to be, as Seneca claimed, one of the most delightful stages of life, a stage that is "full of pleasure if one knows how to use it."[10]

WHILE I WAS WRITING this book, my eighty-eight-year-old mother had a stroke and was banished (by me, as it so happens) to a nursing home. The stroke so weakened the left side of her body that she was no longer able to get out of bed by herself. Not only that, but her ability to swallow was compromised, making it dangerous for her to eat regular foods and drink regular liquids, which might go down her windpipe and trigger a potentially fatal bout of pneumonia. The foods she was served had to be pureed, and the liquids she was given had to be thickened. (There is, I discovered, a whole line of thickened beverages that have been created for people with swallowing problems.)

Quite understandably, my mother was unhappy with the turn her life had taken, and I did my best to encourage her. Were I devoutly religious, I might have attempted to cheer her up by praying with her or for her, or by telling her that I had arranged for tens or even hundreds of people to pray on her behalf. As it was, though, I found that the best words of encouragement I had to offer had a distinctly Stoical ring to them. She would, for example, tell me how difficult her situation was, and I would quote Marcus: "Yes, they say that life is more like wrestling than like dancing."

"That's very true," she would murmur in reply.

She would ask me what she had to do to be able to walk again. I thought it was unlikely that she would ever walk again but did not say as much. Instead, I encouraged her (without giving a lecture on Stoicism) to internalize her goals with respect to walking: "What you need to concentrate on is doing your very best when they give you physical therapy."

She would complain about having lost most of the function of her left arm, and I would encourage her to engage in negative visualization: "At least you have the ability to speak," I would remind her. "In the first days after the stroke, you could only mumble. Back then, you couldn't even move your right arm and consequently couldn't feed yourself, but now you can. Really, you have lots to be thankful for."

She would listen to my reaction and, after a moment of reflection, she would usually respond affirmatively: "I suppose I do." The exercise in negative visualization seemed to take the edge off her distress, if only temporarily.

Time after time during this period, I was struck by how natural and appropriate it is to invoke Stoic principles to help someone cope with the challenges of old age and ill health.

I MENTIONED ABOVE that the stroke made it dangerous for my mother to drink regular, unthickened water. Being denied water made her, quite naturally, start to crave it. She would ask me in a pleading voice for a glass of water, "not thick but from the sink." I would refuse the request and explain why, but as soon as I finished my explanation, she would ask again, "Just a glass of water. Please!" I found myself in the position of a loving son who was continually denying his elderly mother's request for a simple glass of water.

After enduring my mother's pleas for a time, I asked the nurse what to do. "Give her ice cubes to suck on," she said. "The water in the ice will be released slowly, so there is little danger that she will aspirate it."

As a result of this advice, I became my mother's personal ice man, bringing a cup on each visit. ("The ice man cometh!" I would call out on arriving at her room.) I would pop a cube into her mouth, and she would, while sucking it, tell me how wonderful the ice was. My mother, who in her prime had been a connoisseur of fine food and drink, had now become a connoisseur of ice cubes. Something she had taken for granted her entire life—for her, an ice cube had merely been the thing you use to cool a beverage worth drinking—was now giving her intense pleasure. She clearly enjoyed this ice more than a gourmet would enjoy vintage champagne.

Watching her suck appreciatively on ice cubes, I felt a tinge of envy. Wouldn't it be wonderful, I thought, to be able to derive this much pleasure from a simple ice cube? It is, I decided, unlikely that negative visualization alone would enable me to appreciate ice cubes as intensely as my mother does; unfortunately, it would probably take a stroke like hers to do the trick. Nevertheless, watching her suck on ice cubes has been quite instructive. It has made me cognizant of yet another thing that I take utterly for granted: my ability to gulp down a big glass of cold water on a hot summer day.

During one visit to my mother, I encountered the Ghost of Christmas Future. I was walking down the hall of the nursing home toward my mother's room. Ahead of me was an elderly gentleman in a wheelchair being pushed by an attendant. When I got close, the attendant got my attention and said, pointing to her charge, "This man is a professor, too." (My mother, it turns out, had been telling everyone about me.)

I stopped and said hello to this fellow academic, who, it turned out, had retired some time before. We chatted for a while, but during our conversation I was haunted by the thought that in a few decades' time I might have this conversation again, only then it would be me in the wheelchair and it would be some younger professor standing in front of me, taking a few moments out of his busy day to talk to an academic relic.

My time is coming, I told myself, and I must do what I can to prepare for it.

The goal of Stoicism, as we have seen, is the attainment of tranquility. Readers will naturally want to know whether my own practice of Stoicism has helped me attain this goal. It has not, alas, allowed me to attain perfect tranquility. It has, however, resulted in my being substantially more tranquil than was formerly the case.

In particular, I have made considerable progress in taming my negative emotions. I am less prone to anger than I used to be, and when I find myself venting my anger at others I am much more willing to apologize than was formerly the case. I am not only more tolerant of put-downs than I used to be but have developed a near-complete immunity to garden-variety insults. I am also less anxious than I once was about the disasters that might befall me and in particular about my own death—although the real test for this, as Seneca says, will be when I am about to take my last breath.

Having said this, I should add that although I may have tamed my negative emotions, I have not eradicated them; nor is it likely that I ever will. I am nevertheless delighted to have deprived these emotions of some of the power they used to have over me.

One significant psychological change that has taken place since I started practicing Stoicism is that I experience far less dissatisfaction than I used to. Apparently as the result of practicing negative visualization, I have become quite appreciative of what I've got. There remains, to be sure, the question of whether I would continue to be appreciative if my circumstances changed dramatically; perhaps, without realizing it, I have come to cling to the things I appreciate, in which case I would be devastated to lose those things. I won't know the answer to this question, of course, until my Stoicism is put to the test.

One other discovery I have made in my practice of Stoicism concerns joy. The joy the Stoics were interested in can best be described as a kind of objectless enjoyment—an enjoyment not of any particular thing but of *all this*. It is a delight in simply being able to participate in life. It is a profound realization that even though all this didn't have to be possible, it *is* possible—wonderfully, magnificently possible.

For the record, my practice of Stoicism has not enabled me to experience unbroken joy; far from it. Nor have I experienced the higher kind of joy that a Stoic sage might experience, a joy at the realization that his joy cannot be disrupted by external events. But my practice of Stoicism does seem to have made me susceptible to periodic outbursts of delight in *all this*.

It is curious, but when I started experiencing these outbursts, I wasn't quite sure what to make of them. Should I embrace my feelings of joy or hold them at arm's length? Indeed, should I, as a sober-minded adult, attempt to extinguish them? (I have since discovered that I am not alone in being suspicious of feelings of joy.) Then it dawned on me what utter foolishness it would be to do anything other than embrace them. And so I have.

These comments, I realize, make me sound disgustingly self-satisfied, and boastful to boot. Rest assured that the practice of Stoicism does not require people to go around telling others how delighted they are to be alive or about the outbursts of joy they have lately been experiencing; indeed, the Stoics doubtless would have discouraged this sort of thing. Why, then, am I telling you about my state of mind? Because it answers the question you naturally have: Does Stoicism deliver the psychological goods it promises? In my case it did, to a more than satisfactory extent. Having made this point, though, I will in the future do my best to be admirably modest in any public assessments I offer regarding my state of mind.

ALTHOUGH I AM a practicing Stoic, let me confess, in these closing paragraphs, that I have some misgivings about the philosophy.

According to the Stoics, if I seek tranquility, I need to give up other goals that someone in my circumstances might have, such as to own an expensive, late-model car or to live in a million-dollar home. But what if everyone else is right and the Stoics are wrong? There is a chance that I will someday look back on what I will then term "my Stoic phase" and be both baffled and dismayed. "What was I thinking?" I will ask myself. "If only I could have those years back!"

I am not the only Stoic to harbor such doubts. In his essay on tranquility, for example, Seneca has an imaginary conversation with Serenus, a Stoic with misgivings about Stoicism. When Serenus has been among people with normal values—for example, after he has dined in a house "where one even treads on precious stones and riches are scattered about in every corner"—he discovers within himself "a secret sting and the doubt whether the other life is not better."[11] The above comments make it clear that I, too, have felt this "secret sting."

It doesn't help that those who think fame and fortune are more valuable than tranquility vastly outnumber those who, like myself, think tranquility is more valuable. Can all these other people be mistaken? Surely I am the one making the mistake!

At the same time, I know, thanks to my research on desire, that almost without exception the philosophers and religious thinkers who have contemplated life and the way people normally live it have come to the conclusion that it is the vast majority of people who are making a mistake in their manner of living. These thinkers have also tended to gravitate toward tranquility as something very much worth pursuing, although many of them disagreed with the Stoics on how best to pursue it.

When I start having second thoughts about Stoicism, my current practice is to recall that we live in a world in which certainty is possible only in mathematics. We live, in other words, in a world in which, no matter what you do, you might be making a mistake. This means that although it is true that I might be making a mistake by practicing Stoicism, I might also be making a mistake if I reject Stoicism in favor of some other philosophy of life. And I think the biggest mistake, the one made by a huge number of people, is to have no philosophy of life at all. These people feel their way through life by following the promptings of their evolutionary programming, by assiduously seeking out what feels good and avoiding what feels bad. By doing this, they might have a comfortable life or even a life filled with pleasure. The question remains, however, whether they could have a better life by turning their back on their evolutionary programming and instead devoting time and energy to acquiring a philosophy of life. According to the Stoics, the answer to this question is that a better life *is* possible—one containing, perhaps, less comfort and pleasure, but considerably more joy.

I suspect that in coming decades (should I live that long) whatever doubts I may have had about Stoicism will fall by the wayside as the aging process takes its toll. Stoic techniques can improve a life when times are good, but it is when times are bad that the efficacy of these techniques becomes most apparent. If I find Stoicism to be beneficial in my sixth decade of life, I am likely to find it to be indispensable in my eighth or ninth decade. Unless I am an unusual person, my biggest tests in life lie ahead. I will, I think, be glad to have developed an understanding and appreciation of Stoicism before these tests are administered.

It would be nice to have a proof that Stoicism (or some other philosophy of life) is the "correct" philosophy. Unfortunately, the proof offered by the Stoics is unconvincing, and an alternative proof is unlikely to be forthcoming. In the absence of such a proof, we must act on the basis of probabilities. For a certain kind of person—for a person in certain circumstances with a certain personality type—there are many reasons to think that Stoicism is worth a try. Practicing Stoicism doesn't take much effort; indeed, it takes far less effort than the effort one is likely to waste in the absence of a philosophy of life. One can practice Stoicism without anyone's being any the wiser, and one can practice it for a time and then abandon it and be no worse off for the attempt. There is, in other words, little to lose by giving Stoicism a try as one's philosophy of life, and there is potentially much to gain.

Indeed, according to Marcus,[12] it is possible, through the practice of Stoicism, to gain a whole new life.

A Stoic Reading Program

Many philosophical writings are inaccessible to nonphilosophers. This cannot be said, though, of most of the writings of the Stoics. Readers of this book are therefore encouraged to take a look at Stoic primary sources. On doing this, they might discover that their own interpretation of the Stoics differs from mine, and they will certainly discover that in the process of writing this book, there were many nuggets of Stoic wisdom and insight that I had to omit.

Those wishing to read the Stoics would do well to start with the essays of Seneca, especially, "On the Happy Life," "On Tranquility of Mind," and "On the Shortness of Life." These can be found in *Seneca: Dialogues and Essays* (Oxford University Press, 2008). Alternatively, they are available in volume 2 of *Seneca: Moral Essays*, in the Loeb Classical Library. (This volume also has the advantage of being small enough to fit into a pocket or purse. Thus, if readers find themselves at a banquet given by nonphilosophers and the talk turns to inappropriate things, they can slip off to a quiet corner, pull out their copy of Seneca, and read.)

Seneca's letters to Lucilius also merit attention. There are more than a hundred of these letters, and some are of more interest than others. Furthermore, the letters themselves tend to focus on different topics. In Letter 83, for example, Seneca talks about alcohol; in Letters 12 and 26, about old age; and in Letter 7, about gladiatorial contests. (He describes how, during breaks in the show, spectators would yell out to have some throats cut just so there would be something for them to watch.) Many readers would therefore do well to get a book containing a selection of these letters.

Musonius Rufus is worth reading for his practical advice on daily living. The only published translation of Musonius that I know of, though, is Cora Lutz's "Musonius Rufus: 'The Roman Socrates,'" in volume 10 of *Yale Classical Studies* (1947), which is difficult to buy or borrow. Readers are therefore encouraged to visit my author website (williambirvine.com) for information on how to obtain a copy of Cynthia King's translation of Musonius's works. (This is the translation I quote from in this book.)

Readers wishing to sample Epictetus are encouraged to start with his *Handbook* (also known as his *Manual* or *Encheiridion*). It has the advantage of being short, easily obtainable, and philosophically accessible. In the world of philosophical literature, it stands out as a gem.

Marcus Aurelius's *Meditations* is also both accessible and readily available. Reading the *Meditations* can be a bit frustrating, though, inasmuch as it is a collection of disconnected (except for the Stoic theme) and sometimes repetitious observations.

Readers might also be interested in branching out beyond the Stoics. They might, for example, take a look at Diogenes Laertius's biographical sketches of the Greek Stoics. The sketches of Zeno of Citium, Cleanthes, and Chrysippus can be found in volume 2 of *Diogenes Laertius*, also in the Loeb Classical Library. And while the reader has possession of this volume, it might be fun to take a look at the biographical sketch of Diogenes of Sinope, the Cynic. He combines wisdom with humor in a most admirable manner.

Readers might also want to take a look at Arthur Schopenhauer's essays in *The Wisdom of Life and Counsels and Maxims*. Although not explicitly Stoical, these essays have a distinctly Stoical tone. Readers might also be interested in the novelist Tom Wolfe's *A Man in Full*, in which a character accidentally discovers Stoicism and subsequently starts practicing it. Finally, readers can get some insight into the practice of Stoicism under difficult circumstances by reading James B. Stockdale's *Courage under Fire: Testing Epictetus's Doctrines in a Laboratory of Human Behavior*.

Enjoy!

Notes

Introduction

1. Epicurus, 54.
2. Seneca, *Ad Lucilium*, CVIII.4.
3. *American Heritage Dictionary of the English Language*, 3rd ed.
4. Seneca, "On Tranquillity," II.4.
5. Seneca, "On the Happy Life," IV.4.
6. Musonius, "Lectures," 17.2.
7. Seneca, "On Firmness," II.1–2.
8. Marcus, VII.31.

One

1. Diogenes Laertius, "Prologue," I.13–14.
2. Cicero, V.10.
3. Cornford, 5.
4. Navia, 1.
5. Marrou, 96.
6. Diogenes Laertius, "Prologue," I.17–19.
7. Diogenes Laertius, "Zeno," VII.25.
8. Price, 141.
9. Veyne, viii.

Two

1. Diogenes Laertius, "Zeno," VII.2–4.
2. Epictetus, "Discourses," 3.22.
3. Diogenes Laertius, "Antisthenes," VI.3, VI.4, VI.12, VI.15.
4. Diogenes Laertius, "Diogenes," VI.44, VI.71, VI.66.

5. Diogenes Laertius, "Diogenes," VI.35.
6. Dio Chrysostom, "The Sixth Discourse," 12.
7. Diogenes Laertius, "Diogenes," VI.63.
8. Diogenes Laertius, "Crates," VI.86.
9. Arnold, 67.
10. Schopenhauer, II:155.
11. Diogenes Laertius, "Zeno," VII.24, VII.25.
12. Arnold, 71.
13. Diogenes Laertius, "Zeno," VII.5.
14. Diogenes Laertius, "Zeno," VII.40.
15. Kekes, 1.
16. Becker, 20.
17. Veyne, 31.
18. Diogenes Laertius, "Zeno," VII.87.
19. Diogenes Laertius, "Zeno," VII.108.
20. Diogenes Laertius, "Zeno," VII.40.
21. Diogenes Laertius, "Zeno," VII.117–119.
22. Marcus, I.17.
23. Epictetus, "Discourses," I.iv.3–6, along with the accompanying footnote.
24. Arnold, 94.
25. Diogenes Laertius, "Prologue," I.21.

Three

1. Technically, Epictetus was not a Roman inasmuch as he was not a Roman citizen; nevertheless, the Stoicism he practiced was the Romanized form of the doctrine, and for that reason I include him among the Roman Stoics.
2. Seneca, "To Helvia," VII.9.
3. Veyne, 9.
4. Tacitus, 14.53.
5. Tacitus, 15.62–64.
6. Seneca, "On the Happy Life," III.4, IV.4.
7. Seneca, *Ad Lucilium*, XXIII.3.
8. Having said this, I should add that some classicists refuse to take Seneca's comments about joy at face value. The philosopher Martha Nussbaum, for example, points out that Seneca, immediately after offering the above advice to Lucilius, goes on to explain what he means by *joy*: It is not, says Seneca, a "sweetly agreeable" kind of joy; rather, the joy Seneca has in mind is "a stern matter." See Nussbaum, 400. I would

argue, however, that in saying this, Seneca is simply trying to distinguish Stoic joy from related mental states. When, for example, he tells Lucilius not to assume that "he who laughs has joy" (*Ad Lucilium*, XXIII.3) he is distinguishing joy from elation: A person can be elated and can therefore laugh, even though he is not experiencing joy—think, for example, about someone who gains a state of elation by using crystal meth.

9. Tacitus, 15.71.
10. Strabo, 10.5.3.
11. Seneca, "To Helvia," VI.4.
12. *New York Times Index* (1973), 929.
13. Lutz, 15, 16.
14. Musonius, "Lectures," 8.9.
15. Musonius, "Sayings," 49.3.
16. Epictetus, "Discourses," III.xxiii.29.
17. Musonius, "Lectures," 3.1.
18. Long, 10.
19. Arnold, 120.
20. Long, 108.
21. Epictetus, "Discourses," II.xvii.29–31.
22. Epictetus, "Discourses," III.xxiii.30.
23. Long, 91.
24. Epictetus, "Discourses," I.xv.2–3.
25. Long, 146.
26. Epictetus, "Discourses," I.i.11–12.
27. Epictetus, "Discourses," I.xxiv.1–2.
28. Seneca, "On Providence," I. 6, II.2, III.2.
29. Marcus, II.1.
30. Julius Capitolinus, sec. 2.
31. Birley, 37–38.
32. Julius Capitolinus, sec. 2.
33. Marcus, I.8, I.7.
34. Marcus, VII.67.
35. Birley, 104.
36. Julius Capitolinus, sec. 7.
37. Julius Capitolinus, secs. 10, 11.
38. Cassius Dio, 72.33.
39. Birley, 160.
40. Quoted in Birley, 11.
41. Lecky, 292.
42. Marcus, III.6.

43. Birley, 179, 182, 191, 196, 183.
44. Julius Capitolinus, sec. 12.
45. Birley, 149, 158; Julius Capitolinus, sec. 11; Birley, 205.
46. Marcus, VII.61.
47. Cassius Dio, 72.36, 72.34.
48. Julius Capitolinus, sec. 28.
49. Birley, 209.
50. Cassius Dio, 72.35.

Four

1. Seneca, "To Marcia," IX.5.
2. Seneca, "On Tranquillity," XI.6.
3. Epictetus, "Discourses," IV.v.27.
4. Frederick and Loewenstein, 302, 313.
5. Veyne, 178 n 38. This technique has also been called *premeditation of evils* (76).
6. Seneca, "To Marcia," I.7, IX.2, X.3.
7. Epictetus, "Discourses," II.xxiv.86, 88.
8. Marcus, XI.34.
9. Epictetus, "Discourses," III.xxiv.86–88.
10. Epictetus, *Handbook*, 21.
11. Seneca, *Ad Lucilium*, XII.8, XCIII.6, LXI.1–2.
12. Marcus, X.34.
13. Stockdale, 18–19.
14. Seneca, "On Tranquillity," XI.10.
15. Epictetus, *Handbook*, 26.
16. Marcus, VII.27.
17. Seneca, "On the Happy Life," III.3.
18. Seneca, "On the Happy Life," III.4.
19. Seneca, "To Marcia," XXI.1.
20. Marcus, X.34, VI.15.

Five

1. Epictetus, *Handbook*, 29, 48.
2. Epictetus, "Discourses," III.xv.12.
3. Epictetus, "Discourses," III.xxiv.17.
4. For more on this point, see my *On Desire: Why We Want What We Want*.

5. Epictetus, *Handbook*, 14, 19.
6. Epictetus, *Handbook*, 1.
7. Epictetus, *Handbook*, 2, 1.
8. Epictetus, *Handbook*, 14.
9. Marcus, XI.16, VII.2, XII.22.
10. Marcus, X.32, VIII.29, VIII.8, V.5.
11. Marcus, VIII.17.

Six

1. Seneca, "On Providence," V. 8.
2. Epictetus, *Handbook*, 17, 8.
3. Marcus, II.16, X.25, VI.39, III.4, III.16, X.6, III.4, III.16.
4. As the supreme god, Zeus had it in his power to override the decisions of the Fates but usually chose not to do so for pragmatic reasons. In the *Iliad* (16.440–49), for example, Homer describes an episode in which Zeus complains to Hera that Sarpedon is fated to be slain by Patroclus. Zeus is considering interfering with events in order to save Sarpedon's life. Hera implores him not to do this, since it would result in the other gods also interfering with earthly events, which would in turn create great discord among them.
5. Marcus, II.14, III.10.
6. Seneca, "On the Happy Life," III.3.

Seven

1. Seneca, *Ad Lucilium*, XVIII.5–6.
2. Seneca, *Ad Lucilium*, XVIII.9.
3. Musonius, *Lectures*, 19.2–3, 6.4.
4. Musonius, *Lectures*, 6.5.
5. Seneca, "On the Happy Life," XIV.2.
6. Dio Chrysostom, "The Eighth Discourse," 389, 391.
7. Marcus, II.2, V.26, VII.55.
8. Epictetus, *Handbook*, 34.
9. Seneca, "On the Happy Life," X.3.
10. Musonius, *Lectures*, 7.1.
11. Seneca, "On Anger," II.13.
12. Epictetus, *Handbook*, 34.
13. Epictetus, *Handbook*, 34.
14. Seneca, *Ad Lucilium*, XVIII.10.

Eight

1. Seneca, "On Anger," III.36.
2. Seneca, "On Anger," III.36–37.
3. Epictetus, "Discourses," IV.xii.19.
4. Marcus, III.11, V.11, X.37.
5. Epictetus, *Handbook*, 46, 13.
6. Epictetus, *Handbook*, 48.
7. Quoted in Plutarch, "Progress in Virtue," 12.
8. Epictetus, *Handbook*, 50, 47, 46.
9. Seneca, *Ad Lucilium*, XXVI.5.
10. Seneca, "On the Happy Life," XVII.3.
11. Epictetus, *Handbook*, 33.
12. Marcus, V.9.
13. Marcus, XII.6.

Nine

1. Seneca, "On the Happy Life," II.4.
2. Marcus, VIII.19–20, X.8.
3. Musonius, *Lectures*, 14.3.
4. Marcus, V.16, VI.44.
5. Marcus, III.4, IV.3, II.1, VII.5, V.20.
6. Marcus, V.6, IV.32, VI.22, V.1.
7. Marcus, XI.9, VI.39.
8. Marcus, II.1, V.10, XI.15.
9. Marcus, IX.3, X.36, X.19.
10. Lecky, 250.
11. Marcus, V.6, IX.12.
12. Marcus, VIII.7, V.34, VII.28, XII.3, VI.40, VIII.26.

Ten

1. Epictetus, *Handbook*, 33.
2. Seneca, "On Tranquillity," VII.4.
3. Epictetus, *Handbook*, 33.
4. Seneca, "On Tranquillity," VII. 6.
5. Johnson, s.v. "seeksorrow."
6. Epictetus, *Handbook*, 33.
7. Marcus, XI.18, X.30, XI.18.
8. Marcus, III.4.
9. Marcus, IX.42, VII.63, XII.12, IV.6, X.42.

10. Marcus, XII.16.
11. Marcus, XI.18.
12. Marcus, XI.9, XI.13, VII.65, VI.6.
13. Musonius, *Lectures*, 12.2.
14. Epictetus, *Handbook*, 33.
15. Marcus, XI.16, VI.13.
16. Bodhi, 83–85.
17. Epicurus, 8.
18. Musonius, *Lectures*, 14.1–2, 13A.2.
19. Musonius, *Lectures*, 15A.4.

Eleven

1. Musonius, *Lectures*, 10.1.
2. Seneca, "On Firmness," X.2.
3. Seneca, "On Firmness," XVI.4.
4. Epictetus, *Handbook*, 42.
5. Seneca, "On Firmness," XII.1–2.
6. Marcus, VII.26.
7. Epictetus, *Handbook*, 20, 30.
8. Epictetus, *Handbook*, 5.
9. Seneca, "On Anger," III.38.
10. Seneca, "On Anger," III.11. Other sources claim it was Diogenes the Cynic, not Socrates, who was responsible for the helmet joke.
11. Seneca, "On Firmness," XVII.3.
12. Epictetus, *Handbook*, 33.
13. Musonius, *Lectures*, 10.2.
14. Seneca, "On Anger," II.32.
15. Seneca, "On Firmness," XIV.3.
16. Seneca, "On Firmness," XVII.4.
17. Seneca, "On Firmness," XII.3.

Twelve

1. Seneca, "To Polybius," XVIII.4–5.
2. Seneca, "To Polybius," XVIII.6.
3. Seneca, "To Polybius," IV.3.
4. Seneca, "To Marcia," XII.1.
5. Seneca, "To Polybius," IV.2, XVIII.6.
6. Seneca, "To Polybius," V.3, IX.2.
7. Seneca, "To Helvia," IV.1, I.2.
8. Epictetus, *Handbook*, 16.

Thirteen

1. Seneca, "On Anger," I.1, I.2, III.28.
2. Seneca, "On Anger," I.12, I.10.
3. Seneca, "On Anger," I.12–15, II.31.
4. Seneca, "On Anger," II.14.
5. Seneca, "On Anger," II.22, III.31.
6. Seneca, "On Anger," II.25, III.35, II.25.
7. Seneca, "On Anger," III.28, III.27.
8. Seneca, "On Anger," III.33.
9. Marcus, IV.32.
10. Seneca, "On Anger," III.26, III.13.
11. Bodhi, 32, 69.
12. Seneca, "On Anger," III.42–43.

Fourteen

1. Epictetus, *Handbook*, 25.
2. Epictetus, *Handbook*, 23, 14.
3. Epictetus, *Handbook*, 50, 48.
4. Marcus, XII.4, III.4, VIII.1, IV.18.
5. Marcus, XI.13.
6. Marcus, IV.33, IV.19, VI.18, VIII.44.
7. Plutarch, "Cato the Younger," VI.3.

Fifteen

1. Irvine, 31–43.
2. Seneca, "To Helvia," X.6, X.10.
3. Musonius, *Lectures*, 17.5.
4. Epictetus, *Handbook*, 12.
5. Epictetus, "Discourses," IV.ix.2–3.
6. Musonius, *Sayings*, 50.
7. Musonius, *Lectures*, 18A.5.
8. No, I did not make this meal up; at the time of this writing, it could have been ordered at a famous restaurant in Beverly Hills.
9. Musonius, *Lectures*, 18A.2–3, 18B.5.
10. Musonius, *Lectures*, 18A.6, 18B.3.
11. Musonius, *Lectures*, 19.5, 20.3.
12. Seneca, *Ad Lucilium*, XVI.8–9.
13. Seneca, *Ad Lucilium*, XC.19.

14. Musonius, *Lectures*, 20.5, 20.7.
15. Seneca, *Ad Lucilium*, XC.16.
16. Seneca, "On Tranquillity," VIII.9, IX.2–3.
17. Seneca, *Ad Lucilium*, V.5.
18. Epictetus, *Handbook*, 33, 39.
19. Epictetus, *Handbook*, 24, 44.
20. Seneca, *Ad Lucilium*, CVIII.11.
21. Lao Tzu, XXXIII.
22. Seneca, *Ad Lucilium*, V.5.
23. Seneca, "On the Happy Life," XXIII.1, XX.3, XXVI.1.
24. Carus, 72–74.

Sixteen

1. Tacitus, 16.21.
2. Epictetus, "Discourses," I.i.31–32.
3. Seneca, "To Helvia," V.6, VI.1, VI.4.
4. Seneca, "To Helvia," VIII.3, XI.5.
5. Musonius, *Lectures*, 9.10.
6. Musonius, *Lectures*, 9.2.
7. Musonius, *Lectures*, 9.4.
8. Diogenes Laertius, "Diogenes," VI.49.

Seventeen

1. Seneca, *Ad Lucilium*, XII.4–6.
2. Quoted in Plato, *Republic*, bk. 1.
3. Seneca, *Ad Lucilium*, XXVI.2.
4. Seneca, *Ad Lucilium*, XII.9.
5. Musonius, *Lectures*, 17.3.

Eighteen

1. Musonius, *Lectures*, 17.4.
2. Musonius, *Lectures*, 17.4.
3. Seneca, "On Tranquillity," XIV.4–10.
4. Seneca, *Ad Lucilium*, XXVI.6.
5. Diogenes Laertius, "Zeno," VII.28, 31; Diogenes Laertius, "Cleanthes," VII.176.
6. Musonius, *Sayings*, 28, 35.
7. Musonius, *Sayings*, 29.

Nineteen

1. Musonius, *Lectures*, 7.1–2.
2. Epictetus, *Handbook*, 22.
3. Epictetus, *Handbook*, 46.
4. Marcus, IV.49.
5. Seneca, *Ad Lucilium*, CXXIII.3.
6. Seneca, "On Tranquillity," II.4.
7. Epictetus, *Handbook*, 51.

Twenty

1. Lecky, 249.
2. Lecky, 255.
3. Clarke, 133.
4. Marcus, VII.31.
5. Descartes, 16–17.
6. Quoted in Richardson, 4.
7. Richardson, 4.
8. Thoreau, 172.
9. Quoted in Richardson, 4.
10. Richardson, 1.
11. Nussbaum, 4.
12. Sommers and Satel, 180.
13. Furedi, 19.
14. Furedi, 19.
15. Furedi, 16.
16. Sommers and Satel, 136.
17. Sommers and Satel, 133–34.
18. Quoted in Sommers and Satel, 133.
19. Sommers and Satel, 134.
20. Sommers and Satel, 7.
21. Seneca, *Ad Lucilium*, LXXVIII.14.

Twenty-One

1. Jeffreys, 9–10, 12.
2. Jeffreys, 15, 17–18, 39, 230.
3. Hadot, 83n. 18.
4. Seneca, "On the Happy Life," III.2.

Twenty-Two

1. Seneca, "On Anger," II.32.
2. Seneca, "On Anger," III.33.
3. Seneca, "On Tranquillity," XV.3.
4. Epictetus, *Handbook*, 48.
5. Epictetus, *Handbook*, 34.
6. Seneca, *Ad Lucilium*, LXXVIII.14.
7. Veyne, 112.
8. Seneca, "On Firmness," IX.4.
9. Seneca, *Ad Lucilium*, XXVI.5.
10. Seneca, *Ad Lucilium*, XII.4–5.
11. Seneca, "On Tranquillity," I.8–9.
12. Marcus, VII.2.

Works Cited

Arnold, Edward Vernon. *Roman Stoicism*. Freeport, NY: Books for Libraries Press, 1911.

Becker, Lawrence C. *A New Stoicism*. Princeton: Princeton University Press, 1998.

Birley, Anthony. *Marcus Aurelius: A Biography*. Rev. ed. New Haven: Yale University Press, 1987.

Bodhi, Bhikkhu. *The Noble Eightfold Path: Way to the End of Suffering*. Seattle: BPS Pariyatti Editions, 2000.

Carus, Paul. *The Gospel of Buddha*. La Salle, IL: Open Court, 1915.

Cassius Dio Cocceanus. *Dio's Roman History*. Vol. 9. Translated by Earnest Cary. Cambridge, MA: Harvard University Press, 1927.

Cicero. *Tusculan Disputations*. Translated by J. E. King. Cambridge, MA: Harvard University Press, 1927.

Clarke, M. L. *The Roman Mind: Studies in the History of Thought from Cicero to Marcus Aurelius*. New York: Norton, 1968.

Cornford, Francis Macdonald. *Before and after Socrates*. Cambridge, UK: Cambridge University Press, 1962.

Descartes, René. *Discourse on Method*. Translated by Laurence J. Lafleur. Indianapolis: Bobbs-Merrill, 1950.

Dio Chrysostom. "The Eighth Discourse: Diogenes or On Virtue." In *Dio Chrysostom*. Vol. 1. Translated by J. W. Cohoon. Cambridge, MA: Harvard University Press, 1961.

———. "The Sixth Discourse: Diogenes, or on Tyranny." In *Dio Chrysostom*. Vol. 1. Translated by J. W. Cohoon. Cambridge, MA: Harvard University Press, 1961.

Diogenes Laertius. "Antisthenes." In *Lives of Eminent Philosophers*. Vol. 2. Translated by R. D. Hicks. Cambridge, MA: Harvard University Press, 1925.

———. "Cleanthes." In *Lives of Eminent Philosophers*. Vol. 2. Translated by R. D. Hicks. Cambridge, MA: Harvard University Press, 1925.

———. "Crates." In *Lives of Eminent Philosophers*. Vol. 2. Translated by R. D. Hicks. Cambridge, MA: Harvard University Press, 1925.

———. "Diogenes." *In Lives of Eminent Philosophers*. Vol. 2. Translated by R. D. Hicks. Cambridge, MA: Harvard University Press, 1925.

———. "Prologue." In *Lives of Eminent Philosophers*. Vol. 1. Translated by R. D. Hicks. Cambridge, MA: Harvard University Press, 1925.

———. "Zeno." In *Lives of Eminent Philosophers*. Vol. 2. Translated by R. D. Hicks. Cambridge, MA: Harvard University Press, 1925.

Epictetus. "Discourses." In *Epictetus: The Discourses as Reported by Arrian, the Manual, and Fragments*. 2 vols. Translated by W. A. Oldfather. Cambridge, MA: Harvard University Press, 1925.

———. *Handbook of Epictetus*. Translated by Nicholas White. Indianapolis: Hackett, 1983.

Epicurus. "Fragments: Remains Assigned to Certain Books." In *The Stoic and Epicurean Philosophers*. Edited by Whitney J. Oates. New York: Modern Library, 1940.

Frederick, Shane, and George Loewenstein. "Hedonic Adaptation." In *Well-Being: The Foundations of Hedonic Psychology*. Edited by Daniel Kahneman, Ed Diener, and Norbert Schwarz. New York: Russell Sage Foundation, 1999.

Furedi, Frank. *Therapy Culture: Cultivating Vulnerability in an Uncertain Age*. London: Routledge, 2004.

Hadot, Pierre. *Philosophy as a Way of Life*. Edited by Arnold I. Davidson. Cambridge, MA: Blackwell, 1995.

Irvine, William B. *On Desire: Why We Want What We Want*. New York: Oxford University Press, 2006.

Jeffreys, Diarmuid. *Aspirin: The Remarkable Story of a Wonder Drug*. New York: Bloomsbury, 2004.

Johnson, Samuel. *Johnson's Dictionary: A Modern Selection*. Edited by E. L. McAdam Jr. and George Milne. New York: Pantheon, 1963.

Julius Capitolinus. "Marcus Antoninus: The Philosopher." In *Scriptores Historiae Augustae*. Vol. 1. Translated by David Magie. Cambridge, MA: Harvard University Press, 1921.

Kekes, John. *Moral Wisdom and Good Lives*. Ithaca, NY: Cornell University Press, 1995.

Lao Tzu. *Tao Te Ching*. Translated by D. C. Lau. New York: Penguin, 1963.

Lecky, William Edward Hartpole. *History of European Morals: From Augustus to Charlemagne*. New York: George Braziller, 1955.

Long, A. A. *Epictetus: A Stoic and Socratic Guide to Life*. Oxford: Clarendon Press, 2002.

Lutz, Cora. Introduction to "Musonius Rufus: 'The Roman Socrates.'" *Yale Classical Studies*. Vol. 10. New Haven: Yale University Press, 1947.

Marcus Aurelius. *Meditations*. Translated by Maxwell Staniforth. London: Penguin, 1964.

Marrou, H. I. *A History of Education in Antiquity*. Translated by George Lamb. New York: New American Library, 1956.

Musonius Rufus. "The Lectures." In *The Lectures and Sayings of Musonius Rufus*. Translated by Cynthia King. Edited by William B. Irvine. Unpublished manuscript, 2007.

———. "The Sayings." In *The Lectures and Sayings of Musonius Rufus*. Translated by Cynthia King. Edited by William B. Irvine. Unpublished manuscript, 2007.

Navia, Luis E. *Socrates: The Man and His Philosophy*. Lanham, MD: University Press of America, 1985.

Nussbaum, Martha C. *The Therapy of Desire: Theory and Practice in Hellenistic Ethics*. Princeton: Princeton University Press, 1994.

Plato. *Plato's Republic*. Translated by G. M. A. Grube. Indianapolis: Hackett, 1974.

Plutarch. "Cato the Younger." In *The Lives of the Noble Grecians and Romans*. Translated by John Dryden. Revised by Arthur Hugh Clough. New York: Modern Library, 1932.

———. "How a Man May Become Aware of His Progress in Virtue." In *Plutarch's Moralia*. Vol. 1. Translated by Frank Cole Babbitt. Cambridge, MA: Harvard University Press, 1927.

Price, Simon. *Religions of the Ancient Greeks*. Cambridge, UK: Cambridge University Press, 1999.

Richardson, Robert D. "A Perfect Piece of Stoicism." *Thoreau Society Bulletin*, no. 153 (Fall 1980): 1–5.

Schopenhauer, Arthur. *The World as Will and Representation*. 3 vols. Translated by E. F. J. Payne. New York: Dover, 1969.

Seneca. *Ad Lucilium Epistulae Morales*. Translated by Richard M. Gummere. Cambridge, MA: Harvard University Press, 1967.

———. "On Anger." In *Moral and Political Essays*. Translated by John M. Cooper and J. F. Procopé. Cambridge, UK: Cambridge University Press, 1995.

———. "On Firmness." In *Seneca: Moral Essays*. Vol. 1. Translated by John W. Basore. Cambridge, MA: Harvard University Press, 1928.

———. "On Providence." In *Seneca: Moral Essays*. Vol. 1. Translated by John W. Basore. Cambridge, MA: Harvard University Press, 1928.

———. "On the Happy Life." In *Seneca: Moral Essays*. Vol. 2. Translated by John W. Basore. Cambridge, MA: Harvard University Press, 1932.

———. "On Tranquillity of Mind." In *Seneca: Moral Essays*. Vol. 2. Translated by John W. Basore. Cambridge, MA: Harvard University Press, 1932.

———. "To Helvia on Consolation." In *Seneca: Moral Essays*. Vol. 2. Translated by John W. Basore. Cambridge, MA: Harvard University Press, 1932.

———. "To Marcia on Consolation." In *Seneca: Moral Essays*. Vol. 2. Translated by John W. Basore. Cambridge, MA: Harvard University Press, 1932.

———. "To Polybius on Consolation." In *Seneca: Moral Essays*. Vol. 2. Translated by John W. Basore. Cambridge, MA: Harvard University Press, 1932.

Sommers, Christina Hoff, and Sally Satel. *One Nation under Therapy: How the Helping Culture Is Eroding Self-Reliance*. New York: St. Martin's Press, 2005.

Stockdale, James Bond. *Courage under Fire: Testing Epictetus's Doctrines in a Laboratory of Human Behavior*. Palo Alto, CA: Hoover Institution, Stanford University, 1993.

Strabo. *The Geography of Strabo*. Vol. 5. Translated by Horace Leonard Jones. Cambridge, MA: Harvard University Press, 1928.

Tacitus. *The Annals*. Vol. 4. Translated by John Jackson. Cambridge, MA: Harvard University Press, 1937.

Thoreau, Henry D. "Walden." In *Thoreau: Walden and Other Writings*. New York: Bantam, 1962.

Veyne, Paul. *Seneca: The Life of a Stoic*. Translated by David Sullivan. New York: Routledge, 2003.

Index